GW01032704

PETISHISM

KaTHLeen szasz

HOLT, RINEHART AND WINSTON

NEW YORK   CHICAGO   SAN FRANCISCO

Petishism

PETS AND THEIR PEOPLE IN THE WESTERN WORLD

FOR
MY FATHER AND MOTHER,
AND FRANCIS AND MICHAEL,
WITH LOVE.

ACKnOWLeDGMenTS

⊙ ⊙ I SHOULD LIKE TO EXPRESS MY GRATITUDE
to all those who have given me invaluable help and encourage-
ment by supplying factual material or by admitting, and
providing examples to prove, the importance of animal con-

tacts in cases of physically and mentally handicapped children and adults.

In the United States, thanks are due to Frank Dittrich, director, and Mrs. Avis Pfeiffer, editor, *Pet Shop Management*; Neal Pronek, editor, T.H.F. Publications, Inc.; W. N. Chimel, the Gaines Dog Research Center; Dr. Dean C. White, the Institute for Human-Animal Relationships, Inc.; Dr. Boris M. Levinson, Professor of Psychology, Yeshiva University, New York City; Dr. Ross Speck, clinical associate professor of psychiatry, Hahnemann Medical College, Philadelphia; Dr. Elisabeth Enczi, psychiatrist, Manhattan State Hospital, Wards Island, New York City; and my editor, Steven Kroll, at Holt, Rinehart and Winston, publishers.

In England, to the editor in chief of *Pet Trade Journal;* the Home Office for permission to visit one of H.M. prisons; the RSPCA, especially Superintendent James Kerr, who will *not* agree with me; the Church Army, especially Sister Theresa Capel; H. T. Radford, director, Interbro Limited; the Association of Psychiatric Social Workers; the British Council for Rehabilitation of the Disabled; the Institute for the Study and Treatment of Delinquents; the National Association for Mental Health; the National Society for Mentally Handicapped Children; the British Polio Fellowship; the psychological social workers who wrote to me about their experiences; Angus Wells, of Animal News Service; Mrs. Dolly Sewell, who helped with the research, and Mrs. Jean Lane, who typed the material, for her valuable comments.

In Germany, to Dr. M. Tripp and his assistant, Mrs. Eva Loschheim, for their kind cooperation; the Zoologischer Zentralanzeiger; Joseph Class and Rolf Wegner for the invaluable factual material received from them.

In France, to Gabriel Renay, director of the French SPA, and his assistant, Mme. Bijot; Jean Fabre of *Paris Jour*; and my friend Mme. Francoise Biro for the material she collected for me.

In Italy, to Dr. Corrado Trelanzi, director of the Italian SPA.

K.S.

contents

INTRODUCTION

⊙ ◉IN HIS SEARCH FOR IDENTITY, IN HIS STRUGGLE
against total estrangement from a civilization that turns
machines into men and men into machines, the *Homo neuroticus* has reinforced the ties binding him to the animal world

from which, at a certain stage, evolution divorced him. On the one hand, he is progressively discarding the social rules that regulate human behavior without having any conception of the "freedom" he seeks; on the other, he is attempting to raise the animals to his own exalted level. In Western Europe and in America two communities live side by side, intercommunicating and interacting: the community of men and the community of animals or, to be more precise, pet animals. Although man has kept pets since the dawn of his existence, the present form of his relationship to animals is new and as incalculable in its implications as the computer.

It is no easy task to trace back man's relationship to pet animals through the 800,000 years of his history on earth in a brief chapter. Unavoidably, the outcome will be superficial and open to attack by serious historians. Yet to understand the animal fetishism, "petishism," we are witnessing in the Western World today, it is necessary to look back upon the past first because in every phase of man's uneven progress his attitude to animals has been an important, and revealing, feature of the spirit of the age.

In fact the whole subject of human-animal relationships is so vast that every aspect of it deserves to be studied separately. If this were done the result would be a multivolume work, each volume written by a scholar of one particular discipline. There would be a volume on animals in the fine arts from the cave drawings to Picasso; a volume on animals in world literature from the Sumerians to George Orwell; a volume on animals in language: imagery, symbolism, analogies, proverbs; a volume on animals in the world religions; one on animals in philosophy, in psychology, in the modern mass media, in medicine, and so on. But to understand our present relationship to our pet animals and the intense preoccupation with animals in general that has, in the last decade or two, achieved the proportions of a social phenomenon, we have to study not so much the animals as ourselves: the individual, the society he built for himself, and his quarrel with that society.

Any criticism of society usually elicits the answer, "True,

but look how much we have progressed, how much better things are today than they were a hundred years ago." I feel that while in some respects things are indeed better than they were a hundred years ago, in others they are worse. Besides, and this is what I wish to emphasize most strongly, to compare the present with the past is far too comfortable; it is merely a rejection of responsibility and cheap justification of what is still very bad. To me only one comparison can have any validity: that of things as they are with things as they should and could be if we used *all our resources* for the creation of a society in which every potential human being would have the opportunity to grow into a real human being. If I describe only what is bad in our Western World and fail to give due praise to what is good, it is because the bad needs to be changed; the good, once recognized, is on the way to getting better.

The fact that Americans spend 5 to 6 billion dollars a year on their pets and the British well over 100 million pounds, that there are 8 million dogs and cats in West Germany and 16.5 million in France, can be, and often is, ascribed to affluence and one of its side effects, leisure. It may be due to modern methods of advertising that the pet trade and industry record an annual increase of 15 per cent in their turnover and that the circulation of pet magazines and the number of pet books published attain astronomical figures. However, before trade, industry, advertising, and publishing discovered this new and highly profitable market and threw themselves wholeheartedly into exploiting it and creating new needs, the basic need, man's growing dependence on pet animals as an emotional crutch, was already there.

This basic need springs from the same frustrations that drive men to the psychoanalyst's couch, to indiscriminate sex, to alcohol, drugs, and crime: from his alienation from himself and from the society he can no longer control or even understand, from the mental agony of loneliness, from deracination and the anonymity of urban living, from his feeling of inadequacy in a world that demands a moral flexibility and intellectual alertness of which few are capable, and from the breakdown of human communication. In his *Insight and Responsibility*, the American psychologist Professor Erik H. Erikson writes: ". . . it dawns on us that the *technological* world of today is about to create kinds of alienation too strange to be imagined." Is petishism one of them?

When you love children and dogs *too* *much*, you love them instead of adults.

— JEAN-PAUL SARTRE: *The Words*

Echoes of cries of pain reverberate in my heart. Children in famine, victims tortured by oppressors, helpless old people a hated burden to their sons, and the whole world of loneliness, poverty and pain make a mockery of what human life should be.

The Autobiography of Bertrand Russell

Part I
⊙ ⊙ A DOG IS A CAT
IS A PARROT IS A FISH. . . .

CHAPTER 1
THE HISTORY OF PET KEEPING

In the age of magic man sought to control nature through ritual; in the age of monotheism he could dispense with this control by relying on the mediation of a personal god; in the age of quantity man exerts his own will and seeks to control nature himself.

— LANCELOT LAW WHYTE:
The Next Development in Man.

◉ ◉ WHEN APPROXIMATELY 800,000 YEARS AGO, during the first glaciation period of the Pleistocene Age, man's earliest ancestor raised himself on his hind legs and gained a new outlook on his narrow world, the dog's earli-

3

est ancestor, wolf, fox, jackal, or a mixture of the three, was already there. How man and dog met is a matter of conjecture. Perhaps, after having made a copious meal of a captured bitch, replete and sleepy, man gave her puppies to his children to play with. If this is indeed how it happened, his gesture laid the foundations for an alliance that has endured to this day.

The road behind the species man, from the Australopithecus, the pea-brained erect ape, to what we euphemistically call *Homo sapiens*, is relatively short compared with the evolution of animal life on our planet—a good deal less than 1 million years as against 870 million. It is a strange thought, and not one to flatter our inflated ego, that if some quirk of nature had not provided our weak and helpless ancestors with a brain capable of growth, all living creatures on earth would today be safe from total destruction by a few rather decorative, mushroom-shaped clouds.

What caused man's brain to be different from that of other animals is still a complete mystery, but the American physiologist Professor Anton J. Carlson held out at least some hope of a future scientific answer when he said that one day we may find a "new building stone," an "additional lipoid, phosphatid, or potassium ion" in the human brain that will explain it. In the meantime let us accept the hypothesis that the human brain differs in kind, not merely in degree, from the animal brain and this is why it grew as it did. Even if the raw material was there, the question still remains: What caused it to develop by such leaps and bounds?

If we think of the giant intellectual steps forward that man always takes at times of extreme emergency—natural catastrophes, pestilences, wars, anything that threatens to destroy him—it seems at least possible that his relatively rapid development should have been due to the character of the age into which he was born—the Ice Age, with its unimaginable natural upheavals and radical changes of climate. From the day of his appearance on earth, man has lived in an almost permanent state of emergency, and survival has required—as it still requires—the ingenuity only an enlarged brain is capable of.

From the day he teamed up with the new, eminently unattractive, two-legged creature, the dog, sensing the other's potential superiority, trotted faithfully along behind him across the millenia. He shared his master's food and in the early days, when the going was tough, *was* his food. He watched the short, puny hominoid's heroic battle against giant animals, helped him evict the cave bear from its lair, and moved in with him when successive glaciation periods made life in the open impossible. The dog rejoiced with his master when, at last, man discovered fire, and assisted him in bringing home the Sunday joint for roasting. He witnessed man's first attempt at artistic creation, and if he was offended that the paintings on the cave walls represented animals his master feared, hunted, or tried to make friends with, and not he who was by then a member of the family and taken for granted, he might have growled but he never bit.

It may well be that the animal painted on the cavewall assumed a life of its own, became a third image between that living in man's mind and the flesh-and-blood animal he knew. This third image might have been regarded as a mediator between man and his prey, giving man the power to defeat it, and between man and his enemy, preventing that enemy from killing him. Had man then been able to paint heat and cold, water and ice, storm and earthquake, we should have proof that these, too, made part of his magic.

Magic, the ancestor of both science and religion, roots in man's conscious awareness of the Janus-headed Unknown-and-Uncontrollable whose one face inspires terror, the other hope. Survival was a miracle, and knowing his weakness, man could not but ascribe it to some superhuman force that he tried, and still tries to propitiate. But to explain to himself why his magic so often failed, man also invented the force of evil, fighting, and sometimes defeating, the good. From there it was only a short step to his use of that force, with the help of magic, against his enemies.

To earn his keep and his place by the fire the dog made himself useful in many ways. He defended the camping place against predators, accompanied his master on hunting expeditions, and later, when man domesticated some of the other animals and settled down to till the soil, guarded the herd and protected the home.

Some five thousand years ago, when the Sumerians invented the art of writing, replacing our guesses at interpretations of the past with factual knowledge, the dog lived in the towns built by man. It appears from the proverbs recorded in those days that he was not, however, a particularly respected member of the community. "The ox plows, the dog spoils the deep furrows," goes one saying. "The smith's dog could not overturn the anvil; he [therefore] overturned the water pot instead," goes another. But there he was, accepted if not petted and, in many written documents, sharply distinguished from his hated kin, the "kid-devouring wild dog."

Still, for some strange reason even the animals domesticated by man retained their magic. While our prehistoric ancestors turned flesh-and-blood animals into two-dimensional symbols in order to dominate them, in the early civilizations the animals became symbols of other forces man wished to dominate—sun and storm, fire and water.

As his imagination developed, man began to realize that the Unknown-and-Uncontrollable with its two faces, good and evil, existed not only without but also within him. He invested the animals he adored as gods, for the magic powers they possessed and he lacked, with the bright and dark sides of human nature. This twofold identification, the projection of himself into the animals and the borrowing of their powers, caused man's relationship to both his gods and his animals to become ambivalent.

As man's horizon broadened and his chances of survival multiplied, his will to live and, consequently, his fear of death, increased. Realizing that no sacrifice could keep death indefinitely at bay, he aspired to afterlife, the survival of the self, to ensure for himself at least partial immortality. But since he was still strongly identified with the animal world, he shared this partial immortality with the animals. The story of the Flood and Noah's Ark, written down for the first time by the Sumerians, clearly demonstrates that man still regarded the animals as his equals in importance.

In organized society the caveman's magic developed into organized religion with a highly complex symbolism. Statues of animal-gods enthroned in buildings devoted to their cult replaced the wall paintings, but the gods' earthly counterparts, though sacred, were the servants of man. In Egypt the dog-god Anubis enjoyed divine honors, but after their death domestic dogs were also granted divine status. Their bodies were embalmed and buried in dog cemeteries. The cat, ancestor of our alley cat, appeared in Egypt later and was adored as the earthly incarnation of the goddess Bast. Each year a cat festival was held at Bubastis, seat of the goddess, where priests and the faithful mewed in chorus, imitating the voice of the divine animal. This is what the Greek historian Herodotus has to say about the Egyptian cat and dog cult:

What happens when a house catches fire is most extraordinary: nobody takes the least trouble to put it out, for it is only the cats that matter; everyone stands in a row, a little distance from his neighbor, trying to protect the cats, who nevertheless slip through the line, or jump over it, and hurl themselves into the flames. This causes the Egyptians deep distress. All the inmates of a house where a cat has died a natural death shave their eyebrows, and when a dog dies they shave the whole body including the head. Cats which have died are taken to Bubastis, where they are embalmed and buried in sacred receptacles; dogs are buried, also in sacred burial places, in the towns where they belong. . . .

All animals being sacred, but not all animals being used for lowly work, the Pharaohs chose as their own pets the most decorative, the most costly, and the most difficult to tame. In the palace gardens antelopes, monkeys, baboons, and the cat's wild relatives lived peacefully side by side with a large variety of beautiful birds, well-fed amphibians and several species of reptile. The ladies of the royal court surrounded themselves with perfumed and bejeweled cats and lively monkeys, and often wore live snakes as armbands or around their necks. Exotic pets, with a multitude of slaves to look after their welfare, were a badge of rank, and the people were duly impressed by their rulers who lived in such close intimacy with the most feared of the animal-gods.

When the Hebrews marched out of Egypt to find a homeland of their own, it proved easier to shake Egypt's dust off their feet than to shed her customs and beliefs. Much blood soaked the sands of the desert, many heads were broken, before Moses succeeded in making his people accept the wholly abstract, one and only God of whom the poet-Pharaoh Akhnaton had dreamed and who was not to be represented either in human or in animal shape.

The abstract god tolerated no rival, and this put an end to the earlier ambivalent attitude toward god and animal. Deprived of their divinity but retaining their usefulness, the animals were treated by the Jews with humanity and granted, like all those who worked, a weekly day of rest. The myths connected with them were forgotten, and as familiarity with animal-gods was no longer a badge of rank, the possession of tamed beasts as pets lost its attraction. The animals were relegated to their proper place in the scheme of things and served the Jews in their gigantic struggle for survival in the land they could, at last, call their own.

Perhaps because the light of the sun was not so blinding, the dark of the night not so black and wrought with unknown perils, the Greeks had less need of magic for protection and created for themselves a mythology free from the terror of the Unknown-and-Uncontrollable. Their fear of animals was merely physical, and therefore they did not have to raise them to divine status. They created their gods in their own image with all the human failings and virtues but, to make them better than themselves, invested them with supreme power and immortality. The only exception was the lesser god Pan, half-man, half-goat, a combination of man's natural instinct —not yet considered base—and his superior mind. The religious taboos, however, were already at work, and Pan was always rejected by the nymphs he pursued because of his "ugliness."

The Greek attitude to animals was poetic, scientific, and practical. Each god had his or her pet animal, and when in the throes of some eminently human emotion — lust, jealousy, anger, revenge — they would change themselves, the lesser gods, or even mortals who had annoyed them, into animals. Greek mythology swarms with wonderful, imaginary beasts, but these, possibly to prove man's still precarious physical superiority over the animal world, are always defeated by a venerated hero like, for instance, Hercules.

But animals were also an intergral part of everyday Greek life. The Greeks loved horses above all but had a soft spot for dogs as well. Homer movingly tells of Ulysses' dog Argus dying happily when the long-awaited master at last returns.

This highly imaginative people, with their positive attitude to life and great love of beauty in every form and shape, were possesed of an infinite curiosity about everything on earth and beyond it. Their literature, dealing with an endless variety of subjects, from philosophy to politics, from agriculture to strategy, from astronomy to history, from the creative arts to science, includes a large number of books on animals. Among these is Aristotle's ten-volume work, the *History of Animals*, in which he observes that, like people, dogs also dream, as shown by their yapping, whining, and running motions while asleep. Aristotle was also the first to note the extraordinary intelligence of dolphins.

The Romans, a people far less imaginative but vastly more practical than the Greeks, adopted and adapted the Greek mythology, gods, heroes, animals and all, adding them to their own unsubstantial numina, "those who are above." But while the Greeks shared their world with the animals, real and imaginary, the Romans used them and often misused them with the cruelty that always goes hand in hand with superstition and a fanatic lust for power.

Although the Romans were not particularly fond of dogs, they were fond of their possessions, and the house of every well-to-do Roman had a dog posted in its entrance hall. In August of each year, at the beginning of the "dog days," they sacrificed a number of dogs, possibly to be granted safety from rabies, very common then.

The animals all Romans loved, from the rulers to the humble fold, were birds of every description, from the decorative swan and peacock to the singing and talking birds. When parrots were imported from the Eastern provinces they became the pets of the rich, who employed trainers to teach them to talk.

In the course of time, noble Romans developed a taste for exotic animals. Everyone who was anyone established a private zoo or game park. The Roman emperors, as their power grew and their excesses multiplied, began to fill their palaces with increasing numbers of wild animals. They built tiger and lion pits of their own and fed them on convicts condemned to death. Though, in principle, citizens of Rome could only be beheaded, the personal enemies and rivals of the emperors often ended their lives in the lion pit. Of the three Roman modes of execution—beheading, crucifixion, and the lions—some of the emperors preferred the last, perhaps because it reduced the meat bill.

Not to be outdone even by their emperor, the Roman nobles, generals, and statesmen, harnessed tigers to their chariots to impress the plebs, or brought back large numbers of wild animals from their campaigns and made gladiators fight them in the circus. One of these performances, under Emperor Titus, cost the lives of five thousand animals. The number of gladiators killed was not recorded. In the early days of Christianity the armed and well-trained gladiators were replaced with unarmed and helpless Christians. Of the animals killed by them there is no record.

But the Roman emperors and nobles also kept lions, tigers, and other wild animals as pets. Powdered with gold dust and rendered harmless by overfeeding and the removal of sharp teeth and claws, these animals would guard their masters' sleeping quarters, lie at their feet to be caressed and fondled, and follow them about like dogs.

The cream of the Roman intelligentsia, writers and poets, deplored the inhuman practices of their time, but their influence on both rulers and ruled was negligible. Vergilius wrote with tender warmth about animals that, like the wolf and the goose, played an important role in Roman mythology, and Pliny, an admirer of Aristotle, published an encyclopedia of animals that was used as a textbook by zoologists well into the sixteenth century.

> Last week I saw a woman flayed and you will hardly believe how it altered her person for the worse.
> — JONATHAN SWIFT:
> *A Tale of a Tub*

Christianity added new dimensions to man's relationship with animals. To the rational and humane attitude evolved by the Jews was added an animal symbolism more varied and richer than any before. Part of it was inherited from former beliefs, part of it adopted from other contemporary religions, and part of it was new and rather original. The most notable feature of the Christian attitude to animals, however, was its striking ambivalence.

Animals figure widely in the Christian "good magic." Thus the fish, the dove, the lamb, and the wild animals and imaginary monsters in the legends of the saints. The taming of these beasts by holy men and women illustrated man's spiritual superiority to the animal world. But the place animals occupied in "bad magic" was even more important. The Devil was often depicted as some awful monster, an imaginary beast, or a being half-man, half-animal, but it was in the shape of ordinary domestic animals that the Devil was believed to consort with witches and sorcerers in the witch-hunts of the Middle Ages. Any woman who kept a pet animal in her home, especially if she was poor, old, or not quite sane, or was hated or envied by her neighbors, was in danger of being denounced as a witch harboring a "familiar" and, more often than not, would end her days at the end of a rope or at the stake. Usually the pet animal was flayed alive or dipped in oil and burned along with its mistress.

In Catholic Europe the Inquisition executed well over 300,000 witches, but there are no statistics to show how many animals shared their fate. In Protestant England the self-styled witch-finder-general Matthew Hopkins, delivered more than 300 witches to their executioners between 1664 and 1667, receiving a reward of three guineas for each, which accounts for his zeal. The contemporary documents show that almost invariably these unfortunate women kept one or several pet animals, and usually these were the only evidence against them.

The belief in witchcraft was exported to America by the seventeenth-century English immigrants, and in New England, witchcraft was made a capital offense punishable by death. The last and most famous witch trial, at which 20 people were hanged and 2 dogs were accused of witchcraft and killed, took place at Salem in 1692.

But the animals treated as human beings did not fare better than those regarded as embodiments of the Devil. A wide variety of them, from the smallest to the largest, were put on trial and judged for "crimes" committed. Locusts, June-bugs, flies, small birds, mice, frogs, caterpillars, were summoned before the court by the town criers, who had to walk the fields and read the summons to them three times. If they failed to obey the summons, they were tried in absentia. Dogs were tried and executed for biting, bulls for goring people. At the first of such trials, in 1268, a pig was condemned to death for eating a small child, and in 1572 another pig was dressed up in human clothes, then condemned and killed for the same crime.

Another aspect of the Christian attitude to animals was a complete indifference to the fate of these God's creatures, surpassed only by the indifference to the suffering of one's fellow men. In England and France the priests hunted with the lords of the manor, owned and bred hunting dogs, and kept falcons. These privileged animals accompanied their masters even to church, and the falcons would listen to the service perched on the corner of the altar. Good hunting dogs were purchased for fantastic amounts of money, and an army of servants catered to their needs.

It is not surprising that by the end of the Middle Ages dogs were promoted from the kennel to the palace or manor and made to share their masters' affection with all sorts of expensive, decorative, but useless animals outrageously spoiled by the mistress of the house. It was then that the cat, long before demoted from god to mouser, came again into its own as a pet.

While the pets of the feudal lords lived on the fat of the land, the common people were reduced to unprecedented misery. Immobilized by serfdom, terrorized by the Church, martyred by war, hunger, and disease, ignorant, superstitious, and violent, they treated their animals as cruelly as their masters treated them. Next to the witch-trials and public executions, their favorite entertainment was to watch cock-fights, bear baiting, or the ravaging of a bull by dogs, a process practiced in England to tenderize the meat.

The discovery of America enriched not only the treasuries, but also the aviaries and menageries of Europe. The ships brought back parrots, canaries, macaws, parakeets, and many other birds of brilliant plumage. They brought back hitherto unknown members of the cat family—pumas, cougars, jaguars—and a small Peruvian mammal, the guinea pig. The birds and big cats soon joined the ranks of the most valued pets, and as in Roman times, the kings of Europe shared their chambers with wild animals.

North America, up to the Arctic regions, became a huge hunting ground for food and fur animals. The European hunters were surprised to find that the beaver, much valued at home for its fur, was kept by the Indians as a pet, preferred even to their other pet, the dog.

The fifteenth and sixteenth centuries wholly transformed the face of Europe. The human mind, maturing in oppression, demolished the cage of prohibitions confining it. The Renaissance, the Reformation, the discovery of America, were so many stages in the humanist revolution that gained ground quickly because of the discovery of the first means of mass communication—printing.

Gradually, as faith gave ground to knowledge and increasing numbers of people came to know the joys of intellectual exercise, the false beliefs concerning animals began to disappear. The Reformation did away with the legends of the saints and the picturesque monsters of Hell, though, as men are slow to change, it retained the belief in the Devil's incarnation in domestic animals. Even in the Catholic art of the Renaissance, realistic animal portraits began to take the place of imaginary beasts.

However, as the living standard of the population did not keep pace with cultural progress, it was still only the rich who could afford to keep nonworking animals. Manors and palaces were teeming with ordinary and exotic pets, and the treatment of some of these was never equaled in ridiculousness until four hundred years later. Mary Queen of Scots dressed her dog in a blue velvet suit in winter, Henry II of France fed his on bread specially baked for it, and Henry III carried his small dog around in a basket hung about his neck so as not to be parted from it even in church or at political conferences. François I hunted with a trained cheetah, and a tame lion slept at the foot of his bed. Kings and nobles had their own menageries, but it was George II of England who first opened his to the public.

In the sixteenth, but even more in the seventeenth century, European thinkers picked up the thread dropped by the Greek scientists and philosophers, and began to show an increasing interest in animals. Descartes represented the views of the Catholic Church when he declared that animals were mere machines that could neither think nor feel because they had no soul. Leibnitz believed that there was but a difference of degree between man and animal, and the English philosopher Locke held that while animals possessed the capacity both to think and to feel, they were incapable of abstraction.

In America, cut off from the intellectual upheavals of Europe, the relationship between man and animal became again what it had been in prehistoric times. In their effort to build a new fatherland, the colonists depended on animals for survival, especially on horses and dogs. Domestic animals were valued for their usefulness, but only the representatives of the European monarchs and their entourages had the means and the time to keep pet animals.

While in the vast and underpopulated Americas man still lived close to nature, the fast-growing cities of Europe and the new bondage created by the Industrial Revolution divorced man from the skies and the fields. The only animal the urban working population ever saw was a stray dog or cat or a bird in a tree, the only field the battlefield.

The new middle class, however, seeking new ways to enjoy its growing opulence, began to ape the way of life of the upper classes. Not content with buying estates, building country houses, and riding, hunting and fishing like, but not with, the landed gentry, they began to keep pet animals in their elegant town houses. But while the pets of the landowners still retained some of their animal dignity, being allowed, within certain limits, to lead a life befitting their natures, the pets of the middle class lost theirs, without enhancing the dignity of their masters. Eighteenth-century painting gives a good idea of the sticky sentimentality these animals were surrounded with.

Yet the eighteenth century also witnessed the first systematic study of the animal world since Aristotle. *Systemae Naturae* by Carl von Linnee was first published in 1735, and von Linnee, a Swedish naturalist, exerted a profound influence on the European intelligentsia, who were turning more and more from religion to science.

By the ninteenth century, humanist thought had impregnated every domain of European life. The lower classes, excluded from the blessings of civilization, lost patience and, with the help of humanist middle-class intellectuals, organized and formulated their demands. The ensuing improvement of their condition liberated new energies, produced new talents, and created new needs that paved the way for the technological revolution of the twentieth century.

With the lessening of man's inhumanity to man, movements were started in the Protestant European countries — England, Sweden, Germany, — and, not much later, America, to protect animals against man's cruelty. Within ninety years, 125 societies in fifty countries joined in a world organization for animal welfare, counting millions and millions of members.

It may well be that this rapid spread of animal conscious-ness was also due to the teachings of Charles Darwin and the world controversy they aroused. Realizing that far from having been created by God in His own image, he was "created equal" with the other members of the animal world, and proud of having achieved such superiority, man may sud-denly have felt responsible for his lesser brothers. It is all the stranger that while the animals living in man's immed-iate environment were given a new deal, the killing of wild animals continued unabated. As hunting in the fields and woods of Europe became an increasingly popular sport, those wishing to preserve their status took up big-game hunting — more costly and therefore more exclusive, and made attractive by an illusion of danger.

As a result of the nineteenth century social revolution, the lot of the working classes improved to such an extent that the solidarity that brought this about evaporated and the striving for personal advancement turned the workers into petty bourgeois. Just as the middle classes had done before them, they began to imitate the way of life of those more prosperous than they. Their new condition allowed them to share their homes with pet animals, with dogs, cats, birds, fishes. By the middle of the twentieth century, animals had invaded every stratum of Western society.

World War II gave birth to a new type of man. Although the war ended in the defeat of the Western variety of totali-tarianism, in the process certain aspects of it had become accepted as normal and had been admitted into the realm of everyday reality. Actions termed "expedient" that con-flict with the Christian and humanist values that shaped European thought for two thousand years and were re-spected even when not acted upon, had gained civil right and attained their apotheosis in the dropping of the atom bomb.

The mature humanism of the nineteenth century is kept alive today by a mere handful of man and women. It is scorned by those who conform to the letter of a social ethic whose spirit has long been dead, by those who seek desperately for a new set of values, and by those who, having lost faith even in seeking, simply opt out of society. Western man hovers, like Mohammed's coffin, between a past defended tooth and nail by the older generation and fully repudiated by the young, and a future that is frighteningly slow in taking shape.

In this age of transition, immured in giant cities and in a system of obsolete ideas many of which were false even when new, the *Homo neuroticus* is groping for a way out of the intellectual, emotional, and spiritual chaos that threatens to smother him. In his confusion, in his yearning for the natural, the not man-made, he has seized upon what is most easily accessible—the animal. But his alienation is so complete that the natural no longer satisfies him. Instead he perverts it to his own image and has brought into being a community as sick as his own, that of the furred, feathered and scaly people.

CHAPTER 2
PETS—AND THE POTENTIAL ADULTS

In the context of our present pervasive madness that we call normality, sanity, freedom, all our frames of reference are ambiguous and equivocal.

— R.D. LAING:
The Divided Self

◉ ◉ SOME TIME AGO A YOUNG GIRL WAS TRAVELING on top of a London bus reading a newspaper. A large headline on the front page announced the Chinese had exploded another atom bomb. The lady sitting next to the girl read the headline over her shoulder.

18

"I wish they'd stop experimenting," she said to no one in particular, but when the young girl smiled her agreement, she continued, ". . . and start dropping that bomb on each other! Though not until there are enough shelters for animals."

"Why animals?" the young girl asked, perplexed.

"Because animals are innocent. They're not responsible for the state the world is in today. But it's time people got what they deserved."

"And what about children?" the young girl asked angrily. "Are they responsible?"

"Don't talk to me about children," the lady spat at her. "Potential adults, that's what they are! They're cruel and vicious, and in a few years they'll be no better than their parents!"

"There is a great deal of resemblance between the relationship of children and of primitive men towards animals," says Freud in his *Totem and Taboo*. "Children show no trace of the arrogance which urges adult civilized men to draw a hard-and-fast line between their own nature and that of all other animals. Children have no scruples over allowing animals to rank as their full equals. Uninhibited as they are in the avowal of their bodily needs, they no doubt feel themselves more akin to animals than to their elders, who may well be a puzzle to them." The uninhibited avowal of bodily needs is the first thing a human child has to unlearn to prove his superiority over the animal world, and he must indeed be puzzled by his elders who allow their pet animals much that they emphatically forbid him.

Many parents believe that through living with animals, observing them, looking after them, training them, children will acquire a sense of responsibility that playing with inanimate objects would never teach them. At the same time, they will find out in a natural way about certain facts of life that many parents are painfully embarrassed to explain, such as birth, sex, death. However, the reasons parents give for buying their child a pet express their own wishes rather than the reality of the animal's huge importance in the child's life. The Nazis recognized this importance when, as a lesson in emotional discipline, they obliged members of the Hitler Jugend to raise a pet dog and, when they had grown very fond of it, kill it with their own hands.

It is natural that by the time they become parents or educators, adults have forgotten what it means to be a child. In addition to the many causes so well known to psychotherapists, this acquired ignorance of the psychological make-up of a child is due to the brainwashing, begun at a very early age, that we call education. This process, passed down from generation to generation, enables the child, square peg that he is, to fit into the round hole of society by ridding him of the most subversive human traits—love, spontaneity, common sense, and imagination.

A city child born into a family that keeps no pets will learn about the existence of animals from the stories told him and from occasional visits to the zoo. The stories, however, anthropomorphize the animals, giving the child an entirely false idea of their nature, and visits to the zoo are not frequent enough to undeceive him. When the child asks for a pet animal of his own and for the usual educational reasons his parents buy him one, the conflict between the "should be" and the "is" begins.

The fantasies a child weaves around animals do not include cleaning up after a puppy or taking it out regularly. It may be that this much publicized "sense of responsibility" could be taught him with greater and more lasting success if it were connected in the child's mind with a more general sense of responsibility extending to humans.

Nor is the sexual enlightenment a city child gains from his pets of much use to him. In nine cases out of ten he is prevented from relating what he observes to human beings. When he watches with interest as his little dog masturbates, he is told that this is a dirty thing only animals do, good little boys never. When he sees two dogs mating in the street or park, his parents drag him away and hasten to explain that the dogs were "only playing."

A child is rarely allowed to be present when the pet dog or cat gives birth, because it may frighten or disgust him, or fill his head with ideas he is too young for. Even death, the only "fact of life" no one has yet thought of calling "dirty," would remain unrelated to people in the child's mind if he did not work it out for himself, for the desperate attempts of adults to misinform him on every phenomenon of existence, and send him out into the world unprepared, extends to death as well.

Where parents cannot interfere is in the child's physical and emotional relationship with his pet, mainly because they fail to relate its manifestations to their own emotional conflicts that the child strongly reacts to. Nor do they put the blame for the child's often excessive attachment to his pet on their own failure as parents. Yet their rigidly traditional, or just as rigidly applied but book-learned and undigested modern educational methods may force the child to seek refuge in his pet from the artificially cool, or emotionally overcharged, relationship between him and his parents.

In England, where public school education is still directed at producing empire builders, superior beings who can cope with any hardship without betraying the slightest weakness, gentlemen whose emotions are so well disciplined that they never even notice when they cease existing altogether, many sensitive children depend on their pet animals for a free and uninhibited emotional relationship. But in America too children often depend on pet animals for the sense of permanence and security their overpermissive parents cannot give them. The pet is always there. It does not go to work or, in the evening, to social functions like Daddy, or to the psychoanalyst and morning coffee-and-gossip parties like Mummy. It does not come home late at night exhausted and often slightly drunk; it does not quarrel and, most important of all, does not divorce.

Even in the less prosperous and the poor social strata of the affluent Western countries the relationship between child and pet is based not only on love but on need. Where both parents go out to work and come home tired and irritable, the mother to another full-time job—her home—and the father to hurry out for a drink with his friends to forget the frustrations of his job and his marriage, the child is lucky if he has a pet that will listen to him when nobody else does and give him the demonstrative love he needs. Children will not make do with being told they are loved. They want proof.

Whatever a child's background, certain aspects of his relationship to his pet are universal. A child walking his dog is filled with a sense of importance, of power, and a protective superiority nothing else can give him. He will act out on his pet all his primitive impulses—his budding sexuality, his sadism, his curiosity, his need for the reassurance of physical contact. He will take his pet with him into his imaginary world and give it a place in all his daydreams. When playing alone with his pet, he will improvise little scenes in which the two actors, his pet and himself, take a large variety of roles, most often the parts of his father, his mother, and himself.

Parents may be in for a surprise when, as it sometimes happens, they catch their children at play with their pets. The father who found his four-year-old son whipping his puppy dog with a belt and shouting: "I'll make a man of you yet, you sniveling little bastard!," learned his lesson and changed his educational methods. The mother who came upon her little daughter of six lying on the carpet with a purring cat on top of her, moving her little hips and moaning, never again forgot to shut the door between the bedroom and the nursery before going to bed.

In Harlem, New York, a group of Negro children were throwing stones at a cornered, helpless white cat, screaming: "Kill the white man! Kill him! Kill him!" A little farther on a ragged little girl was sitting on the curb with a big mongrel dog next to her. She had a piece of paper on her knees, and holding a colored pencil and his paw in her hand, she was teaching him to draw letters.

"Warmth and loving kindness to animals may coexist with a cold and rejecting relationship with people," writes the American psychiatrist Sherwin M. Woods. However, loving kindness to animals and to people will coexist only if a child is not compelled to love an animal "instead," or "against," human beings but can use his pet as just one more outlet for his spontaneously and uninhibitedly expressed emotions.

In the introduction to the Pelican edition of his book *The Divided Self*, the English existentialist psychologist Professor R. D. Laing says: "We are born into a world where alienation awaits us. We are potential men, but are in an alienated state, and this state is not simply a natural system. Alienation as our present destiny is achieved by outrageous violence perpetrated by human beings on human beings."

Disturbed children are not born but made. A child becomes disturbed through his contact with his alienated parents who "perpetrate outrageous violence" upon him, first by being what they are, then by trying to mold him in their own image. If not treated—and how few of them are—disturbed children grow rings around their injured psyches like trees, and allow the injury to fester until, sometimes a decade or two later, it erupts in a still curable, or already incurable, form. But sometimes the flaw will manifest itself in what is called "antisocial behavior" or "sheer cussedness": delinquency, crime, drug addiction, homosexuality, or just a rebellion without cause (but not without reason) that society then tries to curb by deliberate "outrageous violence." It may also happen that the disturbed child will go through adulthood and old age, apparently functioning normally but in a permanent state of acute unease, often unable to communicate with people and surrounding himself with surrogate people he is not afraid of because they never hurt him.

Psychotherapists have made use of pet animals in child psychotherapy for a long time, empirically and without publishing their experiences. No systematic research in this field has so far been undertaken. Dr. Boris M. Levinson, professor at the Graduate School of Humanities and Social Sciences,

Yeshiva University, New York City, has published several articles and read several papers to psychoanalytical conferences on the use of pets in psychodiagnosis and psychotherapy of disturbed children. It took considerable courage to throw overboard the fear of ridicule and the idol of "professional dignity," but innovators are often laughed at until their achievements put a stop to laughter.

Dr. Levinson holds that a child's attitude to a pet animal will give the therapist many clues to the child's conflict and thus facilitate treatment. He describes, among others, the case of David, an adopted child of seven who was very much disturbed that his real mother had deserted him.

He had threatened to kill his sister Helen (also an adopted child) and himself since he felt that they were both very bad, otherwise they would not have been surrendered for adoption. This in spite of the fact that Mrs. B. (their adoptive mother) had read many stories to David which explained that an adopted child was a preferred child because he had been picked out, while with the natural born child the parents had to take pot luck. However, David did not accept this explanation. He felt that it was not possible for his adoptive parents to love him since there must have been something inherently wicked about him that brought about his desertion. He was convinced that he was taken on approval and that as soon as he misbehaved he would be surrendered.

Although our cat would sleep in her basket on the table, a few sessions passed before David noticed her. Eventually he began to fondle her and later he wanted to feed her. He asked many questions about the cat. Finally, he wanted to know where the cat came from. I explained that we had picked her up in the ASPCA from an abandoned litter. We love this cat very much; so much that my two sons often fight over the privilege of having her in their room at night.

At first David found it difficult to accept the idea that a cat, even abandoned by her mother or owner, could still be loved and accepted by others. After several sessions during which he returned constantly to this subject, he began to consider the possibility that he was actually loved by his adoptive parents. I believe that this was the turning point in David's recovery.

Another way of using a pet in therapy is to introduce one into the home situation, says Dr. Levinson:

With centrifugal social forces rampant in our society today, members of the family often become alienated. The presence of the emotionally disturbed child may be a storm warning that hot fires are burning under the seemingly quiet and placid surface of family living. A child in such a family must have a constant support. He is the hostage of fate. He cannot get up and leave an intolerable situation. He cannot divorce his parents, nor can he prevent a divorce by his parents—which he so much fears. For a child who is afraid to go to school because his parents may leave (as each has loudly threatened to do in his presence) a pet will offer constant solace and will be there to greet him with unconditional joy and warmth.

Dr. Levinson feels that "pet therapy" is particularly useful with nonverbal, severely ego-disturbed children:

It is well known that most children learn about the world and the difference between self and nonself, through the medium of their body. This is particularly true for the autistic child whose contact with reality is most tenuous . . . . It seems to me that if we trained pets to give bodily comfort to the autistic child in his crib, or while he is a toddler, and thus provide constant stimulation throughout his waking hours, it would assuage the autistic child's all-consuming anxiety and help him establish a firmer grip on reality.

Another, very characteristic case was described by a London psychological social worker:

Jimmy, aged 6½, was referred to a therapist for head-banging and "strange" behavior. He acted in a superior and grown-up way, talked about architecture and Tchaikovsky, but did no work in school and made no friends. He was also obsessionally clean and was always washing his hands until they were sore.

After a year of treatment, during which his mother made a lot of progress with the psychological social worker, Jimmy began to be able to play, which he had never done before, and carried around a teddy-bear wherever he went. . . . In treatment he showed great interest in babies and asked for factual information which, with his mother's consent, was given him. However, when he talked about this at home in a very open way, both parents were greatly shocked and father, in particular, was very angry and threatened to stop the treatment. A week or so later, mother noticed that Daisy, the dog, was pregnant and she told Jimmy about it. He wanted to know "who had given her the seed," became intensely interested and very protective towards the dog.

On returning from the Clinic one day Jimmy and his mother found that Daisy was having her pups and had dropped one on the carpet. Jimmy was thrilled, picked up the pup and gave it to Daisy, then watched her having five more. He was enthralled and in no way upset that his hands had got messy. . . . Both parents were delighted with the nice, sensible way in which Jimmy dealt with the event. "There was no nastiness, no smuttiness," they declared. . . . This experience had a beneficial influence on the whole family, and communication between child and parents increased. It helped Jimmy:

a) to relate normally to the outside world, which he found enthralling;
b) to talk to his mother and father about important personal things;
c) to deal with his fears about dirt; both the compulsive hand-washing and the head-banging ceased;
d) he is beginning to respond to his teacher and has done

some sums for him and is no longer hiding under the desk or table.

Dr. Levinson writes:

Maybe some day we shall advance so far in our under-standing of animals and their meaning to human beings that we shall be able to prescribe pets of a certain kind for different emotional disturbances. . . . A child who may shy away from human contact, who is frightened when you touch him and say endearing words because he senses the harshness and rejection beneath the sugary surface, may react well to animals, love them and relate to them. In fact, the animal may trigger in the disturbed, ego-centered child the first breakthrough of concern for something outside himself. . . . The need for definite re-search is indicated.

Sometimes the psychic flaw of a disturbed child stems from his parents' attitude to his pet. An investigation by an RSPCA inspector revealed that many low-income fam-ilies feed their pets at the expense of their children. One family with three small children, for instance, earning 15 pounds a week, spends 30 shillings a week on a large dog and her many puppies, which they do not have the heart to give away. It seems probable that the three children are not only physically but also emotionally undernourished.

A couple of years ago six thousand people signed a petition in an English town pleading for the life of a dangerous dog the Council wished to destroy. In the same year, in the same town, 250 cases of cruelty to children were brought before the court.

A woman in the United States has two sons, one, aged twenty, from her first marriage, and a little boy of two by her present husband. The older boy left home when he was sixteen and has not been heard from since. The little boy is entrusted to a nurse, the mother never picks him up, never kisses him: "He makes her nervous." At the same time she walks around all day with a Chihuahua in her arms that she fondles, kisses on the nose, and takes with her to bed at night.

It is not difficult to foresee that all these children will grow up with psychological problems. Nor would it be surprising if it turned out that the case of vandalism that took place recently in Nottingham had been committed by children of animal-loving parents. What other explanation could there be for the actions of the two lads who broke into a pet shop on a week end, took the fish from the aquariums, and slit them in two with their penknives, wrung the necks of the birds or placed the cages on the floor and flattened them with the bird inside, punched a hole in every tin of pet food, slit open every bag holding dog biscuits, broke the shelves, tore up the books—then defecated in the middle of the floor?

An investigation by the *Sunday Mirror** showed that in England it is often better to be a sick dog than a sick child. Having to pay for the National Health Service, parents will take their children to the general practitioner, even those who could afford a doctor in private practice. If the GP decides that the child needs a thorough checkup, an operation, or hospitalization, appointments have to be made, sometimes weeks in advance. But if you take your pet to any of the free animal hospitals, the Blue Cross or the People's Dispensary for Sick Animals, it will get immediate treatment, impeccable care, and if need be, the most complicated operations in modern, well-equipped operating rooms that would do any human hospital proud. No pain-killing drug or anesthetic available to humans is denied the pets, and there is never a shortage of nursing staff.

But the penalty for being human can be still worse. The following article appeared in the February 1, 1968, issue of the *Daily Telegraph.*

A cat that was X-rayed at a Liverpool children's hospital has caused a mother to complain to the hospital authorities.

Mrs. Enid Parker, 24, of Sunbeam Road, Liverpool complained that she took her son Alan, eight months, to the

*London, June, 1966.

Alder Hey hospital for an X-ray examination and was astonished when a kitten was given priority.

She said last night that she had been waiting for about half an hour at the X-ray department to be seen.

"Two men, who I gather were house doctors, came in carrying a box containing a kitten. They talked with the two women radiographers, and the cat was placed on the table and X-rayed while we waited.

"Then a boy of about 18 months was brought from a ward and X-rayed naked on the same table. I was disgusted. I did not see the table being cleaned or disinfected after the kitten was X-rayed.

"After waiting 15 minutes more my son was stripped to the waist and X-rayed on the same table. One reads of unexplained infectious diseases at hospitals and I do not think it right that cats should be X-rayed in the same places as children. There is, after all, an RSPCA clinic!"

Everyone in England has a *right* to free medical care for himself, but free medical care for pets is, in principle, a service maintained not by the state but by private donations for those who cannot pay veterinary fees. As a result, a great many people who would not even think of going to a private physician gladly pay the fees of a veterinarian in private practice. Nothing could demonstrate the importance of veterinarians today more strikingly than the fact that a man specializing in pets can, after five years of college, immediately obtain a job at £1500 a year plus free accommodation and car, while a medical doctor must, after five years at medical school, spend another year in a hospital at £770-850 a year minus deductions for room and board. But if the medical doctor wishes to buy a practice afterwards, he may not have to pay £8000 for one in the provinces, or £18,000 in London's West End, like the veterinary surgeon.

In America, where they do not believe in "socialized medicine," the disparity between child and animal care is even more appalling. A study carried out by the American Humane Association in 1966 showed that a vast majority of the large

urban communities had no child protective service what-
soever. It showed that a total of twelve states had no responsibility for protecting children in any manner. In some of the
other states, despite the programs that were said to exist,
no service of any kind was performed for the children they
were designed to help. Nor does Medicaid, the much advertised free federal medical service, apply to children. Anyone who has ever lived in the United States knows that "illness means bankruptcy." For those who are already bankrupt, the 34 million American poor, illness means lifelong
disability or death. While America spends approximately
one dollar on its War on Poverty for every *forty dollars* it
spends on the Vietnam War, millions of children, white and
black, die of malnutrition and lack of medical care.

There, too, it is better to be a sick dog than a sick child.
Six hundred and fifty animal welfare organizations, that
do not need Congress to allocate funds for their War on Animal
Poverty but maintain themselves from dog licenses, donations, legacies, and membership fees, watch that animals
should not be reduced to having to live like people. The motto
of the ASPCA (New York) is: "No animal in need of care
is ever turned away." And indeed, its hospital and clinic,
employing fourteen veterinary surgeons, X-ray technicians,
laboratory technicians, and nurses, gives skilled and sympa-
thetic care to 32,000 to 35,000 sick or injured animals a year.
Those suffering from minor ailments are examined in the out-
patient clinic and sent home with a prescribed medicine from a
well-stocked drug room. Others with more serious ailments
are hospitalized, some for surgery in modern, fully equipped
operating rooms, others for extensive diagnostic tests in
the pathological laboratory, and still others for prolonged
treatment under a veterinarian's watchful eye. The therapy
unit administers extra oxygen to patients suffering from
cardiac condition, heart failure, heat prostration, and lung
disorders. Modern dental methods using ultrasonic vibrations remove dental tartar and debris quickly and with
minimum shock to the animal. A beta-ray applicator helps
prevent blindness by bombarding eye growth and inflam-
mations with radiation. Sixty-five ambulances and other

cars drive 700,000 miles a year to pick up injured animals or give treatment on the spot. No effort, no expense, no skill, is spared when it comes to restoring an animal to health, entirely free of charge if the owner is poor.

And if the owner is not poor, he can take his pet to a veterinarian in private practice and pay astronomical fees for a five-minute examination and medicines. He can call himself lucky if he gets away with a bill of three hundred dollars for having his dog's broken leg X-rayed and set in a private animal hospital. He will pay fifty dollars to have his cat spayed, and twelve dollars for the yearly shot his dog has to have.

Children not brought up by their parents—2.5 million in the United States and some 75,000 in England—bear a burden heavier than those living in the family. In their book *Children in Homes*, Kenneth Brill and Ruth Thomas write:

> Keeping pets has been recognized by Heads of Children's Homes for many years as one of the ways of compensating children a little for some things which they have lost when they had to leave their own families. Pets are an additional type of possession and one which calls out the protective qualities of a child. . . . Different people have different ways of trying to make up for feelings of loneliness. A pet (unless it is a dog) is not necessarily company, but at least it is something of your own. What the lonely child misses is someone who specially belongs to him to give comfort and care. It is a generally hopeful sign if a lonely child, instead of getting depressed or aggressive, gives a pet the mothering he wants for himself; and many a child who, in his isolation, has turned to excessive masturbation has been helped by being given an animal which it can tend and play with. Large animals of strength and agility fill the child's mind because they seem so powerful, whereas he himself feels small and weak in a shifting world of unreliable parent figures.

The fact that we still bring children into this world proves that somewhere deep within us, shut off from the everyday reality of "pseudo-events, to which we adjust with a false consciousness adapted to see these events as true and real and even beautiful . . . ," as Professor Laing expresses it, we have preserved a glimmer of hope, an instinctive realization that there must be more to existence than what we are able to encompass, a higher stage of human evolution that will be attained, perhaps, by the next generation. What compels us, as individuals and societies, to suppress that glimmer of hope, obscure that instinctive realization, and proceed with insane deliberation to destroy the children we bear and, with them, the future?

In the United States of America 3 per cent of the population is subnormal or severely handicapped mentally. In Great Britain one in every one hundred children is educationally subnormal and one in every four hundred severely mentally handicapped. The situation is equally distressing in all Western European countries. In France the allowance granted large families to encourage the production of soldiers for the "Gloire" inspires the lowest strata of society—alcoholics, tuberculars, syphilitics, the subnormal, and the just plain shiftless—to breed like rabbits. This, combined with the outlawing not only of abortion but also of prevention, results in an increase in the numbers of mentally, and often physically, handicapped children. In Germany, where the principle of the three Ks, Kinder, Küche, Kirche (children, kitchen, church), still applies in many circles, women bear armies of children, many of them deficient. In Italy and Spain, where the only thing the have-nots have is children, owing not only to the efforts of the Catholic Church to prevent prevention but also to what a poor Spanish peasant woman once expressed as "copulation is the poor man's cinema," the incredible poverty of a large section of the population often results in mental retardation among the children.

Although a great deal is known today about the causes of mental deficiency, there is no way in a democracy—or in a totalitarian Catholic country—to prevent people who will produce subnormal children from having them. On the contrary, by treating abortion as a crime and not making premarital medical examinations obligatory, the churches and governments conspire to maintain a certain quota of mentally and physically disabled citizens. The majority of these are then dropped into the laps of charitable organizations and, with a clear conscience, ignored. "The toll of retardation could be reduced by fully one half if all we know today could be applied successfully everywhere," says Stafford Warren, M.D., assistant to President Johnson in the field of mental retardation. *Why don't we, then?* Because governments everywhere are engaged in infinitely more important projects, such as the development of weapons of mass-extermination, and there are never sufficient funds available to conduct experiments, train enough specialized staff, and establish truly modern schools and institutions.

The use of pet animals in the education of the mentally handicapped, however, requires neither additional funds nor special training. All it requires is patience, devotion, and the courage to do some original thinking.

In the not too distant past, mongoloid children used to die young, usually before the age of fifteen. Today, thanks to the achievements of medical science, they often live to a ripe old age, facing the parents, who often love their problem children more deeply than the others that can fend for themselves, with the painful alternative of giving up their entire lives to their mongoloid child or placing him in an institution.

After having had a gifted and beautiful daughter in her first marriage, a mother gave birth to a mongoloid boy in her second. For the last twenty-five years both she and her husband have arranged their lives in such a way that one of them would always be with the boy. She taught Jean-Luc to read and write and, by singing to him since infancy, has instilled in him a love of music that is still his greatest joy. He never went to school, was never exposed to the cruelty of children, and because he is charming and well mannered and the neighbors and shopkeepers are kind to him, he believes the world is filled with people who can give and accept love.

He is a happy child—he believes he is only fifteen—except for one thing: He has no friends of his own age. When his parents discovered that when alone he was carrying on endless conversations with an imaginary *copain*, they gave him a dog as a companion. Now Jean-Luc has a real *copain* for whom he is responsible and with whom he can discuss his problems. When his mother scolds him and he walks out in a huff, he comes back a few minutes later to tell her that he has consulted his dog, been told his mother is right, and will she forgive him.

But Jean-Luc's parents are no longer young. They have no money to leave him, no close relatives who will look after him when they are gone. What will become of Jean-Luc? Will he, penniless orphan, be placed in a mental institution where, treated as an imbecile, deprived of the love he has been used to, and separated from his dog, he will turn into a human wreck worse than an animal?

Animal lovers, even those who cannot leave a fortune to their pets as so many do, are spared the worry of what will become of their darlings when they are gone. There are pension schemes for animals, various kinds of insurance, charities like the Rest Home for Horses and the Rest Home for Donkeys, and a large number of charitable foundations that take in the orphaned animals and keep them happy and well cared for until they die of old age.

There are a few scattered attempts made by governments and individuals to save the mentally handicapped from the lethal atmosphere of mental institutions and create for them an environment in which they can make use of their limited capabilities and lead a useful and not too unhappy life. But what a small fraction of their number is so privileged!

It has been determined in the United States as well as in Great Britain and the European countries that the use of pets, and animals in general, can show unexpected, but all the more encouraging, results in the education and training of the handicapped. In an American school for retardates, for example, the children named a club they formed after a friendly mongrel and made him its president. The children, many of whom are withdrawn and unwilling to talk to strangers, stroke and hug the dog and whisper their secrets in his ear. They hold parties in his honor, and their teachers find that afterwards the children are able to write down some of the highlights. "Experts in mental health advise the parents of retardates to buy their children pets, and in many cases this has led to remarkable changes in the child. For the first time someone needs, really needs him. The pet becomes dependent on him for love, food, care. This elicits a sense of achievement, a feeling of success in the child. Often his whole outlook brightens and he develops a mental flexibility that prevents him from shutting out a world that seemed to offer no real purpose for his existence."*

A somewhat similar experience was described in *The Times Educational Supplement:*†

The first time I saw the animals: a pony, a donkey, goats, geese, and others, at a residential school I occasionally visit, I made a mental note to take the reception class of seven to nine-year old backward children to see and touch these animals. . . . It is often only by touching things that our children make them into reality. . . .

The children were able to get quite close to them and in their various individual ways to explore and investigate them. Of course, most stroked and patted, one or two timorously advanced a tentative finger. Only firm restraint prevented some more adventurous boys from climbing all over them. . . .

The teacher who came with us wanted full value from the morning. On their return she immediately pinned up a long roll of lining paper, some 20 ft of it, on the corridor wall and set the children to painting. Within half an hour they had filled the paper and were seeking more space. . . . Next morning the creative spirit stirred by the visit was still there, so the teacher proposed cutting

*Stan Gore, *Pet Shop Management*, Mar., 1965.
†London, Sept. 16, 1966.

out in coloured cloth and making an applique. The children went at it with continued drive which kept them going for about three days. . . . When I handed the teacher the photographs I had taken of the visit and of the paintings and sewing, she revived the subject and the children produced a considerable volume of more drawings and written work. . . .

We have frequently had such creative outbursts after visits to unusual places, but I do not recollect such a sustained drive as this.

One American experiment in the training and employment of subnormal youths is so successful that it could be tried out elsewhere as well. Two teachers of mentally retarded children in Chicago, Mrs. Corinne Owen and Robert Terese, felt that the trouble with most programs for retardates was that they were all lumped together on the lowest level of ability. Therefore, with the financial help of a score of parents and the support of the pet trade, they opened the Lambs Pet Shop staffed by mentally handicapped youths. As interest grew in the project and mental health experts joined the board of directors, the Lambs succeeded so well that the staff could be entrusted with increasingly complicated tasks.

The founders watched the pattern of the retardates. Some proved hopeless, but others showed tremendous growth potential. Studies made by Mrs. Delilah White, executive director and chief psychologist of the Dr. Julian Levinson Research Foundation, revealed important changes in retardates who worked in the Lambs Pet Shop.

The young people in the Lambs range from IQ 45 to 85. Opportunities are offered to all of them, commensurate with their abilities. I have made psychological tests of all of these young people when they first started, and recently I re-examined them to find that practically all have shown a rise in IQ. . . . The Lambs is a unique venture. . . . I think it would be wise for the pet industry to support this pilot project to determine if retarded people can function in this field. So far I am very excited about the results we have observed.

The next step in the project planned by the founders—and already partially achieved—is the Lambs Ranch, a large pet center with 150 to 200 retardates working and living there. The center will include a pet shop with grooming facilities, an exhibition area, an aviary, aquarium, cattery, kennel, and classes on the selection and training of family pets.

Physically handicapped children are, in some ways, worse off than the mentally handicapped because they are fully aware of their infirmity and cannot help but compare themselves with the more fortunate children around them. Modern science, the combination of medicine, technology, and psychiatry, has done a great deal toward improving the condition of these children and, where they cannot be cured, to help them live with their disability and still find joy in life. Here again, pet animals can have a decisive influence on the improvement of a child's condition or, where that is impossible, on his acceptance of it.

An account was published in the British press of a thirteen-year-old polio victim who had lost all interest in life until his parents bought him a dog. From then on, in order to be able to play with his dog and take it out, he was more than willing to make the required sustained effort without which he might never have been able to leave his wheelchair.

In an article on Larchmoor School in England, run by the National Institute for the Deaf, Paula James writes: "These sadly handicapped souls take their first faltering step when their headphones pick up the cheerful chirping of the school's pet budgerigar, Joey. He is their passport to the world they have never known: the world of sound."

An American physiotherapist working with spastic children has also had very favorable experience with pet animals. She writes:

Spastic children can be taught to use and control their limbs sometimes to a surprising extent. This, however, involves a tiresome routine and an effort children are not always willing or able to make. One family bought an aquarium and the spastic child was given the task of feeding the fish. Within a few weeks the little girl, who was fascinated by the fish, had mastered the movements necessary to open the package of fishfood, take out the required amount, and drop it in the aquarium. A little boy who consistently refused to use his legs because he often fell and hurt himself, achieved wonders when his father bought him a puppy. He forgot his fears and followed around the little dog from room to room, stumbling, falling, creeping and, sometimes, walking. In addition to the progress made, both patients achieved a degree of independence, stopped demanding constant proof of love from their parents, and found assurance, pride and happiness in looking after their pets. Also, the pets helped them greatly in communicating with their healthy brothers and sisters because they now had a subject of conversation equally interesting to all.

It is easy to understand that in the often overcrowded and understaffed schools and institutions for the mentally or physically handicapped the keeping of various pets should present an apparently insurmountable problem. Looking after the animals would mean additional work, and many of the mentally handicapped would have to be watched when playing with the animals lest, giving way to a destructive impulse, they should harm them. Still, I believe the results would be well worth it. A handicapped child has so few moments of happiness. The presence of an animal, even if it cannot be touched, like a bird or a fish, could make up for so much he misses.

In the children's ward of every hospital the matron is God. The responsibilities of the matrons are tremendous, and in many cases, out of sheer self-defense, they deliberately stunt their sensibilities. The large majority of these matron-Gods ban pets from the children's wards, using hygiene as an excuse or an unwillingness to burden the nurses with additional work. Yet wherever it has been tried out, doctors, matrons, and nurses alike have had to concede that far from making their tasks more difficult, the presence of pets relieved the strain. Sick children cannot be expected to keep themselves occupied or to keep quiet when their condition demands it. Even healthy children get bored with toys and picture books and, when bored, will go to any lengths to attract the attention of adults. But things that move can be watched endlessly, and as imagination weaves fantasies around them, the children are taken out of themselves and forget their pain or discomfort.

Many parents believe that every children's ward should have two or three large aquariums on wheels and a few cages with singing or talking birds suspended on wall brackets. With very little effort the bleak hospital with its restless, unhappy little inmates could be transformed into a fairy-tale world of happy children and, for once, unharassed nurses. It is astonishing that although pets are widely used in all animal-loving countries both educationally and therapeutically, this should be done only on an *ad hoc* basis. The effects are not systematically observed, and the results remain unpublished. But if experiences were recorded, they might inspire a scientific investigation that would yield results beneficial to both those in charge and their charges.

In his book *The Nonhuman Environment*, Dr. Harold F. Searles writes:

I believe that one of the major phenomena of adolescence, . . . one of the greatest achievements of this phase of human living, is the maturing person's becoming committed to his status as a human being. Not only does the boy become a man, and the girl become a woman, but each becomes more deeply *human*, and aware and accepting his or her human status vis-à-vis the nonhuman environment, than had been true before. In this transitional period he turns his greatest interest from the world of Nature, and of other nonhuman things, to the world of his fellow human beings.

Going through a transitional phase, adolescents are particularly sensitive people. An intelligent parent, an inspired teacher, an enthusiastic champion of a "cause," can easily channel their lively imaginations and still confused emotional drives toward something truly believed. Adolescence gives society the last chance to make or break a person, to offer him a place within the boundaries of the "nation" or push him out on the fringes among the "expendables."

The adolescent mind is essentially a mind of the *moratorium*, a psychosocial stage between childhood and adulthood, and between the morality learned by the child and the ethics to be developed by the adult. It is an ideological mind — and indeed it is the ideological outlook of a society that speaks more clearly to the adolescent who is eager to be affirmed by his peers and is eager to be confirmed by rituals, creeds, and programs which at the same time define what is evil, uncanny and inimical.*

Adults, on the whole, are well aware of this malleability and use it in the way they think best — best for the adolescent or best for themselves.

Armed with a slogan they themselves know is false, that kindness to animals leads automatically to kindness to man, the innumerable animal welfare organizations in the West go all out to recruit the young into various societies, clubs, and groups of "animal defenders." The first Bands of Mercy — groups of children and adolescents — were formed in Victorian England by members of the aristocracy in whom hunting had developed a tender love of animals. The movement rapidly spread to the Dominions and to America. The Industrial Revolution in England and the conquest of the continent of America gave rise to a split moral code, a double consciousness that, while reacting violently to cruelty to animals,

*Erik H. Eirkson: *Childhood and Society*, W.W. Norton & Company, Inc., New York, 1964.

ignored, or rationalized, cruelty to human beings. In the eyes of the ruling classes the slave trade, child labor, the extermination of the American Indians, the misery of the lower classes, the bloodshed of colonization, were "historical necessities." However, since Christianity has deliberately fostered a sense of guilt in those under its influence, people quieted their bad consciences by displacing compassion from man to animal and thus salvaged their virtue and self-esteem.

The tremendous social changes of the last one hundred years, two world wars, and the vertiginous progress of science have speeded up the process of alienation. Having lost the anchor of religion and simultaneously, but not because of it, his identity, man has no respect for the "human-ness" in himself or in others and has become more coldly and purposefully cruel than before. Today, his overwhelming preoccupation with animals is no longer a symptom of displaced guilt but a desperate attempt to preserve at least some food for his "soul" in a materialistic world that rejects love and drives those it cannot cure of it into lunatic asylums.

Animal welfare is the only remaining domain where love and compassion are not controversial issues, and its popularity with the "nation" increases with the increase of the number of problems from which it is essential to divert public attention. The earlier this diversion of emphasis occurs in youth, the better.

In 1965-66, the RSPCA enrolled 6000 children in the headquarters group and formed ninety-six groups in the branch areas. Forty-eight hundred and sixty-four talks were given by the society in schools, youth clubs, and similar organizations. Four hundred and twenty schools participated in the annual essay competition, submitting 52,000 essays on animal subjects. *The Animal World* magazine for young people has a circulation of 52,000 per month. Some 2000 films were sent out by headquarters, branches, and auxiliaries to schools, youth clubs, and the like, resulting in 4200 showings.

The American Humane Association provided, in 1966, material for 1.7 million children, about 4 per cent of all children through secondary school level. Its animal program was shown on thirty-two television stations, and thousands of youngsters were recruited into various Junior Humane Groups. About 10,000 children a month learn about animals on visits to the ASPCA, or from ASPCA teachers on field trips, in schools, and community groups.

In 1966 the American Humane Association printed 1.5 million publications. Its series on the care of pets attained a distribution figure of 6 million. Seventy thousand pieces were printed for the Be Kind to Animals Week; publications for humane slaughter totaled 20,000. Mailing and correspondence increased by 1968 by 225 per cent. Publicity in magazines and newspapers climbed up to almost 250 million words, and 700 radio and television stations used AHA material. About its work for children the association's annual report for 1967 says the following: "The Children's Division marked another year of progress, too. We published four new technical manuals, participated in numerous meetings in all parts of the country and provided consultation services to humane societies, to juvenile courts and to other agencies."

Throughout Europe and America, children's programs on radio and television acquaint youngsters with the world of animals and teach them how to be decent human beings — in relation to their "lesser brothers." The press omits no gory detail when describing cases of cruelty to animals, and usually the articles are illustrated with nauseating pictures of the victims.

These campaigns are highly commendable and, on the whole, probably successful. Yet their main achievement lies in preventing adolescents from turning their "greatest interest from the world of Nature, and of other nonhuman things, to the world of [their] fellow human beings," from developing their potential qualities in the interest of mankind, from taking the more difficult road, that of accepting responsibility for their fellow men.

The beautiful and healthy romanticism and adventurousness of adolescents that, as we see from movements like the Peace Corps, the Voluntary Service Overseas, the Task Force, still exist and can be encouraged or discouraged, will often squander itself in *negative* romanticism and adventurousness, like membership in a delinquent gang or collective drug taking, only because it is not made aware and channeled toward a worthwhile "cause." Even the dreams of heroism and self-sacrifice inspired by the reading of literature and history in school are diverted from their proper course when, by moving examples and the promise of medals and awards, adolescents are encouraged to risk their lives for the sake of animals.

Headlines like "Boy, 16, Drowns Saving Dog" (which, naturally swam ashore), or "Boy, 15, Gets 11,000-Volt Shock Saving Squirrel," or the tear-jerking description of a twelve-year-old boy who ran into a burning house to save a cat, or of two boys of thirteen who jumped into a fast-running river to save a duckling, may appear rewarding to the publicity departments of the animal welfare organizations but should elicit loud protests from the public. If they do not, we have one more link in the chain of evidence showing that respect for animal life grows in inverse ratio to respect for human life.

While tremendous efforts are made and huge sums collected and spent to instill in the young the love of animals, little is being done on a similar scale to teach them to love their fellow men regardless of race, color, creed, social class, age, or nationality. Nor can anything be done on these lines as long as the glue holding human communities together—the family, the ethnic group, the class, the gang, the political party, the various armed services, the nation—is a mixture of fear and hatred, an aggressive sense of inferiority and a false sense of superiority, a combination directed against every other human community. Were this glue removed by some miracle, the entire structure of modern society would crumble. Therefore, to preserve at least some appearance of undiscriminating humanity, we substitute in the education of the young the harmless love of animals for the subversive love of human beings.

CHAPTER 3
PETS AND THE "EXPENDABLES"

Der Mensch is gut; gar nicht so roh,
Doch die Verhältuisse die sied reicht so!
—BERTOLT BRECHT:
Die Dreigroschenoper

⊙ ⊙ THE HUNGARIAN HUMORIST FRIGYES KARIN-
THY, who would have achieved world fame had he not written in a language read by little more than ten million people,
once said, when asked to define in one sentence the greatest

imaginable human misery: "To be a poor, old, sick, thiev-
ing, ugly, stupid, Jewish, Negro woman." Although he said
it during the Great Depression, the definition is still valid
in our affluent societies.

Writes Dr. Searles: There is a great proclivity on the
part of human beings, even adult human beings, for the
development of prejudicial attitudes towards groups of
other human beings, prejudicial attitudes which include
the conviction that these groups of their fellow men are
really subhuman, really more animal than human. Such
prejudicial attitudes, to which I believe we are all in some
degree drawn, betray our own unconscious lack of sure-
ness that we ourselves are fully and unmistakably human.
We all have some tendency, great or small, to project
onto fellow men who are members of other racial or religious groups, or who are hospitalized with psychiatric
illness, or who in some other respect can be looked upon
as alien to ourselves, the less-than-human creature which
we unconsciously believe to reside in us.

The same applies to the abstraction called "nation," a
collective term describing those to whom its priests — the
governments—appeal at times of domestic or international
emergency. The "nation" does not deny that the poor, the
old, the mentally or physically disabled, minorities such
as Negroes, Gypsies, or Jews, and its offenders are *in* society.
It denies only that they are *of* society. Depersonalized and
kept within invisible barriers that only the "nation's" court
jesters—psychologists, sociologists, and the illustrious members of the social conscience club—are allowed to penetrate
if, to prevent contamination, they wear the protective clothing
issued to researchers and charities, the poor, the old, the
mentally or physically disabled, the minorities and offenders
form a single less-than-human community. Despite the spora-
dic efforts of the well-intentioned visitors, this community
is so prolific that it is becoming an increasingly severe threat

to the "nation's" delusion of grandeur. Sooner or later it
will have to turn its inward eyes outward and face it.

To the *Homo neuroticus*, in whom fear of death and the
death wish are equally balanced, old age is odious because
it reminds him of the reality of death he is always trying
to unsubstantiate into an intellectual game. His revulsion,
and the guilt engendered by that revulsion, are reflected
in every facet of our Western attitude to the old. Governments, social organizations, charities, and medical science
deal with the "aged citizen" as if "the old" were a different
species whose longevity is a scientific and social achievement to be proud of but, at the same time, an economic and
emotional burden neither the individual nor society can
be expected to carry. One of the rules of being "civilized"
demands that the old be treated with charitable consideration, but nowhere is it pointed out that they have, at the
very least, the same *right* to food, proper care, and affection
that we so generously grant the animals living among us.

Nothing could illustrate this discrepancy better than the
letter published in the November 19, 1967, issue of the *Sunday Express* in London:

My mother, my small corgi dog and myself went by
train to spend a day at Rye. During the morning my mother
spotted a pretty kitten sitting on a doorstep and she went
over to stroke it. The cat jumped at her and clawed her
hand very badly indeed.

She was bleeding profusely so I took her to the nearest
chemist shop. They told me they were too busy to do anything and sent us to the St. John Ambulance Station further
down the road.

Here we were met with kindness, but the officer on
duty was quite rightly reluctant to take the responsibility
as he said a scratch like this could have serious consequences
and that my mother required an immediate injection
against tetanus. He recommended us to go to a surgery

at the bottom of the road, saying there were about four doctors there and one of them was sure to be on duty. There, we were told that the doctors had a very busy morning and could do nothing else for anyone. We were directed to the Rye General Hospital — quite a bus ride out of the town.

We proceeded to the hospital. Again they were exceedingly kind but told us (at this I was open-mouthed!) that they did not give tetanus injections at their hospital and mother would have to go to Hastings! My mother by then had given up and just could not be bothered to do anything further.

My sister at Rye dressed the wound extremely well and we started to walk back to town. On our way back a Staffordshire bull terrier, without warning, sprang on our small corgi and bit a hole through his ear. We were told where the nearest veterinary surgeon was to be found.

Within 10 minutes my dog was receiving attention, an injection plus dressing of the wound.

The one thing that scared me about all this was that my mother could have died — and this is a fact, had she been infected by the scratch. But no risk was taken with my dog!

In Great Britain today 1.3 million people above the age of sixty-five live alone, 300,000 of them in abject poverty. Another 1.6 million are lonely, though not alone, and some 400,000 are residents in institutions — residential homes, psychiatric and other hospitals, nursing homes, etc.*

It follows that the overwhelming majority of the "old" can also claim membership in the less than human community by being poor, and a large percentage by being physically or mentally sick. The Psychiatric Rehabilitation Association, having done research in six British cities, revealed that in the poor areas of the cities the percentage of mental illness is three times the national average.

*Jeremy Tunstall: *Old and Alone*, Humanities Press, New York, 1966.

By 1975, 10 per cent of the American population will be over sixty-five. Already today, 50 per cent of the elderly, some 8 million men and women, exist below minimum standards of decency. Since mental illness is not only more frequent but also more severe among the poor in the United States as well, and many of the poor there are Negro, the species "old" often has a quadruple claim to membership in the less-than-human community.*

It is strange but nonetheless true that man, abandoned by his fellow men, should often seek and obtain help from the animals. Thus today the spreading custom of pet keeping helps a large number of lonely men and women to retain their identities as members of the human race in the face of the "nation's" efforts to deprive them of identity.

To the old a pet animal is not merely the last, paper-thin wall separating them from the self-rejection they fall victim to when they no longer have the strength to withstand the powerful pressure of social rejection. To an old person a pet animal means much more. The dog, cat, or budgerigar is an old person's accomplice with whom he shares the guilty secret that he is not *really* old within his wasted frame.

With their children, with the authorities, the social worker, doctor, nurse, priest or minister, old people are cautious enough to play the role cast for them. Only when alone with their pet animals do they relax and allow themselves to be what they really are—rebellious victims of a physiological process that can perhaps be slowed down but not halted. This physiological process succeeds where Christianity has failed for almost two thousand years; it succeeds in separating the product of the "original sin," the slowly disintegrating body, from the ageless and therefore unaging spirit.

A pet does not know the difference between old and not old. To an animal the person who provides food, care, and affection is never a burden, never a problem, never an unperson whose only duty to the rest of humanity is to die as quickly and as unobtrusively as possible. A pet never

*Michael Harrington: *The Other America*, The Macmillan Co., New York, 1962.

shames an old person into concealing the bodily needs he has been taught, since infancy, to conceal. It does not frown upon the flickering sexual urge that compels old men to follow mini-skirted girls, or upon the old woman whose womb, warmed by the cat in her lap, recalls the man who entered, the children who left her body. The pet shares the old person's greed for food, warmth, and companionship. It does not openly display boredom or impatience when having to listen to reminiscences often told, or to the lessons learned from a long, alienated life. The pet fulfills an old person's need for the unequivocal, for the natural and simple, for the unsophisticated joys he has denied himself in adulthood when, in order to "fit in," he had to repudiate the child, the adolescent, the youth, he once was.

The pet animal, dog, cat, bird, or fish reassures an old person because it has remained the same dog, cat, bird, or fish he remembers from his childhood; it has not "progressed," it has not, in any way, been transformed by the achievements of the technical civilization that make the old feel as lost, as uncomprehending, and as frightened as a creature from outer space dropped onto our planet would feel.

The only people with whom the old have a real rapport are the world's natural existentialists, small children whose umbilical cords have not yet been fully cut and who, therefore, neither fear nor desire nonexistence. But a child's very inability to perceive his elderly friend's dominant preoccupation—the *when* and *how* of death—and his demand for the attention an old person wrestling with the ultimate problem cannot give, make that child a less desirable companion than an animal.

A fairly characteristic example of an old man-animal relationship is the case of Mr. S., although its details may be more extravagant than many. At the age of sixty, Mr. S. lost his wife after thirty-five years of a marriage that was just beginning to calm down into contentment after the innumerable crises caused by his infidelities. A year later Mr. S. started an affair with a widow ten years younger than himself but would not marry her. At sixty-five he retired

with a decent pension but continued to earn as a part-time
accountant. He kept his apartment spotless, read, listened
to music, watched television, and as a hobby, took up cooking. He often invited his daughter and her family for ela-
borate meals, enjoyed giving presents, and was a happy
man loved and respected by his mistress and his family.

At the age of seventy he suffered two terrible blows: his
mistress died of cancer and his eyesight began to fail rapidly.
Since he could no longer read or watch television, he adopted
a mongrel bitch from the ASPCA for company. He treated
Lila, the dog, with the same consideration and affection
he had shown his wife and mistress. Lila slept on the other
side of the double bed and ate her meals at the table, sitting on a chair opposite Mr. S. The daughter laughed at her
father's "new girl friend," and her children adored Lila.

Soon, however, Mr. S.'s eyesight deteriorated to such
an extent that he could no longer fend for himself, and his
pension would not cover the cost of hired help. His daughter insisted that he move in with her, offering him a room
and bathroom of his own. He accepted with great reluctance,
on the condition that Lila could come with him.

It did not take long before the daughter's attitude to her
father began to change. She regarded him as an old man
and bossed him as she bossed her children. Unconsciously
but systematically she began to destroy her father's individ-
uality. She did not allow him in the kitchen, though cooking was still his favorite hobby. She did not let him stay
up late and listen to music, although he had always been
a bad sleeper and was used to staying up until after mid-
night. She prevented the children from spending much time
with him because she did not want him to "infect" them with
his unorthodox views and his "immoral" interest in women.
When he joined in the conversation at table, she fidgeted
and betrayed such anxiety that even Mr. S., who was now almost blind, could not fail to notice. He took to eating in his
room with Lila, but even that was not as it had been because
his daughter would not allow the dog to sit on a chair. She
stopped his walks with Lila and the children after the children

told her one day how they had watched Lila being mounted by a dog, a sight they had found both exciting and hilarious. When Lila showed signs of pregnancy, she declared that the dog would have to be given away or destroyed.

By then Mr. S., now seventy-five, had become an emaciated old man whose hands shook and who hardly opened his mouth. He began dropping things, spilling food on himself, sitting around all day alone in dressing gown and slippers and usually unshaved, speaking in whispers to Lila. When someone entered his room — without knocking, of course — he looked so guilty that his daughter made a habit of coming in unexpectedly to catch him at whatever he was doing. She succeeded. One day she caught him masturbating, with Lila sitting at his feet and watching with interest.

Trembling with rage, she called him a "filthy old man," accused him of having sexual relations with the dog, and unable to stop herself, let loose the avalanche of resentment stored up since her childhood, when, as her mother's confidante, she had learned every detail of her father's affairs. Two hours later, in spite of his desperate entreaties, she took Lila to the ASPCA to be destroyed.

When she returned, nervous and with a bad conscience, she found her father bathed, shaved, and fully dressed, his face alive and smiling. He told her he was going for a walk, and she was glad because, as she said, after months of vegetating he was at last behaving like a normal human being.

Mr. S. did not go very far. He took the elevator up to the twentieth floor and without hesitation stepped outside through the window in the corridor.

Old people living in municipal flats are usually not allowed to keep dogs or cats, but they may be permitted a budgerigar or an aquarium. Although not nearly as satisfying a companion as a dog or cat, a talking bird creates at least the illusion of intelligence. Even the most lonely old people living alone do not feel their exclusion from society entirely if they can at least pretend that being alone is of their own choosing. As long as they can look after themselves and whatever pet they are allowed to keep, they do not realize that a verdict has been pronounced on them and that, punished for being the victims of time, they have been deprived of their humanity the way a politically unreliable person in the United States is deprived of his passport.

The sadistic severity of the punishment for intruding on the consciousness of the not-old—understandable only in the context of human alienation — does not hit them until, unable to fend for themselves any longer, the "old" are incarcerated in homes, hospitals, or mental asylums. The process of dehumanization begins when they have to give up the last thing that, by depending on them, made them feel independent—their pet. Some, like the retired army officer of seventy-four who gassed himself *and* his dog, prefer physical death to the living death of the humane, charitable institutions.

It is a curious fact that the people fighting that the poor and the old be allowed to keep their pet animals in municipal flats as well as in institutions are not the social organizations dealing with those categories but the *animal welfare* organizations. Yet the Samaritans, the Church Army, and the Salvation Army know of a large number of cases in which those to whom they represent the last refuge would commit suicide if they were not worried about the fate of a pet animal, their last link with life.

If the German philosopher Von Humboldt judged the ethical maturity of a nation by its treatment of animals, we are today justified in judging the degree of alienation of a people by its treatment of the aged. Glancing over the map of Europe from east to west and from south to north, we are presented with a strange and surprising geography of alienation reflected in two characteristic symptoms, the treatment of the old and the attitude toward animals.

In the Catholic and Greek Orthodox countries—the Soviet Union and her satellites at the eastern end, and the Mediterranean countries in the south, where religion is a living force, agriculture outweighs industry, and the living standard is accordingly low—the old, even if they do not hold the purse strings, live out their lives as full members of the family, the neighborhood, their class, and society. They may be respected or badly treated by their children, but they are not excluded from the human community and left with animals as their only companions.

In the center of the map we have a Catholic country, France, and a predominantly Protestant country, Germany, where religion is no longer equivalent with faith, where agriculture equals industry and the living standard is high. Here we witness a rapidly increasing separation of the species "old" from the rest of society, and parallel with it a conspicuous growth of the animal cult.

At the northern and western tips of the cross are two Protestant welfare states, Sweden and Great Britain, where religion has been replaced by a philosophy of Christian-humanist tolerance loudly proclaimed but rarely applied, where industry far outweighs agriculture and the standard of living is the highest in Europe. In these countries the old are nonpersons, statistical factors, a small figure in the national budget and the balance sheets of the charitable organizations while, at the same time, animals are anthropomorphized and raised to the rank of *consumers*, the golden calves of every industrial society.

Once swallowed up by the gates of institutions, the old are delivered defenseless into the hands of individuals who can make life hell, purgatory, or just a vale of tears for them. If animals of the most obscure Western zoo were treated as the aged are in some of these institutions, public indignation would shake the very foundations of the state. But then animals remind us, at most, of our distant past and not of our not so distant future, so they do not have to be excluded from our consciousness.

In America, where the scrap metal of national minorities has been melted down into the valuable alloy of "one nation" but the cultural heritage of the immigrants has not, as yet, been completely annihilated, every shade of European living is represented. This also manifests itself in the attitude to the four "expendable" categories—the old, the poor, the mentally and physically disabled, and the criminals. Still, the over-all picture is that of loneliness and rejection:

> One opinion study cited by the Senate Report documents the feeling that these problems of age and the aged should be taken care of by the Federal Government. Washington was listed first as the place with responsibility; state governments were second, employers third, and the family fourth. . . . At first glance this might seem to be callous indifference. And indeed, it does reflect an America obsessed by youth and frightened by age and death. The old, in such a land, are to be kept out of sight and mind.*

America, too, hides away its aged poor in nursing homes, county homes, hospitals, and mental asylums, where, in Christian charity, they are taught to look forward with yearning toward the inevitable, the liberating embrace of death. Dr. Searles writes:

> I have seen a number of instances in which a schizophrenic patient had evidently succeeded, for many years, in staving off the eventually overwhelming psychosis, chiefly through the maintenance of a relationship with a dog, a dog that provided the individual with the companionship, the love, and the assurance of being needed by the individual which were unobtainable from the available human beings. . . . One such patient revealed, upon the outbreak of his schizophrenic psychosis, a capacity for psychological insight which his family members had never suspected; one of the statements now made by this man who had been, they felt, entirely contented with what had been in actuality a life almost incredibly desolate as regards human relationships and rendered supportable mainly by a faithful cat, was: "People should love *people*, not *cats.*"

But cats, dogs, horses, and other animals, *not* people, are what people love throughout the Western world. While

*Ibid.

responsibility for the old and sick is shifted onto governments and charities, hundreds and hundreds of animal welfare organizations, supported by the same people who refuse to look after their aged family members, keep old and sick animals in a luxury few humans can afford. The Miss Macindoe, who died in November, 1967, presumably of cancer, and who left half of her £116,485 estate to the Royal Free Cancer Hospital, could have, had she loved *people*, found better use for the other half than a gift to the RSPCA "for the care and comfort of horses in their old age."

Saint Hubert's Giralda, a sanctuary and shelter for dogs and other creatures of the animal world, established by Mrs. Geraldine Rockefeller Dodge in the hills of Morris County, New Jersey, could serve, with few alterations, as a model old people's home. "In addition to its concept of alleviating the suffering of animals, in caring for the unwanted and abandoned, it has a second phase of endeavor. That is, education of the public, particularly young people, in an appreciation of animals and their care . . ."

The reception area of this beautiful shelter opens into a main hall of which are the private offices, clerks' rooms, radio dispatch room, dispensary and examination room, and kitchen. All the interior walls of the kennel area are a marble aggregate-faced cinder block of a bright and cheerful tan color, the offices and other rooms have walls of ceramic tile. Dim, dark corners have no chance with flourescent lighting overhead and wide windows at ceiling height. Each kennel has a pulley-operated door to an individual outside yard, and thermostatically controlled fans turn off and on automatically to keep an even temperature. Comfortable resting and sleeping places are provided for the animals and plenty of space for indoor exercise in bad weather. Three ambulances patrol a ninety-square-mile radius, and some nine thousand calls per year come through the radio dispatch. The animals handled here range from dogs and cats to rabbits, ducks, chicks, raccoons, and monkeys.

Another even more luxurious establishment, the Small Animals Centre of the Animals Health Trust, looks after the dogs, cats, and birds of England. The Nuffield Foundation gave £40,000 for laboratories, the hospital appeal raised £31,500, Lord Nuffield made a personal donation of £10,000, an anonymous donor sent another £10,000, and the rest was raised by Lady Stainer and her ladies committee with the help of the Kennel Club and from donations. The first of its kind in the country, the center will be the best and the largest in the world.

Whether we realize it or not, beauty is as necessary to us as oxygen, and yet the overwhelming majority of human institutions, state and charitable, from orphanages to prisons and from maternity homes to geriatric wards, completely disregard this need and thereby reduce their inmates to spiritual starvation.

What Dr. Searles says here about schizophrenic patients is valid for every institutionalized and hospitalized person, young or old, healthy or sick, normal or mentally ill, innocent or criminal:

> Beauty is here of far more than merely aesthetic significance. I think it not too much to say that a schizophrenic patient who has gone through many months of living in a drab, and even ugly, disturbed ward of a hospital has suffered the additional trauma . . . that this drabness and ugliness has become an integral part of himself. . . . Contrariwise, whatever of beauty we can bring to him may be of great and lasting benefit to his personality.
>
> . . . for example, patients should be freely allowed to cherish non-human objects for 'sentimental' reasons, as a small child does, irrespective of the so-called practical value of these objects. They should have much greater access to animal pets and plants than is now generally the case. . . .

The American psychiatrist Dr. Ross V. Speck writes:

> The idea of using dogs, cats, and other pets as a means of therapy for the mentally ill is not a new one; however, no systematic study has ever been undertaken. . . . Cer-

tain state hospitals now allow their patients to keep pets in the wards of the hospital. Some physicians even refer some of their more difficult patients to pet adoption agencies. In New York City, there is such an adoption agency which caters to the therapeutical effect of pets on people with physical or mental illnesses, or who are depressed or even have suicidal tendencies.

In Germany, too, various hospitals have begun to introduce pets into the wards to study their therapeutic effect on patients spending long periods in hospital, and the mentally sick. At first they tried pigeons, ducks, pheasants, squirrels and aquariums, and the results were so promising that one of the largest psychiatric clinics installed a veritable zoo in its park. The zoo has become the favorite place not only of the patients but also of the doctors and nurses. The latter are amazed at the beneficial effects the contact with animals has upon the patients.

But brightly painted walls, gay curtains, pretty lampshades, earphones that work when you want to listen to music would also help to relieve the drabness and thus do away with one of the punishments running concurrently with the principal one—institutional life.

Sister Teresa, matron of a London Church Army Hostel for Women, has never read Dr. Searle's book, but having spent almost thirty years of her life among society's orphans, she has found out for herself how important the nonhuman environment is to those irreparably damaged by the human environment.

The hostel houses 130 women of all walks of life, mostly middle-aged and elderly. Some go out to work, others are unable to do so. There are among them former prisoners, women released from mental institutions, retardates, drunks, drug addicts, freaks, women for whom rejection has become a way of life and whom acceptance would now destroy, the usual jetsam and flotsam of society.

The dormitories are bright and clean, and in each there is at least one picture on the wall. The huge lounge is furnished with comfortable armchairs with low tables between them; there is a radio, a television set, bookshelves, an aquarium, and two birdcages, one with a canary, the other with a parakeet. In the tiny garden there is a pond with goldfish, a turtle among the plants, and a rabbit hutch with two rabbits. In the house there are two cats and two dogs, Bob and Willie.

The women are very fond of these pets, play with them, talk to them, and often do without the little luxuries that would give them pleasure in order to buy delicacies for the animals. The best loved among them, however, is Bob, a half-Labrador, a big, affectionate animal, always ready to give emotional support to whoever needs it. When Sister Teresa has to raise her voice to one of the women, Bob will immediately take the side of the culprit, sit next to her, lick her hand. One has only to read the Christmas cards he receives from his many mistresses to see how deeply they appreciate the warmth they can accept without fear and suspicion only from a dog. These women, who rarely talk to one another and are very reticent about themselves, confide their secrets to Bob, who can be trusted not to gossip, not to judge, not to preach. For Bob is no do-gooder. Nor is Sister Teresa. What the two of them offer is not tolerance—which implies a superior-inferior relationship—but unconditional acceptance. To Sister Teresa the women in her charge are not sick people or sinners but the victims of an alienated society or of their own mental and psychological makeup.

Sister Teresa knows there are two things without which a human being cannot remain human for long—beauty and freedom. In a recess in the corridor she has installed what she calls a "beauty corner," a lovely carved table and chair with a bowl of fresh flowers on the table. These two pieces of furniture are not there to be used but to be looked at and enjoyed whenever someone feels the need to forget, for a moment, the ugliness of life.

The mentally ill and physically disabled are themselves another category of people exiled to "reservations" to be kept alive on a starvation diet but otherwise ignored. The schizophrenic social mind that rejects the idea of euthanasia even in the case of Thalidomide babies, mongoloids, and incurables—no matter how desperate their spiritual and physical suffering—and goes into a St. Vitus dance at the very mention of abortion or the sterilization of criminal psychopaths, enthusiastically sends healthy young men to the battlefront to lose life, limb, or mind and allows millions of children to be mentally, morally, and physically damaged in the slum culture of poverty, characterized by disease, neglect, cruelty, racial and religious discrimination, bad schools, and cold charity. It then entrusts the survivors of its tender care to the ministrations of the Social Conscience Club without, however, providing sufficient funds for its activities.

Fortunately, and this is why the species man has not yet disappeared from the earth, there are, in every society, individuals whose undefeatable spirit resists victimization and instills in others the will to fight. Here, too, animals have a part to play:

One of the school lecturers employed by the RSPCA reports how he has been able to help by talks on animal welfare to bring light into minds darkened by psychological disturbances. He went recently to a hospital where psychopathic patients are accommodated. On his arrival he had the moving experience of being locked in each room he entered. Eventually he arrived at the ward where he was to talk to the patients.

These particular patients had started a "Wild Life" club and were making fine efforts. They had guinea pigs, hamsters, fish, and were in the process of obtaining pet mice. They had an excellent library.

The pets were housed in a spacious hutch providing roomy and clean compartments. The hutch resembled a large doll's house. The club is at present limited to ten members and any member breaking the rules is expelled from the club and must go to the bottom of an extremely long waiting list for new members.

Each month the members elect a new Chairman, Treasurer and Secretary. . . . Discipline has shown a marked improvement since the inception of the club.

Patients in the hospital had looked forward keenly to the visit made by the Society's lecturer and they expressed the wish to receive further talks from him.*

Dr. Dean White, founder and secretary of the Institute for Human-Animal Relationships in New York, has been handicapped all his life. As a child he contracted polio, and at the age of twelve he fell off a horse in Texas and broke his back. Wheelchair and crutches notwithstanding, Dr. White has built for himself a happy and active life, the secret of which he is determined to share with others.

The purpose of the institute is "to benefit humanity by the use of pets. . . . To create a new kind of therapy: the treatment, help and even recovery of the handicapped, the shut-in, the geriatric, the troubled in mind and spirit, and the delinquent who has become antisocial for the want of love." For twenty-five years the institute has placed pets in the homes of lonely old people, of only children, of mentally subnormal and physically handicapped people, in geriatric wards and all sorts of institutions, to help both the people who enjoy the presence of these pets and the animals themselves, usually strays picked up by the ASPCA. Dr. Richard H. Hoffman, one of America's leading neuropsychiatrists and president of the institute, believes that pets provide a motive and often a means of recovery and has great confidence in their therapeutic value.

Dr. White quotes the case of an eleven-year-old boy, prisoner of a congenital illness. The boy did so poorly in his studies that he was believed to be mentally retarded. When the institute gave him a pet dog, the responsibility and pleasure of looking after it helped him make a breakthrough, and today, in spite of his illness, he is able to keep up with his classmates.

*The Animal World, 1966.

Another example is that of a woman in her seventies who felt she was too old to do anything but sit on a park bench, full of memories that made her cry. She ate poorly, stayed inside most of the time, and began talking to herself and to imaginary friends, since she had no real ones. In giving her a nearly grown pup, the institute gave her a new lease on life. She takes daily walks with the dog and through it has made friends with other dog owners. She is happy and occupied and no longer feels she is an unwanted has-been.

Recently, the Institute for Human-Animal Relationships has opened a library, where data and information on the value of pets to people are available to the psychiatrist, the medical doctor, veterinarian, social worker, and others.

A letter to the British Polio Fellowship's *Bulletin* has brought a number of replies, two of which I should like to quote.

. . . as a farmer's daughter I grew up with animals but now, in my 60s, I am alone and reduced to one canary. She is my great joy and companion, almost human. She enjoys the fireside and radio. . . . She also enjoys TV and takes her stand on the arm of a chair expecting me to notice her. Smiled on, she sings. She likes the Sunday service especially. . . . Only today, on TV, Blue Peter showed some cats. She fled with a shriek to safety but later a parrot was introduced so I called her to "look" which she did, and liked him. Yes, animals can and do recognize things they are used to. She has become a real tennis-fan and looks round the set to find the people as they disappear. We have our meals together, she will never start before I sit down. Sometimes, when I have forgotten to fetch her she was still waiting but when she saw that I had a cup of coffee in my hand that satisfied her and she made a dash for the seed. . . . So you can gather what this bird means to me. . . .

After my wife, Pussy has become the most important thing in my life. She keeps me company on the odd occasion when my wife has to go out. From the first thing in the morning, when she comes into the bedroom, till the last thing in the evening when we pat her good-night, she is everything for us. Her coquettish little ways, her toilet, and her schemes to get us to play with her especially on the lawn where she can leap and run to her heart's content, are a pleasure to watch. Some time ago she jumped, evidently, on a piece of upturned glass and badly cut one of her forepaws. She came limping in to ask for our help. It took months (and the help of a vet) to get her right, and for a long time we were very worried about her. But she is all right now. . . .

There is also the case of Mr. P.A. who, at the age of forty-four, was recovering from his third, near-fatal coronary in twelve months. He was told he would never work again. Wrapped in despair, he lay in his bedroom gazing out into the wintry garden when, suddenly, he heard a bird sing. He began wondering who looked after the birds when they were sick and suffering, and this started a train of thought that led to a life of purpose and happiness for him.

As soon as he was able to get up, he nailed a notice to his front door: "Bird Sanctuary." Soon people began to bring sick and wounded birds to him to cure, and with infinite patience and tenderness he was able to save them. To feed the inmates of his sanctuary he sold, gradually, all his possessions. When there was nothing left to sell he called a public meeting, which was attended by seventeen bird lovers. Together they founded the Birds' Welfare and Protection Association, which today has 170 members and is a registered charity. Since its founding it has given treatment to 5322 birds.

"People in ill health," Mr. P.A. told the journalist interviewing him, "should look round to find something useful to do. Now that I have the birds to worry about, I don't worry about my health. If I had given way to self-pity I'd have been dead by now. This is what life is about, isn't it? People being of service to others, whether it is human beings, animals or birds. . . ."

A polio victim, Ross G. Crockett of Logan, Utah, has been paralyzed from the waist down for the last thirty-nine years. His philosophy, "As long as my arms and brain will work that is all I need," saved him from accepting expulsion from society as an invalid. He designed his own home so he could move around in his wheelchair without help and has earned a prominent name in his community as a tropical fish breeder, musician, and photographer. Almost every room in his house holds a beautiful aquarium. He has raised hundreds of kinds of fish over the years and has helped many youngsters and handicapped people to get started in the now second most popular hobby in the nation. He has been visited by several doctors, who, after experiments, have found that tropical fish aquaria in hospitals, particularly mental institutions, cut down as much as 50 per cent on sedation as a result of their calming effect.

In the distant future, when the human race will have learned to make use of all its wonderful gifts and will experience the world with Dr. Laing's "innocence, truth and love," historiographers will illustrate their reconstruction of our present attitude to the old and disabled with one of Bernard Shaw's "rules" in the Preface to *The Doctor's Dilemma:* "In legislation and organization, proceed on the principle that invalids, meaning persons who cannot keep themselves alive by their own activities, cannot, beyond reason, expect to be kept alive by the activities of others. . . . The man who costs more than he is worth is doomed by a sound hygiene as inexorably as by sound economics. . . ."

While the Catholic Church makes it very clear what offenses are covered by the term "sin" and the religious "penal code" has remained unchanged for nearly two thousand years, the term "crime" is often vague and subject to interpretation and the punishment is frequently determined by factors totally unconnected with the offense, such as the momentary mood of the public, politics, the composition of the jury, the judge's likes and dislikes. The people who are never consulted at this stage are the experts on the human soul — psychologists, sociologists, and educators. Being perpetually engaged in the study of society and its members, they are, of course, deprived of objectivity by their insight into the causes of crime and knowledge of the offenders' mental and psychological makeup and put their faith in prevention and cure rather than in retribution.

To pronounce sentence, on the other hand, it is enough to be familiar with the penal code described by the British psychiatrist Dr. Michael Balint as "a queer mixture of old superstitions, remnants of religious ordinances and retributive tendencies, fair common sense, hard thinking, sound empiricism, some sentimentalism and sadism, reckoning with hard facts, etc., etc., and also logistic hairsplitting." And once sentenced to imprisonment, regardless of whether the institution is called Borstal, remand center, open or closed prison, the offender is, as an additional punishment rarely put into words and then only in the form of denial, expelled from the "nation" for all his remaining years and welcomed to the army of "expendables."

In his article "Penal and Total Institutions"* E. Clay, principal officer at Pentonville Prison, London, compares closed prisons to mental hospitals. In both, "the staff look upon the inmates as inferior beings, and therefore the role of inmates is on the lowest level of the institution." In both, "all are classed the same, irrespective of the social status attained prior to admittance to the institution," and in both, "the loss of liberty and the taking away of personal clothes and effects leads to a loss of identity."

Since no psychologist to date has traced back the offender's aggression against society to traumata suffered in early childhood through association with pet animals, it is regarded as perfectly normal that even the most hardened criminal should, if the opportunity arises, form a strong emotional relationship with nonhuman living creatures. The case of Robert Stroud, the Birdman of Alcatraz, has been made famous by the publication of his biography and the film made

*Prison Service Journal, Oct., 1967.

from it, but though he may be the only prisoner to have become an internationally accepted authority on bird diseases, the prisons of the world house a large number of lesser "birdmen" and "fishmen." One, a man serving a life sentence in an English maximum security prison for having killed three policemen, realized a childhood dream when he was allowed to build a fish pond he has peopled with goldfish bought with the 8s. 6d. he earns weekly by operating a towel-making machine.

In other prisons there are fish tanks or aviaries, and in one open prison the inmates have established a bird sanctuary where injured birds, brought in from the outside for treatment, are looked after by the prisoners. In some of the less-crowded English prisons, inmates are allowed to keep one small bird, a canary or budgerigar, in their cells for a standard charge of £1, intended to deter those who would neglect their pet after obtaining it. Cage and bird food have to be purchased from the prisoner's earnings.

In the United States, too, several prisons allow the inmates to keep pets. Before the authorities came to the conclusion that a harmless hobby like looking after an aquarium might have a beneficial effect on prisoners by relieving one of the principal causes of unrest—boredom—the inmates of Indiana State Prison had been keeping guppies secretly for thirty years, even though they were invariably flushed down the lavatory when the guards found them. Today, the prisoners keep fish tanks in their cells and have formed a "Fin and Gill Aquarium Club," which is, from time to time, granted the privilege of listening to experts who, invited by the warden, advise and discuss with them the problems of fish breeding.

Although prison inmates may enjoy looking after an aquarium or aviary because it is an occupation that breaks the drab routine of institutional life, the individual prisoner cannot establish a genuine relationship with an animal that belongs to all and thus belongs to no one. G.I. pets, introduced to the prison by the "authorities" as a sort of occupational therapy, cannot arouse the same feelings as even the humblest pet, a spider or a mouse or a sparrow or a pigeon, found, fed, and trained by the prisoner himself, especially if it has to be kept hidden from the guards. A bird that comes to pick up the crumbs put out for it on the windowsill is a living link with the world outside, and any animal, even a beetle, that shares the prisoner's cell relieves his loneliness. Talking to it seems natural to him, whereas if he talked to himself, he would feel he was going insane.

The loss of identity experienced by the inmates of total institutions, prisons, mental hospitals, and temporarily, of ordinary hospitals, as a result of the loss of liberty and the taking away of all personal effects, is an exceedingly complex emotional state. Even the most antisocial being, a gangster or drug peddler or a person committing acts of violence, *has* a relationship with society, and whether he knows it or not, his rejection of his fellow men has its roots in a powerful unfulfilled desire to belong. The moment he is locked up in an institution his relationship to society ceases because society no longer exists, nothing that is real to him exists, nothing is real except the institution within whose walls every little thing assumes inordinate significance and every conflict grows larger than life size. Few offenders, unless they are psychopaths, are so completely hostile to the world that there is no one, not even a woman or child, they can love. In prison that woman or child loses reality, and the prisoner is more aware of this on visiting days than at any other time when, in his imagination, he invests them, and his relationship with them, with a beauty they do not possess. As everyone who has ever spent a day in prison knows, in this environment even the inanimate objects are hostile and no human being can be trusted. Only an animal is not an enemy because it cannot in any way be blamed for the prisoner's predicament. As a result, animals provide the only outlet for positive emotions—affection, compassion, kindness.

During a discussion following a lecture on animals given by an RSPCA superintendent at a London prison for long-term convicts, the inmates spoke with obvious pleasure about the pets they had had as children and those they owned "outside." They were sincerely indignant at the modern methods of rearing, like factory-farming and broiler houses, and none of them found it strange that they who had committed serious offenses against human beings should grow almost tearfully sentimental about the fates of animals.

One of them related that during a previous sentence he had served at an open prison he had smuggled two pigeons, a rabbit, and a frog into his cell. He was heartbroken when the guards discovered the small zoo and, as he said, "transferred" the rabbit and the frog. He was allowed to keep the pigeons, which, when he was released, he gave to one of his fellow prisoners. He told how the pigeons used to perch on his shoulder and how, when he came in from work, they hopped around him in joyful welcome. It was interesting to watch the prisoners' faces during these conversations. The previously rigid features relaxed, the dull eyes sparkled, and they laughed freely, childishly, at the stories.

It is difficult to imagine the possibility of rehabilitating an offender, that is, of providing him with a new, changed identity, in an atmosphere where the society he is supposed to rejoin as a useful member has lost all reality for him. But even if this could be accomplished, the released offender, relearning the reality of the "extramural" world through the painful experience of being rejected by it, would soon almost certainly revert to his preconviction "outsider" identity and feel more justified than ever in his attitude toward those who have abandoned him.

In a certain sense the imprisoned offender relives his childhood. He has no responsibility because his every move is regulated. The issues he has to make up his mind on are simple. Taking sides is no problem, for whatever his relationship with his fellow prisoners, whether he agrees with them or not, he is always on their side against the prison staff. His relationship to animals is that of a disturbed child who mistrusts all adults.

It might be worth trying to make use of pet animals, as a child psychiatrist makes use of them in his approach to the disturbed child, to break down the offender's stubborn resistance to those accepting and accepted by society, and his rejection of any human relationship not based on defense or aggression. Unfortunately, to keep a pet in a prison cell is a privilege, and whether that privilege is granted or not depends on the guards. The guard is not concerned with the offense or crime committed. Having heard everything, he no longer reacts to anything but the prisoner, and since he is responsible for discipline and nothing more, he is occupied only with the prisoner's behavior while in prison and not with his rehabilitation. A hardened criminal who has served several sentences and knows exactly how to get on the guards' right side may win privileges more easily than a man who, having committed a less-serious offense, is serving his first sentence. With a murderer the guard knows where he stands, and if the murderer is a nice guy and behaves himself, the guard may even show him extra leniency. An embezzler, on the other hand, especially if he is an educated man, may present a problem for the guard, and unsure of himself, he may turn nasty. The treatment, like the sentencing, of an offender, is frequently influenced by factors totally unconnected with his offense, his behavior, and his character, and therefore privileges that could in many cases pave the way toward rehabilitation are often granted to the most cynical, who would laugh at the social worker or psychologist trying to reform them.

The French SPA is aware of the importance a prisoner attaches to his pet. They take in the pets of an offender sentenced to prison, and until he is released, they write to him about and often visit him on visiting days to talk with him about the animal he has left behind. By doing this service, the French SPA keeps a small door open between the hated reality of institutional existence and the feared reality of the world outside. This small door may, in some cases, make all the difference between rehabilitation and recidivism.

When Iain Scarlet, editor of the new magazine *Linkup*, which hopes to establish a two-way communication between Britain's prison population and the community at large, was trying to obtain funds for his publication, he said, in a moment of discouragement: "I honestly think that I would have done better to appeal for money to start a magazine helping dogs and cats to communicate!" Finally, in January, 1968, the first issue of *Linkup* appeared on the newsstands, full of interesting articles—and poems—written by people inside and outside the prison walls.

It is worth noting that the editor, who has been in prison twice for passing bad checks, devoted seven of the magazine's fifty-six pages to animals. On the first page he put a photo of the lioness Elsa with her mistress lying next to her, her head resting on the animal's flank. The caption read: "We were all Born Free. . . ." There is a three-page article by the naturalist Peter Scott on a rare English bird—with photographs. A full-page photo shows a little boy holding a kitten and behind him stuffed birds behind glass. A full-page article describes the effects of oil dumping on sea birds, and there is a full-page story entitled "Requiem for a Dog."

The love of animals is one thing the community would readily admit having in common with "jailbirds." Undoubtedly it is one of the subjects well suited to promoting two-way communication.

CHAPTER 4
PETS AS A "CAUSE"

> I have a pet budgerigar which has a swing in its cage. I have made a practice of disconnecting its swing each Sunday and not putting it back into use until Monday morning. Is this in accord with strict Christian principle?
>
> —"This England" column, *The New Statesman*, 1967

◉ ◉ IN HIS PREFACE TO *THE DOCTOR'S DILEMMA*, G. B. Shaw writes: "There is in man a specific lust for cruelty which infects even his passion of pity and makes it savage. Simple disgust at cruelty is very rare. The people who turn

sick and faint, and those who gloat, are often alike in the
pains they take to witness executions, floggings, operations,
or any other exhibition of suffering, especially those involving bloodshed, blows and lacerations." Bernard Shaw was
a virulent antivivisectionist, perhaps not so much because
he loved animals but because of his dislike and contempt
for people. But since he was also a brilliant man, he suspected
the emotional roots of his fellow vivisectionists' belligerence
almost as much as his own real motives, and his rantings,
though probably highly effective in a certain circle at a certain time, sound supremely unconvincing today.

The lumping together of all laboratory experiments conducted on animals under the gory but misleading heading
vivisection has a very definite purpose, and any modern
advertising agency using depth psychology to find the sales
gimmick with the greatest public appeal would be proud
to have invented it. For the innocent, or not so innocent,
public the word "vivisection" conjures up the image of a
white-coated Frankenstein monster cutting up a screaming, helpless animal tied to an operating table. The violent
but complex emotions thus aroused turn against the scientist,
and the gentle animal-lover, who has never seen an animal
experiment and has never bothered to find out to what extent
they have contributed to the saving of human lives, bliss-
fully indulges in fantasies whereby the vivisectionist is tied
to the operating table and dissected alive, preferably by
himself.

Many surgeons who are known to have performed delicate operations on animals before operating, with spectacular success, on people could, if they wished, publish in book
form the bloodthirsty epistles they have received from members of this eminently humane society, letters in which the
writers threatened to kidnap the surgeon's children and do
unto them what their father had done unto innocent animals.
To quote from one:

Sir, or should I say, Monster!

The Marquis de Sade, one of the filthiest creatures that ever lived, was a paragon of virtue compared to you. He, at least, obtained his base sexual pleasures from torturing people who could decide for themselves whether or not to submit. You, on the other hand, use helpless animals for the satisfaction of your perverted, sadistic sexual desires. Do you enjoy masturbating with hands dripping with the innocent blood of vivisected animals? Do you get an unholy thrill from listening to their screams and watching their writhing bodies?

Who, do you think, is fooled by your protestations that the monstrous deeds you perform on the only living beings still worthy of love, beautiful, intelligent and faithful dogs, will, in time, benefit mankind? Can you tell me how many of the conclusions arrived at through animal experiments apply to humans? Why, if your aim is indeed to help humanity, do you not experiment with humans?

No, Sir. You are not concerned with people. Behind all the scientific blah-blah lurks a filthy and cunning mind that has found a legal—and to some idiots, respectable—outlet for the lowest sexual drive imaginable: the pursuit of pleasure by the infliction of maximum pain.

You will not get away with it for long. Some of us, who are tired of pious words that achieve nothing, are getting ready for action. One day soon we may tie your ugly, stupid and faithless wife, compared to whom the humblest mongrel is a thing of perfection, to the operating table, and when she lies screaming, covered in blood and excrement, we may invite you to show you what benefit "mankind" has gained from your filthy, sadistic sexual indulgences.

A passionate anti-vivisectionist

Although it is evident that the antivivisection societies, like other organizations, have their more fanatical supporters, one wonders how their other members can bring themselves to endorse Shaw's mediaeval and antihuman tenet that ". . . if you cannot attain knowledge without torturing a dog, you must do without knowledge." One wonders how many of them agree with the woman who, on March 12, 1967, wrote to the editor of the *Sunday Citizen:* "Many people like me believe that no animal experiment at all should be permitted. No human life is worth saving at such an expense."

And how many more can agree with the Right Reverend Monsignor LeRoy MacWilliams, who, in 1963, testified before a House subcommittee on vivisection in Washington? "St. Thomas, the great doctor and theologian, warns us about the proper use of animals lest they appear at the Final Judgment against us," Monsignor MacWilliams said. "And God himself will take revenge on all who misuse His creatures."

The fantastic achievements of medical science, especially since the Second World War, have indeed cost the lives of millions of animals, and millions more will perish to bring about the near-miracles mankind can expect in the next few decades. Those who screamed murder when the Western newspapers published pictures of animal experiments carried on in the Soviet Union did not stop to think of the purpose of those experiments. By replacing his worn-out organs from a spare-parts bank, and by giving him various hormones, science will, one day soon, enable man to live, if not forever, at least for two or three times the number of years he can optimistically expect to live today. What antivivisectionist would refuse a chance to live longer because the prolongation of his life demands the sacrificing of animals?

The term "antivivisectionism" does not make very clear that its champions are concerned only with the sufferings of animals. On the contrary, it might mislead people into believing that the League or Union of antivivisectionists is also campaigning against lethal experiments—not necessarily medical—carried out on political prisoners in the Communist countries, Negro prisoners in South Africa, Vietcong prisoners in South Vietnam, and vice versa, and so on. It might get people concerned with human beings to join, under the misapprehension that antivivisectionists are fighting for "a limit to the pain which may be inflicted" on the men, women, and children killed, maimed, tortured, starved, or physically and mentally destroyed by indifference, neglect, or political gamesmanship throughout the world.

When an antivivisectionist or, for that matter, the supporter of any other animal welfare organization, is asked why he devotes his life to the protection of animals rather than to the protection of people, the answer will invariably be: "Because people can look after themselves, and those who cannot are looked after by the state and a great many charities while the animals are helpless and it is our duty to protect them."

Only an imbecile, or one filled with a blind hatred for his fellow men can ignore that in the world we live in the overwhelming majority of people are helpless victims of the schizophrenic system that reigns—with slight methodological differences—over the entire earth. By brainwashing the multitude and sparking off outbreaks of mass insanity during which sanity is regarded as treason, this system has, in a brief fifty years, murdered over one hundred million human beings, not counting those killed in "peacetime" for various reasons in various ways.

In the June 25, 1967, issue of the *Sunday Mirror*, Anne Allen writes:

> As I try to write this my cat curls himself over my desk, pushing my pen with his nose and making little dabs at the paper. It is difficult to imagine a living creature looking more perfectly contented. A few months ago he was run over, but the vet did a really wonderful job and Crumpet is as good as new. . . .
>
> Now, I love this cat. Not to put too fine a point on it, I am dotty about him.
>
> But he is only a cat.
>
> Yet, he received medical help more quickly than the dreadfully wounded children of Vietnam. . . .
>
> The babies of Vietnam are being blasted and burnt. But many of them get no relief from pain at all. I do not in the least care whose side it is that you hope will win

the war. I know only that the women and children are
losing it.

So far one million children have been killed or wounded.

In the last 3,500 years there have been just 230 years
of peace in the so called civilized world. Only 230 years
without men being torn from their homes, without violent death in battle, without burnt homes and crops, without
terror in the night. What can it be that drives men from
one war to another? What possible reason do we have
for accepting this senseless waste?

We accept it because instead of being taught, or even
allowed, to think, to develop our capabilities, to become
human—for *we* are the missing link between the primates
and man—we are conditioned to absorb ideologies that
are, with unfailing regularity, invalidated by history, and
obey rules that, in every society and at every epoch, serve
only to supply human skulls as building stones for the houses
of worship dedicated to the world's wielders of power.

Let animal lovers be reassured, however. The system
that divides mankind into races and nations, classes and
political parties, minorities and religious groups, and various
categories within each, and then incites them to kill one
another, putting the blame for the mutual extermination
on the "aggression" and "territoriality" we inherited from
our hairy ancestors, would not even dream of allowing animals to share our fate. On the contrary, it begs us to be kind
to animals because cruelty to them *might*, just *might*, lead
to cruelty to men.

In his book *All Heaven in a Rage*, E. S. Turner quotes the
March 9, 1964, issue of the *Manchester Guardian:* "The fact is
that an increasing contempt for lower forms of life may be
leading us, especially in an agnostic age, to a contempt for
man himself. *How big a step is it from the broiler-house to
Auschwitz?*" (Italics mine)

But the Russians are not to be outdone. The April 6, 1967,
issue of the London *Times* quotes the Moscow *Literary Gazette* in its campaign for legislation to penalize cruelty to ani-

mals. "The *Literary Gazette* states that the time has come for action because *in the final analysis cruelty to animals breeds cruelty to each other among men.*" (Italics mine) To prove that "cruelty to each other among men" has not yet been bred, four young men who killed a swan in Moscow's National Park were condemned to *ten years in prison,* not for cruelty to animals but because their deed was an offense against the dignity of man.

In the United States some 650 animal welfare organizations, the major ones with branches in every state and in other countries, and as many pet clubs as there are animal species kept as pets, vie with one another in protecting the dignity of man. One cannot but admire the wholehearted zeal with which the unpaid workers of these voluntary societies labor so that America's pets may enjoy the "four freedoms" denied so many men.

Almost all these societies advocate the spaying or neutering of cats and dogs to prevent surplus breeding and to facilitate the task of the humane societies that cannot cope with the stray animal population. There are today more than ninety million dogs and cats in the United States, and puppies and kittens are bred at the rate of ten thousand an hour. The organization most active in this field is the Friends of Animals, Inc., a voluntary society founded and run by a beautiful and impressive young woman who has so far devoted ten years of her life to the spaying and castrating of animals. The society also fights for humane slaughter, against cruel sports—and against the ASPCA.

Another important organization—the Animal Welfare Institute, New York—specializes in preparing animal protection bills and lobbying for them. During the 1966 session sixty-two bills concerning animals were introduced into the New York State Legislature, of which four were enacted as laws of the state of New York. Of those one provides that it shall be unlawful for any laboratory or institution approved under the public health law to purchase any dog or cat for experimental purposes unless the seller provides sufficient proof of ownership of the animal. Another outlaws bullfight-

ing, cockfighting and dogfighting within New York State.
It also makes it illegal to bait an animal or cause an animal
to be in combat either with another animal or a person. At
the last minute an exception was made for "animals in exhibition of a kind commonly featured at rodeos."

True, bullfights were not invented for queasy stomachs,
and one can imagine a more inspiring sight than two cocks
with razor blades tied to their feet cutting each other to
pieces. Still, it is difficult to understand why ritualistic games
involving animals should be outlawed when ritualistic games
involving human beings are not only allowed, not only encouraged, but glorified as shining examples of American, and
by now also British and European, manhood. Are boxing, free-
style wrestling, and such more palatable and less likely to
arouse man's base instincts because the men engaged in
them get paid while the animals do not? Are the sheriff, the
criminal, the spy, the psychopath, who shoot, knife, strangle,
beat to a pulp, or commit the most sophisticated acts of
cruelty on the movie or television screen wading knee-deep
in technicolor blood and brain, less obscene, because it is
only "make-believe," than the *torero* who runs quite considerable risks or the Mexican or Puerto Rican have-nots
who watch a cockfight, the cheapest form of entertainment,
and who may even win a few pennies if their animals win?

The question to be answered is: Do animal lovers protest against cruelty to animals and not against cruelty to
human beings because they feel that animals are more important than people, or do they protest against cruelty to animals
because it is incompatible with the dignity of man? It would
be interesting to get at the truth hidden behind all the undis-
guisedly emotional or falsely rational claptrap on this subject.

"Clarity and distinctness are not criteria of truth," says
the prominent British philosopher Karl R. Popper, "But
such things as obscurity and confusion indicate error. Simi-
larly, coherence does not establish truth, but incoherence and
inconsistency establish falsehood." Nothing could be more
obscure, confused, incoherent, or inconsistent than the explan-

ations given for Western man's obsessional preoccupation with animals.

The most interesting—and perhaps the largest—of the animal protection societies is the American Humane Association, which campaigns against cruelty to animals—and children. Of its forty-page *Yearbook* for 1964-65, a page and a third are devoted to children.

The National Association of Child Protective Agencies is the children's division of the American Humane Association. With its affiliated societies for the Prevention of Cruelty to Children, it functions in three major areas: 1) to better conditions for the neglected child; 2) to give protection to the abused child; 3) to readjust social relationships for the delinquent. It also engages in special research projects—financed by grants. In 1966 a survey was conducted into the status of child protective services on a grant of $10,800 from the Child Welfare Foundation of the American Legion, and another project to assess the needs of children who are victims of sex crimes was pursued on a $210,000 grant from the U.S. Children's Bureau, a federal organization. In one year the AHA found 662 newspaper reports on parents who beat, burned, drowned, stabbed or suffocated their children, usually under four years of age. According to experts, if all cases of the "battered baby syndrome" were reported, the total would exceed 10,000 a year. Many doctors suspect that more U.S. children are killed by their parents than by automobile accidents, leukemia, or muscular dystrophy.

In 1866, Henry Bergh, a wealthy American, founded the American Society for the Prevention of Cruelty to Animals. Seven years later, in 1873, a New York social worker, Mrs. Etta Wheeler, came across a little girl being cruelly treated by her foster parents. She suggested to Henry Bergh that the little girl could be regarded as an animal and be given protection by the ASPCA. Bergh brought the case to court and won. Mrs. Wheeler then proposed that a society should be founded to prevent cruelty to children. The ASPCC, founded by Bergh in 1874, was the first of its kind in the world. Frederick Agnew, an Englishman visiting America, was so impressed by this society that in 1882 he organized a society in Liverpool for the prevention of cruelty to children. From this grew the NSPCA two years later.

Animal welfare still appears to precede child welfare in many Western countries, but it has to be conceded that the animal welfare organizations have a much easier task. The spaying of female cats and dogs is regarded as a social service, while abortion and sterilization are crimes. In addition, the humane organizations are licensed to "put down" homeless, sick, or simply unwanted animals while children cannot be so easily disposed of even when neither their parents nor society wants them. Unwanted animals end in the city pounds, unwanted children in Borstals, prisons, or mental hospitals.

Although private individuals donate huge sums annually to the various American animal welfare organizations, the general attitude to stray animals is more practical than sentimental. The strays, though decency and hygiene demand that they be either adopted or destroyed, are, like the four categories of "expendables," excluded from the "nation" proper, while *pet* animals, economically consumers and psychologically consumed, are an integral part of it.

The founders, directors, sponsors, and leading lights of the animal welfare organizations, unsalaried champions of the "cause," are usually well-to-do people who need an interest in life, an occupation without too much responsibility or emotional involvement, or people who are glad of the free publicity this role affords them, or people who find this the easiest way to prove how Christian, how democratic, and how tolerant they really are. Indeed, animals are often less disappointing "protégés" than people. Animals are less likely to "bite the hand that feeds them" than, for example, are slum children, who may not respond to Christian tolerance with the humility and gratitude expected of them.

The multitude of voluntary workers, predominantly women, get a great deal from joining an animal welfare organization. Loneliness, not only in old age but in middle age, is a world problem, and it rests more heavily on Americans than on the members of any other nation, even when it is not combined with sickness or poverty. In America, to survive psychologically, you have to "belong," and if you belong to an animal charity, the sense of importance, the companionship, and the status gained far outweigh the effort demanded.

A hunt for stray cats, as described in *The New Yorker*, provides more fun than, let us say, tea at Schrafft's with a dull cousin, and the common purpose creates, even if only for a few hours, a warm feeling of solidarity and "togetherness" that one can hug to oneself and take home on a cold winter evening. Those who, justly or unjustly, blame others for their loneliness find a guiltless outlet for their aggressions when, incensed by the sad fate of animals, and identifying with them, they can freely voice their hatred of their heartless, cruel fellow humans.

Mrs. R., a childless widow of fifty, works two afternoons a week for an organization whose aim is to "raise the cat's position in the scheme of contemporary civilization." Her marriage with a much older but wealthy man had been rather unhappy, and his dislike of children and absolute refusal to have any deprived her of even that emotional outlet. Mrs. R. alleges that she loves animals but has never yet offered to adopt a stray cat or dog. On the other hand, she is indefatigable in ferreting out cases of cruelty to pets and persecutes the cat owners until they wish they had never been born. She has a unique collection of press cuttings dealing with cruelty to animals, and though she keeps it a secret from her fellow workers, she writes hundreds of impassioned letters to newspapers, congressmen, and senators demanding stricter penalties for cruelty to animals. She also writes threatening letters to scientists experimenting on animals, and to the animal welfare organizations, attacking them for their complacency and lack of commitment. In her will she has set aside $100,000 to be divided among ten families whose child will have lost its life in an attempt to save the life of an animal.

Mr. L. is a writer who was never able to sell his novels until, ten years ago, he wrote a volume of short stories, every one of which had an animal as its hero. The success of the volume and the fame it brought him would have been ephemeral had he not been elected chairman of an animal welfare organization that sent him on lecture tours, placed his stories in magazines and newspapers, made him appear on television, and turned him into a social lion, a king among animal writers. Mr. L., incidentally, deserves this prominence; not only does he have a genuine love for animals, he is also a very gifted writer. Today he no longer has to write about animals to be published.

Mrs. W. is a nice, dumpy Jewish woman with a large, noisy, happy family. Since her grown children left home to get married and she and her husband exchanged their house in Brooklyn for a modern flat on Third Avenue, she has acquired a lovely little toy poodle. Some time ago she joined an animal protection organization, mainly to make new friends in the new neighborhood. As a voluntary worker she has associated with the "best people," and the proudest moments of her life are when, before or after a meeting, one of her co-workers drops in for a cup of coffee. Mrs. W. sincerely loves animals, but then, being a person of infinite kindness, she loves everyone and everything—Jews, Gentiles, Negroes, rich and poor, adults and children, dogs and cats and, since her small grandson keeps them as pets, even mice.

In France, animal protection societies spring up like mushrooms to keep pace with the spreading fashion of pet keeping. However, because the French are considerably less sentimental than Anglo-Saxons, the efforts of these societies do not achieve the desired results.

The most important of these organizations is the Société pour la Protection des Animaux (SPA), with twenty-six branches in the country, more than 28,500 members, 10 inspectors, and some 300 voluntary workers. Apart from fighting cruelty to animals, the society tries to prevent an animal population-explosion by making the Pill (made specially for animals) obligatory. They may encounter no difficulties from the authorities, since mongrels and alley cats cannot be said to contribute much to making France a first-class military power.

Then there are others of some significance. Les Amis des Bêtes owes its considerable popularity to the charming and enthusiastic veterinarian Dr. Fernand Mery, who has innumerable radio talks and several books on animals to his credit. The secret of his success is his sincerity and human warmth and a love and understanding that are not confined to animals but include human beings as well. The "Brigade de la Défense des Animaux" is kept alive by the journalist Jean Fabre, whose interesting and colorful column in *Paris Jour* is read by everyone, animal lover or not. The OBAB, Society against cruel slaughter, is headed by a militant woman, Mme. Gilardoni, who is responsible for the law prohibiting certain ways of killing animals. The project "Happy Animal Village Prize," founded by Mme. Marianne Gilbert, might also be adopted in other countries. Mme. Gilbert awards an annual prize of 5000 new francs (approximately £ 350) to the community that has the happiest animals. She herself has adopted several mistreated animals, one of which, the donkey Lilou, is even included in her will.

Well aware that French breasts do not exactly overflow with the milk of human kindness, the propaganda of the animal welfare societies centers around two basic themes: *cruelty*, because it appeals before it appalls, and *famous people*, because if Brigitte Bardot, Charles Aznavour, George Brassens, and France's other idols show kindness to animals, their fans would be ashamed to do less.

One would not be far out in saying that in France the humane treatment of animals is an intellectual rather than emotional problem and of significance only to the well-to-do, sophisticated layer of the population that is proud of French cultural supremacy and wishes to preserve it. For the rest, animals are useful, and often loved creatures, but love, where it exists, is restricted to one's own cat or dog and does not extend to animals in general. On the whole, uninhibited in their enjoyment of the pleasures of life and free in the expression of love and hate, the French do not have to use animals as substitutes, as objects of displaced emotions. Nor are they given to mysticism, which, elsewhere, is often at the bottom of the "much ado about animals."

The German Tierschutzbund, which consists of 485 societies comprising more than 400,000 animal lovers, developed from the first Society for the Protection of Animals founded in 1837. Its present chairman has the following ironic remarks to make about it: "When the National-Socialist revolution took place, its government passed in 1933 a German law for the protection of animals. . . . The Head Union of Animal Protection Societies, although it had its offices in Frankfurt, had members in every part of the German nation as it then was. In 1940 it became possible for this Federation to become autonomous . . ."*

The Italians, strongly emotional and very articulate as they are have even less need for substitute love-objects and causes than the French. Their love and respect for life and their healthy fear of death, untainted by mysticism in spite of their religious upbringing, are reflected in their treatment of animals. The idea of killing the multitude of stray cats in their towns has little appeal for them, and to apply birth control to animals when they themselves are compelled to have large families whether they want to or not is not a project they can take seriously. Besides, it is better to be overrun by cats than by rats.

The Italian Society for the Protection of Animals is an organization attached to the Ministry of the Interior and its inspectors are regular policemen. The society's small headquarters in Rome, headed by the cheerful and warm-hearted Dr. Trelanzi, makes every effort to arouse nation-wide interest in the fate of animals but with little success. In principle, the Church disapproves of cruelty to both animals and men. But since her first concern is to ensure her own survival, her second to combat everything that smells of socialism, and only her third to protect human beings — *which* human beings is determined by Vatican politics — she

*ISPA *News*, Mar., 1966.

has little time and energy left to worry about the fate of animals.

Animal welfare organizations the world over agree that as far as animal protection is concerned, Great Britain is far in the lead. The Annual Charities Register for 1966 lists 28 animal charities, but there are a great many more animal welfare societies and clubs maintained from membership fees, legacies, and donations.

While the report of the Charity Commissioners for England and Wales for the year 1964 disclosed that many millions of pounds collected by the registered 55,000 social welfare charities were lying idle because "over the country as a whole many trustees experience difficulty and frustration in finding proper uses for their income . . . or it is being accumulated because trustees lack the machinery for identifying those who are genuinely in need of the benefits they can offer," the animal welfare organizations have no such problems. It is absolutely impossible to guess—and even less possible to find out—how many millions of pounds the British animal welfare organizations collect and spend each year, but a few examples should give one a general idea of the amounts involved.

The RSPCA, which publishes its balance sheet, had in 1965 an income of £1,109,528 from legacies and other sources, and in 1966 £703,337 from legacies and £448,050 from other sources.

The Royal Society for the Protection of Birds, which has twenty-eight bird reserves spread over nine thousand acres in Britain, launched, in May 1967, an appeal for £100,000, a sum needed for four new reserves.

In 1964 millionaire Jeremiah Green put the finishing touches on his 2500-acre Jerry Green Foundation Trust Animal Sanctuary for the Care and Protection of Stray and Unwanted Dogs, which had cost him £500,000 and which he hopes to follow up with a string of Sanctuaries across Britain as a memorial to his golden spaniel Rusty, who died in 1962.

The running of the first sanctuary costs £6000 a year, which by now, is probably provided by the trust's large membership, who "contribute to the great cause for which the trust was formed."

In the fiscal year 1965-66 the Wood Green Animal Shelter for Abandoned Animals collected from subscriptions, legacies, donations, and other sources, £35,773,11.9.

The Sheffield branch of the RSPCA used a legacy of £12,000 and raised an additional £16,000 to build a new animal shelter for 150 dogs, 150 cats, and various small animals, warmed by infrared heating and providing electrically heated beds for dogs.

A few other animal welfare organizations that advertise almost daily in the national newspapers asking for legacies, deeds of covenant, or donations are the National Anti-Vivisection Society, the Pine Ridge Dog Sanctuary, the League Against Cruel Sports, the National Canine Defence League, the People's Dispensary for Sick Animals, the Donkey Sanctuary, the Home of Rest for Horses, the Battersea Dog's Home, and the International Council Against Bullfighting.

These often long and eloquent advertisements appear side by side with, or rather, inserted between, the appeals of organizations that are not, as one would naively suppose, financed by the state, but dependent for their existence on legacies, deeds of covenant, and donations: the Children's Society, the National Society for the Prevention of Cruelty to Children, Dr. Barnardo's Homes, the Mental Health Research Fund, the Mental Health Trust, Cancer Relief, the Imperial Cancer Research Fund, the British Heart Foundation, the Chest and Heart Association, the Royal National Institute for the Deaf, Oxfam, the Greater London Fund for the Blind, the National Society for Mentally Handicapped Children, the War on Want, the Royal Society of Surgeons, and so many others that it takes a four-hundred-page book to list them.

It would be interesting to find out why the people who bequeath their entire fortunes, or part of them, to their own pets or to animal charities do so. The Law Report in the

January 26, 1966, issue of *The Times*, dealing with a legal battle between two animal charities for a legacy, offers at least one answer.

A Mrs. Phyllis Helen Satterthwaite (whose name was once a household word in lawn tennis circles) died in 1962, leaving an estate of £50,000 to be divided more or less equally among nine animal charities. The will was made in 1952, when she was already a widow and her only confidant was an official of the bank where she kept her account. "She told him that she *hated* all human beings and would leave her money to animals; and she asked him to get a list of animal charities."

The motive "hatred," a term covering a large number of thwarted emotions, passions, or even perversions, underlies the activities of many animal lovers whether they know it or not. Why a human being should be reduced to loving animals *only* is a question to which Dr. Theodor Reik offers a convincing reply in his *Masochism in Sex and Society*. "The instinctual aim of those phenomena, which we designate as social radiations of masochism, is the satisfaction of aggressive, ambitious, and vindicative impulses. The rehabilitation of an offended self-esteem and sense of dignity, the gratification of an unsatisfied pride, is connected with the fulfilment of violent and imperious desires. . . ." Later he says: ". . . so great is the power of phantasy and anticipation that he can go even beyond the space of his own life if those wishes are not to be granted him in his time." Hence the legacies.

In an alienated society things rarely are what they seem to be, and the British, while sharing the false consciousness with which Western man experiences the world, add another dimension to it by being "more equal than others."

"Our capacity to think," says Professor Laing, "except in the service of what we are dangerously deluded into supposing is our self-interest, and in conformity with common sense, is pitifully limited; our capacity even to see, hear, touch, taste and smell is so shrouded in veils of mystification that an intensive discipline of un-learning is necessary for *anyone* before one can begin to experience the world afresh, with innocence, truth, love."

It took a long time, the conquest, the ruling, and finally the loss of an empire, for the British people to put together, like a mosaic, the image it cherishes of itself, from sonorous words like "fairness," "tolerance," "humanity," "common sense," "decency," "loyalty," "courage," all specific "British" virtues. Even those who are aware of the falseness of this image believe that it was true in the past, is not, but should be, true today, or will be true in the future. Those who reject it altogether as false in the past, the present, and the future seek desperately for another *true* image or, like many young people today, feel that any image, true or false, national or individual, and even the need for an image, is restrictive and that the fluid mass of thought, emotion, impulse, and instinct that bubbles inside us should be given the freedom to create its own shape, a shape that cannot be imagined because it has never yet been allowed to evolve.

Afraid of the bottomless chasm that separates what they *are*, or believe they are, from what they *could be* if they learned to "experience the world afresh with innocence, truth, love," most people close their eyes. Instead of reaching for what is more than they are, they bend down to those compared to whom they are *more* even as they are, and form a nation of "animal lovers." There are many examples of, and causes for, the deliberate displacement of love from its natural object, man, to the substitute object, the animal. The causes will be discussed shortly; a few examples are given here.

"The Queen was driving. Prince Andrew was at her side. And suddenly—emergency! A black and white terrier dashed out in front of the car wheels.

"The Queen swerved the car violently, jammed on the brakes . . . and missed the dog by inches.

"And when the dog's woman owner went over to apologize, the Queen said she quite understood. She had dogs of her own, she said, and knew how they would run about when off the lead. The Queen added that she was very glad she had been able to miss the dog. . . . Prince Andrew was thrown forward in the emergency stop, but his safety belt saved him from injury."*

Both the Queen and Prince Andrew could have been killed, and not even a funeral cortege of fifty-million animal lovers could have brought them back to life. But in the memory of the nation she would have survived as the greatest Queen that ever was.

Not only the RSPCA, but everyone who read about it, was filled with horror and indignation when a member of the Road Safety Committee of the town of D. advised motorists not to swerve to avoid dogs. "If people could be persuaded to drive straight over the dog if necessary, a lot of injury to humans could be avoided. . . . We have become so sentimental about animals that a motorist will instinctively swerve to miss one — and probably fail to appreciate that a bus queue is on the pavement. . . . Five of 42 accidents in the district in one month were due to dogs. It made my blood boil." Shortly after this stormy meeting, a woman in D. put on her brakes suddenly to avoid two dogs playing in the street and ran into a queue of children waiting before a cinema, severely injuring seven of them. Everyone was sorry, but few besides the parents felt that there was something basically wrong in the driver's innerved reaction.

In these cases the people involved risked their lives and that of others unpremeditatedly, instinctively. There are, however, other cases of people risking their lives deliberately to save an animal, driven by a "false consciousness" of duty and a genuine need for the satisfaction felt after a selfless act of kindness. But often the same people who will run into a fire to save a cat, climb 2300 feet down a steep cliff to rescue an injured dog, pretend to be blind and deaf for fear of "getting involved" when a fellow human being is in trouble. The case of RSPCA Inspector N., whose story

*Sunday Mirror, London, Aug. 14, 1966.

was published in the press, deserves to be recorded here because it is such a striking illustration of displaced humanity.

Inspector N. is in his late forties. During the war he was captured by the Japanese and as their prisoner had ample opportunity to find out the meaning of cruelty and starvation. "As a prisoner of the Japanese I realized what cruelty is and ever since I have done my best to try and prevent as much suffering as possible," he says.

One would think that a man who feels so strongly about cruelty would join a social welfare organization and devote the rest of his life to the fight against cruelty to man in whatever form it manifests itself. But that is not what Inspector N. did. Instead, he went to work for the RSPCA to fight against cruelty to animals. Why? Does he identify himself with the suffering animals because, as a prisoner of the Japanese, he was as helpless as an animal, and does he identify all human beings with the hated Japanese because he feels that deep down they are all alike? Or does he feel he came so near to death in the Japanese prison camp that the life he now risks is but a shadow life not worth preserving?

More spectacular, though less involved, is the case of the two English ladies who, their missionary zeal awakened by the horror stories of returning tourists, traveled to Venice to improve the fate of the town's 28,000 stray cats. They came, they saw—they lost. Even the Italian SPA did not react well to British interference in the country's animal affairs, for no one likes to be treated as a "barbarian" on his own home ground. To the people of Venice, especially those who do not profit from the tourist trade and are, consequently, appallingly poor, the two well-to-do ladies' obsession with cats appeared rather ridiculous, while the cultured Venetians, proud of their city, could not quite understand why the two kind ladies ignored the beauties of this unique place and paid attention only to the matted fur of stray cats. One wonders to what extremes of cold dislike and contempt for the Italian people their love of animals drove these two crusaders.

But the salaried employers, voluntary workers, and supporters of animal welfare organizations are not all people to whom "whatever goes on two legs is an enemy; whatever goes on four legs, or has wings, is a friend."* There are among them those who once not only loved their fellow humans but loved them too well. People, for instance, who devoted decades of their lives to win, for the dispossessed, a place in the sun.

If *The Suspect Generation*† who, like Philby and Maclean, were in their twenties during the 1930s both in Europe and America and were driven "left" as a protest against Fascism (strangely enough, the *Observer* does not even mention the terrible social conditions that drove more decent people "left" than the protest against Fascism) were indeed investigated "with the utmost caution and delicacy," it would not be surprising if a large number of them were found to be active champions of the animal cause. Those who were, in those days, motivated by love and compassion, by honest indignation and a passionate desire for justice, lost the illusion that mankind can be "saved" and long ago turned away from the "cause" in disappointment and despair.

Mr. R., who was an ardent socialist in his youth, devoting his every free minute to the study and later to the teaching of Marxism, became so disgusted when his study group walked out on him after the first wage rise, or preferred a football match to the "Capital," that after years of vain attempts he gave up and turned to those more easily saved, the animals. Today, at fifty-five, he is a man of means, the owner of a small zoo, and an active supporter of the RSPCA.

When Mr. R. discovered the hopelessness of "saving the world" by means of an ideology that even its creator regarded merely as a "working hypothesis," he could have tried to "save" his neighbor by giving practical help when it was needed. Had he, and others like him, done that, he might indeed have contributed to the transformation of society he so passionately desired. But soured by his disappoint-

*George Orwell, *Animal Farm*, Harcourt, Brace and Co., New York, 1954.
†*Observer*, London, Oct. 8, 1967.

ments, Mr. R. turned his back on man, and all his love and
compassion, his honest indignation and passionate desire
for justice, today serve the "cause" of suffering animals.

Others again divert their social consciousness to animals
because doing things for people is too great a responsibility.
Miss E., twenty-four, became a vegetarian as a protest against
factory farming. She eats neither meat nor fowl—though
she eats dairy products and fish!—and yet takes no active
part in the fight to outlaw broiler houses. When a friend
asked her to donate an hour or two of her time each week
to visiting lonely old people or children in hospitals, she
raised her hand as if to ward off a blow.

"Oh, no, I couldn't do that!" she cried. "They might become
attached to me and expect me to go on visiting them. What
if I get tired of the whole thing? No, that would be too much
of a responsibility."

"But what good do you think you are doing to the chick-
ens by your negative protest?" her friend asked Miss E.

"What good? I don't know. . . . It may not help the chick-
ens much, but it does something for me. Not eating meat
has, somehow, restored my self-esteem. . . ."

Since most British animal welfare organizations add to
their attraction by enrolling aristocrats, politicians, church
dignitaries, and other famous people as sponsors and directors, they also get social climbers to work for them. Before
a suffering dog, all class differences crumble. Where but
in the bosom of an animal charity can a maiden schoolmis-
tress, the widow of a butcher, a bank clerk, an elderly li-
brarian, or a still active old-age pensioner, hobnob with the
nobility?

"Lady X. told me yesterday . . ." is a wonderful opening
gambit when one wishes to get acquainted with a neighbor,
and "Lord Y. and I discussed the problem . . ." earns one
more respect among one's fellow men than a long life of hard
work, decent living, and true kindness. But many don't have
even this ambition. The pride and interest of the British
people in their aristocracy is such that the "addicts" who buy
every newspaper and magazine specializing in gossip about

the upper classes are uplifted merely by breathing the same, air, once in a while, with their exalted "betters."

There are a great many other reasons why people choose to work for an animal welfare organization rather than for one dealing with human beings, but whatever the reason, in ninety cases out of a hundred animals are a substitute "cause" and those devoting their lives to them would be much happier if they could love, and be loved by, human beings rather than animals.

Let us quote here a speech to the jury delivered by the late Senator Vest of Missouri in a court action for damages in the killing of a dog. The suit was for two hundred dollars, but after listening to this speech the jury raised the amount to five hundred dollars, and asked the judge if the defendant could not be imprisoned or more severely dealt with:

Gentlemen of the Jury!

The best friend a man has in this world may turn against him and become his enemy. His son and daughter that he has reared with loving care may become ungrateful. Those who are nearest and dearest to us, those whom we trust with our happiness and our good name, may become traitors to their faith. The money that a man has he may lose. It flies away from him when he may need it most. Man's reputation may be sacrificed in a moment of ill considered action. The people who are prone to fall to their knees to do us honor when success is with us may be the first to throw the stone of malice when failure settles its cloud upon our heads.

The only unselfish friend a man may have in this world, the one that never deserts him, the one that never proves ungrateful or treacherous, is his dog.

A man's dog stands by him in prosperity and poverty, in health and sickness. He will sleep on the cold ground when the wintry wind blows and the snow drives fiercely, if only he may be near his master's side. He will kiss the hand that has no food to offer, he will lick the wounds and sores that come in encounters with the roughness of the world. He guards the sleep of his pauper master as if he were a prince.

When all other friends desert, he remains. When riches take wings and reputation falls to pieces he is as constant in his love as the sun in its journey through the heavens. If fortune drives the master forth an outcast into the world, friendless and homeless, the faithful dog asks no higher privilege than that of accompanying him, to guard him against danger, to fight against his enemies, and when the last scene of all comes, and death takes his master in its embrace and his body is laid away in the cold ground, no matter if all other friends pursue their way, there by his graveside will the noble dog be found, his head between his paws and his eyes sad, but open in alert watchfulness, faithful and true even to death.

Rarely can one read a more tragic indictment of human relationships in our day and age, or a more dramatic proof of our alienation from ourselves, from our human environment, from the entire race of which we are a part.

Those who have chosen animals as their "cause" have, for their own psychological comfort, reversed their values. They can boast of being "humane" without having had to pay the stiff price it costs to become simply "human." It is a strange thought that by discarding that insignificant little letter "e" that obscures, distorts, falsifies, and belies the meaning of the original word, and by living up to that meaning, we could change the world around us.

Part II
◉ ◉ THE FURRED, FEATHERED, AND SCALY PEOPLE

CHaPTer 5
PETS AND THE YAHOOS

... the Yahoos were known to hate one another more
than they did any different species of animals ...

—JONATHAN SWIFT:
Gulliver's Travels

⊙ ⊙ WHETHER WE REALIZE IT OR NOT, THE ALIENS
from Outer Space are already with us. Intelligences superior to ours, they have taken up quarters in the minds of the
young, imparting to them the essence of their philosophy:

that freedom is total self-acceptance and the unrestricted exploitation of the self's every potentiality, and that nothing is sacred except life and every member of one's species is a church in which it should be adored. Through the mouths of the young they ask uncomfortable questions the older generations construe as attacks upon their "values" and answer with hostile demagogy, widening the gap between themselves and their children.

Why, the Aliens ask, can the *Homo neuroticus* not apply his—admittedly inferior—intelligence to the simple process of living? Why does he engage generation after generation in the ritual killing of millions of his species and, preparing to be killed, systematically anesthetize his physical, intellectual, emotional, and spiritual self? Why does he create and obey a multitude of antilife taboos that dull his capacity to distinguish between love and hate, fear and hope, joy and misery, sanity and madness, affinity and diffinity?

The young, made increasingly aware of their alienation by these new ideas but not yet ready to build them into a way of life, have set off on a journey of discovery into their being. However, pulled up short by the umbilical cord tying them to their parents, they have turned off on a side road leading not to the goal—their unalienated self—but merely to *alienation from alienation*. In the psychological ambience achieved, they negate the categorical imperative that makes man rebel against what he cannot adjust to and place themselves *outside* the alternatives of god or ape. No longer captive but not yet free, they are *nowhere*, but precisely because they are where they are and no longer where they were, they have a better chance of ultimately reaching *elsewhere* and of finding the answer to their questions than have their elders, who believe they are *somewhere* in this "best of all possible worlds."

That best of all possible worlds, the Aliens think, is a surrogate reality from which the all-embracing taboo on being *human* has banned everything genuine, including the genuine will to survive. It is a world of surrogate values, surrogate ideas, surrogate emotions, and surrogate relationships. But since man's relationship with animals is exempt from taboos in the modern world, he cheats both his society and himself by anthropomorphizing them and turning them into surrogate objects of his suppressed humanity.

In Western man's life the anthropomorphized animal plays the role of the "other" in every imaginable interpersonal relationship. As a substitute child, friend, lover, it is an outlet for both the positive and negative impulses that, due to a variety of taboos, cannot be expressed toward the human object. A pet animal can be the socially sanctioned recipient of various kinds of love, but as shown by the many cases of cruelty to animals, it is also an outlet for man's aggression. The "humanization" of animals is often a means toward the "dehumanization" of people one hates or wishes to punish or, as in the case of front-line soldiers or prisoners, it can be a life belt to cling to in one's own dehumanized state.

Some animal species are easier to substitute for human beings than others. As Dr. Desmond Morris says in *The Naked Ape*: "The popularity of an animal is directly correlated with the number of anthropomorphic features it possesses." This helps to explain the astonishing number of dogs and cats in the affluent Western countries.

Outside the group, or groups, with which the *Homo neuroticus* is on a footing of surrogate loyalty, all other humans are Yahoos, whom, in his ambivalent way, he despises. The Yahoos, says Jonathan Swift, are "cunning, malicious, treacherous and revengeful. They are strong and hardy but of a cowardly Spirit, and by Consequence insolent, abject and cruel."

In his third Reith lecture, Professor Edmund Leach gave a more modern definition of the Yahoo:

What *we* are, or what the *other* is, will depend upon context. ... If anything in my immediate vicinity is out of my control, that thing becomes a source of fear. This is true of persons as well as objects. If Mr. X. is someone with whom

I cannot communicate, then he is out of my control, and I begin to treat him as a wild animal rather than a fellow human being. He becomes a brute. His presence then generates anxiety, but his lack of humanity releases me from all moral restraint, the triggered responses which might deter me from violence against my own kind no longer apply.*

History has shown us the truth of this, and we find ample proof of it every day of our lives in our personal experience and in the newspapers. Every group of humans deprives another group or groups of their humanity. The colored man, black, brown, red, or yellow, the Gipsy, the poor, the Communist, the young, are, to the white man in America, and increasingly in England, not of his "own kind," and the same is true the other way round. There is, however, a *universal negative* on which all subspecies of the *Homo neuroticus* agree and which, at the most, triggers off verbal violence. *Nobody* hates animals, although some hate those who do not love them.

Thus, everybody has his favorite Yahoo, but the group of subspecies White - Rich - Protestant - Anglo-Saxon regards all other subspecies as Yahoos and finds its equals only among the aristocracy of *other animal species* including, but not restricted to, Gulliver's Houyhnhnms. The collective designation of these animal aristocrats who "are endowed by Nature with a general Disposition to all Virtues," is Pets.

Jonathan Swift must have been very widely read in Europe as well as in America during the eighteenth and nineteenth centuries, for the history of those times appears to have been strongly influenced by Mr. Gulliver's views. Although the French Revolution and the American Constitution produced truly inspiring declarations of the rights of man, stating unequivocally that all men are born free and equal—a declaration reiterated 159 years later, in 1948,

*Reich lectures on the BBC in 1967.

by the United Nations, but still not put into practice—the Thirteenth Constitutional Amendment prohibiting slavery in all areas within the jurisdiction of the United States went into force only in December, 1865. In the British Empire slavery was abolished over three decades earlier, in 1833.

These dates that marked the end of one form of slavery but no more than scratched the surface of the *institution* of slavery, are also interesting in the context of human-animal relations. The first law in the history of the world that recognizes the "rights of animals" was passed by the British Parliament eleven years before the abolition of slavery, and the Society for the Prevention of Cruelty to Animals was founded nine years before it. However, law is law and men are men. When, upon ascending to the throne Queen Victoria granted the SPCA a Royal Charter, the East India Company's exploits still included slave trading—with the tacit approval of the Empress of India's Government—and men continued illegally to be almost as cruel to animals as the system was, legally, to them. Children under ten were excluded from the mines only in 1842 but were allowed to work a ten-hour day in the textile factories until 1878. In 1891 the legal age of entry became eleven, and in 1901, twelve, but in 1918 there were still fifteen thousand children under the age of fourteen working in factories. During these decades the animal protection societies campaigned energetically for the education of children—the same children—to be kind to animals.

In America, where people were somewhat less sentimental about animals and were also reluctant to imitate the British, from whom they had only recently won their independence, the Society for the Prevention of Cruelty to Animals came into being only in 1866, one year after the prohibition of slavery, and crowning the protracted efforts of the wealthy humanitarian Henry Bergh. Two years later this man of good will included children among the animals to be protected, but child labor in certain areas, though officially abolished, has not been eradicated to this day.

Bergh's motto was that "men will be just towards men when they have learned to be charitable towards animals." Since then charity to animals has grown into a religion, complete with fanatics and heretics, but justice to men, the great illusion for which so many gave their lives in the nineteenth and early twentieth centuries, has degenerated into a political slogan that today no one would even give a fig for.

Those who fought for the first law protecting animals and the numerous laws thereafter campaigned only for the *humane* treatment of animals. They knew better than to ask that animals be treated as *humans*. But even today, in the affluent West, countless thousands would gladly change places with the protected animals, wild or domestic, or with the millions of the genus pet, whose opulent living standard ordinary mortals cannot even dream of attaining. How well the animal-loving *Homo neuroticus* knows what Mr. Gulliver must have felt when, after his last journey, he returned to the bosom of his family: ". . . I must freely confess, the Sight of them filled me only with Hatred, Disgust and Contempt; and the more, by reflecting on the near Alliance I had to them." After trying vainly for five years to adjust to the society of the Yahoos, Mr. Gulliver bought himself two "pets," two young horses whose company made his life, if not more happy, at least more bearable.

The rejection of human beings and their replacement by pet animals can take several forms, depending on the conscious or unconscious causes of the rejection and the measure of "hatred, disgust and contempt" experienced.

An extreme case was that of Adolph Hitler, who had millions of human beings murdered and countless of his own followers assassinated if he suspected them of treason, but was so attached to his dog, Blondie, that he would, even during the last weeks of the war, come out from his "bunker" at the risk of his life to let Blondie run around in the fresh air for at least fifteen minutes each day. However, one does not have to be a mass-murderer to cause the destruction of one's fellows. An infinite number of ordinary people who expend all their positive emotions on animals contribute, by their hatred, contempt, or mere indifference, to the oppression and physical or psychological annihilation of human beings.

On a cold winter morning Mrs. Y. took the No. 5 bus to Fifth Avenue. She sat down on the wide seat in the back next to a gentleman of her own subspecies. Under her elegant fur coat, Mrs. Y. was clutching a tiny Chihuahua. From time to time the little animal raised its head and licked her chin, whereupon Mrs. Y. bent down and kissed it on the snout. At Fifty-ninth Street a young Negro girl took the seat next to her. Mrs. Y. rose and moved over to the gentleman's other side. "I can't stand their smell," she said to him in a low voice. "They should not be allowed to sit with us!"

Mrs. Y. expressed the attitude of millions in America, an attitude that one has learned to accept as an American Fact of Life without, if one has an iota of sanity left, understanding it. It is made even less comprehensible by the circumstance of a large percentage of Americans living happily in the closest physical intimacy with a wide variety of pet animals from dogs to snakes, completely oblivious to their smell and their habits.

Mr. L., an English businessman living in the country, is another Mr. Gulliver. To get away from the world of Yahoos, he has entrusted his business to a manager and devotes his life to looking after old donkeys that have outlived their usefulness, and other unwanted animals he buys from their owners. He has 8 dogs, 8 cats, 4 goats, 10 old horses, a goose, a duck, a bantam, 30 pigeons—and 135 donkeys who enjoy, under his care, leisure and luxury they had never known.

Mr. L. rises at five-thirty in the morning to feed his "family," and in winter, before going to bed, he wraps up his donkeys in blankets lest they catch cold in their heated shed. When one of them falls sick, he never goes to bed at all. His Old Furred and Feathered People's Home costs Mr. L. approximately eighty-five pounds a week, and he and his wife have not gone on holiday for twelve years because he would not entrust his charges to anyone. A while ago council officials told him he could qualify for a tax rebate if he kept pigs for slaughter. "I told them I'd like to fatten *them* up in a sty for a few months and slaughter *them*!" the humane Mr. L. says proudly.

In December, 1957, after the Hungarian uprising, a young Hungarian couple arrived in New York. He had spent the last five years in prison for the crime of being an "aristocrat," and she had been deported to a godforsaken little village where she worked in a kolkhoz, driven to distraction by the constant persecution of the local party secretary. Liberated by the revolution but physically weakened by their experiences, they had escaped barefoot across the border, having lost their shoes in the knee-deep snow.

A wealthy American couple who had long before reduced their contacts with the hated and despised Yahoos to the necessary minimum were asked by the refugee organizations to take the young couple under their wing. In the prevailing atmosphere of sympathy for the "freedom fighters," it would have been impossible to refuse, and the young people were duly invited to dinner.

After having offered her guests an aperitif, and without bothering to ask them even a single question about themselves, the lady of the house began immediately to talk about the subject closest to her heart, her dog. The subject was sitting in the center of the carpet, surrounded by walls covered with photographs and oil paintings immortalizing every stage of his life, from puppyhood to ripe old age. He exuded an intolerable smell, his eyes were opaque with cataract, his tongue hung out from between toothless jaws, and he had a tick that almost tore his head off his neck.

The lady complained bitterly that the veterinary surgeon she paid two hundred dollars a visit could do nothing for her darling, and even the British specialist she had brought over at the expense of four thousand dollars had been unable to help. She was so worried she could neither eat nor sleep, her whole life was in ruins, and her doctor and analyst were in despair.

The young Hungarian, who had had dogs of his own and was genuinely fond of animals, looked at the poor wreck with great compassion, then turned to the lady and, assuring her of his sympathy, said: "If you really love your dog, the kindest thing you could do for him would be to have him put to sleep." The lady turned white as a sheet, jumped up from her chair, and collapsed in a dead faint. After taking her to her room with the help of the servants, the host returned to the lounge and told his guests curtly that he and his wife were in no mood for dinner and as the young people were unfamiliar with New York, they would do best to leave immediately before it turned quite dark.

Elderly people often come to dislike their fellow men, those who reject them as well as those who show them "charity." They will often cut themselves off completely and, brooding, will turn their—at times justified—dislike into passionate hatred and malice. The only living creatures they feel they can trust, and for whom they develop an often pathological love, are pet animals. Usually their pets are dogs, cats, budgies, or canaries, but sometimes these "familiars" are more outlandish animals like goats, donkeys, turtles, or even monkeys or alligators.

Some people, like Miss R.F. who died in 1966 of a disease caught from dogs after her resistance had been weakened by malnutrition, will deny themselves not only luxuries but the barest necessities for the sake of their beloved pets. Miss R.F. had twenty-three dogs in her incredibly neglected and filthy cottage, but had, for twenty years, refused to see her only relative because he did not approve her mode of living. A similar case is that of a man of sixty, living in a derelict hut with fifteen dogs, five rabbits, and twenty pigeons who has completely outlawed himself from civilization for the sake of his animal family.

Sometimes married couples will turn away from mankind to devote their lives to creatures they consider more worthy of love. On the program *Man Alive* the BBC interviewed some of these couples.

Mr. and Mrs. R. own a fox and thirty-one cats that cost them approximately eighty pounds a month. Their pets keep them so busy they have no time for people nor wish for social contact. They cook their pets three fresh meals a day; the fox likes dog food —not the tinned variety, of course —and the cats favor rock salmon, chicken, and rabbit. They have recently moved to a house away from the main road because it is safer for their pets, and never go on vacation.

Another couple collects abandoned and crippled cats. They have no children and never wanted any. The cats are their family, and they would be prepared to give up everything for them. They would go hungry rather than let their pets starve or be given away. When the interviewer asked them whether they would put themselves out just as much for people, they replied they would not, there are enough charities and organizations to take care of people. They feel people have a responsibility toward animals and owe animals a good life because they have domesticated and exploited them.

Wealthy Yahoo-haters can spoil their pets while they are alive without denying themselves anything and when they die can leave their loved ones well provided for.

A Melbourne manufacturer left £80,000 to his old cockatoo, two Leghorn fowls, and animal charities and not a penny to the wife and two daughters he had deserted fifty years before. An old lady in England left £22,000 to her poodle. Another left £1000 to her two donkeys and the rest of her £31,000 fortune to the RSPCA. A widow, whom her neighbors believed to be penniless, left an estate of over £12,000 to her cats and a retired architect left £2000 for the upkeep, care, maintenance, and happiness of his cat and over £4000 to animal welfare organizations.

In Louisville, Kentucky, two ladies inherited an estate worth $115,000 from a *goat*. The goat, called Sugah, had been the pet of an old lady who left her entire property to it. When Sugah died at the age of seventeen, the property was handed over to the testator's two nieces.

In San Francisco a rich old spinster left a trust fund of $1350 for her parakeets and, to make certain that no Yahoo should profit from her death, bequeathed the rest of her money, $162,857, to the SPCA and $3000 to the Defenders of Furbearers.

Another American lady provided in her will for the continued care and comfort of her parrot, Louise. The parrot was to live in the house for the rest of its life, food was to be taken to it twice, and brandy once, a day. In time the houses on either side fell to ruin and had to be demolished, but the local authorities had to leave Louise's house standing because a clause in the will forbade them to touch it. Until the roof caves in and kills her, Louise will still be enjoying her daily snifter of brandy.

There are, however, people who do not wish their beloved pets to survive them. Among these was Miss Frances Pickney, a veteran campaigner for animal welfare who died on Christmas Day, 1967 at the age of sixty-six. She decreed in her will that her pet animals should be humanely destroyed. Her solicitors and the RSPCA tried to get a stay of execution for her three donkeys, a pony, and three cats, but they were finally put down by a veterinary surgeon, who thought Miss Pickney had made the right decision. She knew no other home would be as good as hers. After the first article about the will was published in *The Times*, the people looking after the doomed pets were flooded with offers of homes for them.

Swift does not tell us how Mr. Gulliver solved his Yahoo problem. Did he throw out his family and share his life with his horses, or did he learn to tolerate them in the end? And how did he bequeath his fortune? Kindhearted as he was, he probably provided for his family, but there can be no doubt that he left the bulk of his estate to his horses and an annuity for the groom with the provision that he continue to serve the noble Houyhnhnms as long as they lived.

Except in war, when the taboo on cruelty to human beings is lifted, man is expected to keep his sadistic impulses within civilized limits. Fortunately, society is rather leni-

ent in judging what is civilized and what is not, mainly because it can distract attention from its own systematically
practiced cruelties through such liberalism.

Mental cruelty, though frowned upon, is admitted, and
no one is more surprised when it leads to violence than the
powers that be. Discrimination against minorities, for instance,
is excused, because "everyone has a right to his opinions,"
and so is cruelty by omission: the withholding of everything
that makes life bearable from people considered "too lazy
to help themselves." The branding of children born outside
wedlock as "illegitimate" and treating them as second-class
citizens all their lives is admissible. The caning of "legiti-
mate" children in English public schools, if done by compe-
tent persons for educational reasons with canes correspond-
ing to the specifications laid down by the government, is
positively cheered.

Physical cruelty and violence, on the other hand, have
to be "sublimated"; they can be engaged in only *by proxy* —
by watching the most obscene acts of cruelty performed
on the stage and on the television and cinema screens or,
even more satisfying because real, by watching newsreels
or reading detailed reports in the newspapers on the most
bloodcurdling cases of crime. Unable to "sublimate," some
people seek substitute objects for their destructive energies. "Cruelty to animals may be characterized by the per-
petrator as uncontrollable rage, justified sport, necessary
evil, or even sadistic perversion, but this much insight never
extends to a recognition that the real objects of this mis-
treatment are human figures toward whom such behavior
could not be exhibited," says the American psychiatrist
Karl A. Menninger.

Fox hunting, fishing, wild-game hunting, are not only socially accepted outlets for cruelty; they are considered gentle-
manly pastimes. Although the animal welfare organizations
never cease to protest against them, one wonders if they are
not preferable to the letting loose of aggression on its real
object: a wife, a neighbor, a political opponent, a foreigner, or

simply a person whose color, shape of nose, or opinions one does not like.

The bullfight, favorite target of the animal lovers, is a much more sophisticated form of "sublimated" cruelty because, although there is a substitute object, the bull, there is also a real object, the *torero*. Although the audience delights in the *torero's* skill, the beauty of his movements, the elegant game he plays with death, the ecstatic pleasure and satisfaction felt when he is gored is not one iota less powerful than when he kills the bull. The same is true for the rodeos so popular in America, for lion taming in the circus, and for the duel between man and man-eating shark as forms of entertainment.

However, there are many people who prefer to "sublimate" in their own particular way, who dislike the "togetherness" of the blood sports and despise the "voyeurism" of the bullfight and other similar performances.

To this category belongs the young Englishwoman of twenty-three with a husband and a small son whose hobby is painting horses. She is so successful at her hobby that many of her paintings are exhibited. Her profession, on the other hand, is to slaughter horses at the local abattoir. From the age of three she had watched her father killing animals at his own abattoir, and at seventeen she was granted her own slaughterer's license. In the last six years she has dispatched thousands of animals by shooting them with a bolt-action humane killer or a .32 single-shot pistol. She kills old, sick, and injured animals, she kills horses that their owners no longer want but don't want anyone else to have, she kills pit ponies that can no longer work, she kills food animals. Had she been born a boy, she would have made a first-class executioner. The rational explanation would be the same: "To pull the trigger of the gun is not pleasant — but it has to be done."

Another case is that of the old lady who, to put an end to fox hunting, advertised in her local paper promising ten shillings — and travelling expenses — for every fox cub brought to her. She then puts these cubs to death with chloroform to save them from being torn to pieces by the hounds. Her "humane" campaign deeply shocked the master of the fox-hounds who said: "I don't think this lady realizes just how much suffering she causes. If she does, she must be terribly hardhearted." For of course hounds never hunt cubs. They don't run well enough.

Professor Menninger* tells of a man locally famous for his episodes of horse whipping. "He would tie the poor beasts (usually mares) close to a post, and protecting himself behind a specially erected scaffolding, he would club them until their screams brought neighborhood arousal and, ultimately, his arrest. Repugnant as such a scene is, it is not difficult to visualize how this man's mother treated him as a child, and how the horse-whipping scenes represented a displaced revenge in unvaried form. (This inference was substantiated.)"

Still another case, where the substitution was much more obvious, was that of a German woman living on the outskirts of a small town who used to catch stray dogs, tie them to a post in her garden, and starve them to death. The woman's husband, father of her two children, had first imperceptibly, then rapidly, begun to change sex. He grew fat, developed large breasts, and became so obsessed with womanly pursuits—cooking, cleaning, washing, and needlework—that he gave up his office job and took employment as a cook and general factotum in a family with several small children and where the mother was expecting another child. He was so happy in his work, so good with the children, so reliable and solicitous, that the family put up with the dreadful scenes made by his jealous wife, who, though she might have known better, accused him of having an affair with his employer. The torturing of dogs began when, to escape from his wife, who beat him, kicked him, and several times slashed him with a kitchen knife, the poor man moved away. The authorities, alerted by the neighbors, interfered only when the

*Karl A. Menninger: *Psychoanalysis and Culture,* "Totemic Aspects of Contemporary Attitudes to Animals," International Universities Press, Inc., N.Y., 1951.

woman, no longer satisfied with substitute victims, began to torture her children.

Sometimes the mildest people will beat or kick a pet animal in a moment of uncontrollable rage directed not against the animal but against a human being, a member of their family, their employer, or any person against whom they might wish to commit an act of physical violence. The animal, however, is not necessarily a substitute for a person; it may be just an outlet for pent-up aggression, for a general feeling of intolerable frustration that, were the animal not handy, might result in suicide.

The penniless husband of a rich American woman was begrudged nothing except cash, but he did have to quit his job because his wife hated to be alone and, also had to play father to her two Chihuahuas. He was so much in love with his young and very beautiful wife that for years he put up with her every whim. While her infatuation lasted, she allowed him to put the dogs out of the bedroom when they made love, but after a while she stopped this practice and only let him chase them from the bed. In time even that was no longer allowed, although the presence of the two tiny beasts that yapped, jumped on him, and licked his neck when he took his wife into his arms made him impotent. When, as a final humiliation, he was banned from the bedroom and made to take the two dogs for a walk twice a day, he lost his head and in a fit of fury kicked one of the dogs down a flight of stairs. The animal broke its neck, and, before divorcing him, his wife reported him to the SPCA. He was taken to court for cruelty, heavily fined, and, with the connivance of his wife and her friends, crucified by the newspapers that described him as a monster—and a pimp.

The well-known English veterinarian Buster Lloyd-Jones relates a fantastic story of substitution in his charming book *The Animals Came in One by One*. The British, the world's most animal-loving people, did their best, even in the darkest days of the war, to keep their pets. Only when it was absolutely unavoidable did they have them put down. However, at the beginning of the war the newspapers featured dachshunds as "wicked, cowardly, treacherous, evil German sausage dogs, opposing the gallant British bulldog" and people began to unleash their hatred for the Germans on these unfortunate animals, to throw things at them, chase them, and kick them. Their owners, too, were persecuted as unpatriotic German-lovers.

He also tells another story that would deserve psychiatric investigation. Once a month he used to visit the kennels of a young woman breeding dachshunds. One day before going down to the pigsties where several of the dogs were kept, he noticed some goat kids in a paddock and stood for a moment admiring them. He was busy checking the dogs when suddenly he heard terrible sounds, yelping and screaming, coming from the paddock. When he ran out, he saw that about a dozen dachshunds were attacking the kids and tearing them to pieces, while the owner looked on with amusement. "Leave them to it," she said, "that's what the kids are for. The dogs are enjoying themselves."

Certainly there is something strange about animal lovers who own pets that have to be fed live animals, yet reptiles and amphibians are gaining in popularity throughout the West. According to *Libre Service Actualities*, a revue of consumption, there are five thousand reptiles kept as pets in France. A German animal-importer writes that an estimated fifty thousand reptiles and amphibians are imported annually for the pet shops. How many of the approximately one million exotic pets in England are reptiles and amphibians would be difficult to establish, and even in America we know only that a reptile dealer who sold four thousand boa constrictors in 1966 sold twelve thousand in 1967. If these animals lived on tinned foods, it would be easier to estimate their numbers. There are enough of them, however, for the animal welfare organizations to print and distribute leaflets dealing with their feeding and care, and for the pet-book publishers to produce a separate book on the keeping of each species.

A man who, after watching a television program, decided to keep snakes as pets, has an eight-foot-long Indian python that weighs twenty-eight pounds, and a five-foot-long boa constrictor. They live on rabbits that have to be fed to them live. In order to be able to do this he probably has to "de-animalize" the rabbits and pretend to himself that they are "things," in exactly the same way people "de-humanize" those they want to destroy. Others feed their snakes live mice or frogs, kept by many people as pet animals, or tiny chicks. People who keep alligators feed them live fish, birds, and small mammals or, for a delicacy, newts or salamanders. If the pet is a newt or salamander or chameleon, the owner does not have to overcome a severe inner resistance unless he has a particular fondness for insects, for these pets thrive on live flies, moths, meal worms, or small crickets. *The Pets Cookbook* gives detailed instruction as to the modes of feeding.

One wonders why antivivisectionists and animal lovers in general, who protest so vehemently against the use of mice in medical experiments that might benefit the human race, never raise their voices against the feeding of live mice to pet snakes, and why those who campaign against factory farming do not mind the feeding of one-day chicks to amphibians.

Some people are addicted to power as others are to drugs, but while drug addiction destroys the person involved, power addiction not only corrupts the sufferer but often destroys others, sometimes entire nations. When the craving for power is combined with brilliance or some particular gift, it may produce extraordinary achievements, but combined with a small mind and lack of imagination it leads only to frustration.

The lust for power is one of the most dangerous human traits and, if it cannot be sublimated, will seek victims among the defenseless, human or animal. How widespread it is can be deduced from the number of bullies, sadists, and criminals among us, but under certain conditions even the unlikeliest person, the mildest, shiest, most modest little man may turn out to be a power addict.

A middle-aged shipping clerk, so insignificant as to be almost invisible, used to hit his wife on any pretext, just

to show her who was master of the house. He would, however, never even speak a harsh word to his sixteen-year-
old daughter. He was inordinately proud of her because
she was doing well in school. He wanted her to go to college.
The home situation changed only when the girl decided to
leave school and take an office job to earn money and become independent. The father raged and begged her to change
her mind, but to no avail. From then on he took to drink,
and when drunk he used to beat both his wife and his daughter. Alerted by their cries, the neighbors often called the police but since no bones were broken and the women refused
to lodge a complaint against him, the police had no power
to interfere. Unable to act out his power complex vicariously
through his daughter, the man now turned to his pets, half
a dozen rabbits he kept in a hutch in the yard. When drunk
he would stand in front of the hutch, his arms outstretched
and, to the amusement of the neighbors, deliver long and
loud speeches to his rabbits. "You, my rabbits, who know
who I am," he would shout, "look on passively while your
lord and master, a man born to rule the stupid, weak and
dishonest masses, and guide them towards a life of peace
and dignity, is mocked and humiliated by superiors and colleagues who do not even deserve to lick his boots, and by
his own daughter whom he raised in his own image, but
who throws away the power he has placed in her hands to
become an animal, like her mother. . . ." He would go on,
sometimes for an hour or more, until the neighbors, tired
of his antics, would forcibly lead him back to his apartment.

Another case concerns a factory worker of about thirty-
five, red-haired, cross-eyed, who lived with his dominating
mother and never had a girl friend. He was an active trade-
unionist and greatly despised the "bourgeois" who were
unable to discipline their pets. He had a Doberman pinscher
whose training gave his life meaning. He would take the
dog out on the commons every night after work and teach
it obedience so strict that the dog would even leave its food
to obey a command. The man had achieved his successes
in training by tying a thin wire around the dog's neck under
the collar, so when he pulled the leash, the wire cut into

the animal's flesh. He himself never buttoned the collar of his shirt and never wore a tie because he could not tolerate anything tight round his neck.

It is more than probable that most people who choose the training of animals as their profession are acting out an unconscious craving for power. One trainer, who specialized in the training of police dogs, had given up schoolteaching for the sake of this new profession. He had taught at an elementary school where he had been known as a strict disciplinarian and was well liked by the headmaster because of the excellent performance of his class. His relationship to the children was that of a sergeant to new recruits; he demanded absolute obedience and would mete out the severest punishments, usually canings, for the slightest infringements of the rules. The children were terrified of him and dared not complain, even to their parents. But his reign came to an end when one of the boys got into such a state that he had to be taken to a child psychiatrist. The psychiatrist reported the child's "confession" to the headmaster who, unwilling to dismiss a good schoolteacher, warned him, in a private conversation, to change his methods. Rather than give up the deep satisfaction of his absolute power, the motive for his having chosen teaching as a career in the first place, he decided to resign. He found substitute, and perhaps even more satisfactory, objects for his power lust in the Alsatians that became model police dogs under his hand.

Pet-shop owners and dog breeders have a great many stories to tell about the preferences shown by certain types of people for certain types of pets. They all agree that men of short stature or weak character will almost invariably buy large pets: bulldogs, Alsatians, Great Danes, Doberman pinschers or, if their circumstances allow it, large exotic pets like cheetahs, ocelots, leopards, margays, sometimes chimpanzees or alligators. Ownership of such animals gives them a feeling of power, a self-confidence that may even help them stand up to a bossy employer, a dominating wife, or contemptuous children.

CHAPTER 6
PETS AND THE TABOOS

Freedom is inconceivable as long as the biological development of man is suppressed and dreaded.

—WILHELM REICH:
The Mass Psychology of Fascism

◉ ◉ IN THE COMMUNIST COUNTRIES IT IS SAID that "most things are prohibited but what is allowed is compulsory." This may be told as a joke, but Western man knows from experience that far from being a joke, it is a statement of fact valid everywhere.

In the Catholic countries, where the state keeps God alive for its own convenience, society is held together by religious prohibitions and compulsions that are, on the whole, less crippling to the inner man than the nonreligious social taboos of the Protestant countries. This is due mainly to the universal complicity of Catholics to circumvent them. In the Anglo-Saxon countries these taboos—some, but not all of which, are identical in England and America—create a reign of terror. Those brought up to obey them react by retreating into themselves and avoiding any kind of "involvement" with their fellow humans or, like many Americans, by clothing the intimidated inner man in the convincing disguise of a well-adjusted, constructively aggressive, outer man.

In a society where man's sanity depends on the extent to which he can protect himself against the stress of everyday living, he has learned to "play possum," to pretend even to himself that apart from the "presence" required for functioning as a cog in the social machine, he is bodily as well as emotionally nonexistent. Instead of consciously experiencing the enlivening interaction of body, instinct, emotion, and imagination, he excludes this from his consciousness and uses his body as a tool to perform a set of actions—those required for his own survival and those required for the survival of the race. Sometimes the inner man cheats the taboos by focusing his emotions on a surrogate object—an animal—that can be relied on not to harm, hurt, disappoint, or reject him or to demand more than he is allowed, able, or willing to give.

In *The Animals Came in One by One*, Buster Lloyd-Jones talks about his overwhelming love of animals from early childhood. His father had been a "strict and rather awesome man," obsessively convinced of always being right and just as obsessively determined to have "perfect" children. He hated any display of weakness, including illness, which he simply ignored, and when his seven-year-old son contracted polio, he regarded it as a rebellion against his authority and turned away in disgust. Of his mother Buster Lloyd-Jones says: "She was utterly unsentimental and never mothered us

in the accepted sense. . . . There were times when we would
have given a great deal to be spoiled. . . . She was a great
one for Good Works as, indeed, was my father. They divided
up the local Good Works equally between them, my father
taking Chapel . . . the Boy Scouts and the Red Cross, my
mother Orphans, Dr. Barnardo's Homes, Sick Visiting and
Overseas Missions."

In this case the taboo on showing love, and the compul-
sion to bring up their children as socially acceptable freaks,
drove the parents to Good Works where emotional involvement could easily be avoided and drove the son to find in
animals the surrogate objects for all that was best and most
genuinely human in him.

The American psychiatrist Dr. Ross V. Speck, who works
with disturbed families in their homes, likes the pet animals
to be present at sessions because he finds they often reflect
the feelings of the family members. In one case, Dr. Speck
reports, the father would pet the dog, or pick it up and carry
it around in his arms when upset. He had acquired the dog
immediately after the death of his favorite child, a daughter,
and was on very bad terms with his two sons, whom he be-
littled or ignored. When this family was asked to fill out
so-called "interaction forms" for research purposes, the
father demanded that the forms also be filled out on the
dog. It was evident that at the time his dog was more important to him than his sons. Had the social taboos not prevented
this father from openly mourning his little daughter until
the terrible heartache caused by her loss abated, he would
certainly have turned for consolation to his wife and divided
the extra love between his sons.

Many parents disappointed in their children will anthropomorphize a pet animal, unable or unwilling to face their
own responsibility for the way their children turned out
to be. A couple who had entrusted their daughter, practically from the day she was born, to servants, baby-sitters,
or mothers-in-law while they traveled or went out every

evening to have "a good time" found, to their surprise, that at the age of six their daughter was utterly unmanageable. The child would not allow herself to be kissed or petted, had tantrums when they talked to each other in her presence but would not reply when spoken to, screamed each morning when she had to go to school and each night when she was put to bed. When her mother slapped her, she bit her hand. They bought the child a puppy for Christmas, but the little girl kicked the dog and refused to play with it. The mother took pity on the small animal and became so deeply attached to it that she stayed home every evening, afraid to leave it alone with her child. Her affection for the puppy drove the little girl to such outbursts of violent rage that the parents decided to send her away from home. The child went to live with an unmarried aunt, who spoiled her outrageously but helped her to adjust to school life. The parents remained alone with the dog.

From then on, nothing was too good for the dog. They ordered every newspaper that had a pet column and religiously followed the advice given by every columnist. They bought their dog the best meat, fed it vegetables, stewed fruit and candy, gave it vitamins every day and a tranquilizer when it slept badly, took it to the veterinarian once a month for a checkup, and had its teeth examined every six months. They collected a veritable library of dog books and a chest of drawers full of collars and leashes in every color and style, dog coats for every season, shampoos, sprays, brushes, combs, and a variety of dishes. The dog slept in the little girl's bed, which was opened for it at night and made in the morning. In winter an electric blanket was left switched on all day in case the dog wanted a snooze.

When the dog was ten years old and the little girl sixteen, two things happened. The dog was run over by a car and died, and the girl became pregnant by a much older, married man. Deeply distressed by the loss of their darling and in dire need of consolation, the parents begged their daughter to come home to live. They made no reproaches. On the contrary, they offered to adopt the baby when it was born and look after it. The daughter, who had quarreled with her aunt about the pregnancy, accepted her parents' offer and moved back into her old room. But surrounded by the innumerable mementos of the departed dog and having to listen to her parents' endless stories about it, she became more and more depressed and in the sixth month of her pregnancy tried to kill herself by slashing her wrists in the bathtub. Her life was saved, but she lost the baby.

In New York the son of a professional couple got involved with a gang of hoodlums and, after an unsuccessful robbery, was arrested and sent to a corrective institution. The parents were convinced that apart from not spending enough time with the boy, they had given him everything—a nice home, a good education, generous pocket money. They could not understand how he could have betrayed their trust. In court they admitted they never checked his movements. At nine o'clock in the evening he was always home, and they never even asked the name and address of the classmate at whose house, allegedly, he was studying every afternoon. When the judge reprimanded them for neglecting their parental duties, both mother and father were deeply offended and blamed everyone but themselves for what had happened.

From then on, the father took an unreasonable dislike to his son's dog. He would not tolerate its presence in the living room but chased it out into the kitchen. When the door was left open and the dog returned to its accustomed place on the rug near its absent young master's chair, the father, an otherwise mild man, would grab the leash and beat it savagely. In his calm moments he knew his rage was directed not against the dog but against his son, but emotion was stronger than reason. After a few weeks, when it became clear that sooner or later he would kill the dog, his wife took the animal to the SPCA, asking them to find a home for it or have it destroyed.

The family of a gentleman farmer in England was envied by the entire neighborhood for the happy and relaxed atmosphere of their home and the warm, friendly relationship between the parents and their three young sons. When the sons went to boarding school, as was traditional in the family, the situation changed dramatically. The couple, who had always lived in affectionate, though undemonstrative, harmony, began to grow away from each other and have increasingly bitter quarrels. Although she never said so, the mother resented being deprived of her children, felt she had lost her *raison d'être,* and blamed her husband for her unhappiness. He, on the other hand, convinced that he had done *the right thing* but missing his sons, blamed his wife for the deterioration of their marriage and spent more and more time with his horses and dogs. They moved into separate bedrooms, and the husband got into the habit of driving each night to the village pub with his two favorite dogs and returning only at closing time. Left completely to herself, jealous of her husband's dogs, and knowing his aversion to cats, the wife began to fill the house with kittens, bringing home a few every time a neighbor's cat had a litter. The couple's hostility communicated itself to the animals. The dogs and cats were constantly fighting, and as the husband took the side of his dogs and the wife of her cats, they and their pets started eating and spending the evenings in separate rooms.

By the time the three sons came home for their first holiday the separation was complete, the parents no longer even spoke to each other, and the boys were constantly made to choose between the two hostile camps. The parents, who had never learned, and in the past never needed, to analyze themselves and discuss their problems with each other came to believe that their estrangement was caused by his love for dogs and hers for cats. To spite one another both became so obsessively preoccupied with their pets that they paid hardly any attention to their sons. From then on, the boys did their best to avoid spending their holidays at home, accepted invitations from their friends, or asked to be sent to holiday camps. A few years later the parents divorced, but by that time the wife had become an "eccentric" who lived only for her thirty odd cats and the husband a taciturn, bitter man who talked only to his dogs. The three boys were saved from the consequence of their parents' madness by having one another, but after graduation all three emigrated to Australia.

In Germany, a young couple had a baby girl the same day their Alsatian bitch had her first litter of four lovely puppies. The owners gave away three but decided to keep one, in the hope that having a child of her own, the Alsatian would not be jealous of her mistress's baby. Intelligent parents with a second child are usually very careful not to make the older one jealous, give it just a little more love than before, and make it feel it has a share in the ownership of, as well as the responsibility for, the new baby. This young couple applied the same principles to their pet, encouraged her to come close to the baby while they, themselves, treated the puppy with the same tenderness they showed their own child.

However, instead of forming one big happy family, as they intended, the Alsatian tried to adopt the baby as her own and completely neglected the puppy. She refused to suckle it, growled when it tried to feed, and when the puppy insisted, she bit it. At the same time she barked and whined so loudly when her mistress tried to feed her own baby that she had to be locked out of the room. One day, when the young mother left the Alsatian to watch the baby while she prepared her orange juice in the kitchen, the animal dragged the child from its cot and tore open its throat. The strange thing was that instead of blaming the Alsatian for killing their child, the couple blamed themselves for having had the child in the first place. They would not allow the dog to be destroyed, treated it from then on as if it were their daughter, and never had another child.

Married couples, or widows and widowers, whose children have grown up and left the home, often adopt pet animals to fill their empty lives. If for one reason or other they feel guilty toward their children, they are apt to make up for their real or imaginary failures by overindulging, overspoiling, their pets.

A woman of sixty whose married daughter, the mother of two small children, lived nearby, was practically in bondage to a little toy poodle. In her youth she had been very pretty and gay, always the belle of the ball, and her whole life consisted of preparing for and going to parties. Her way of life remained unchanged even after the birth of her daughter, a sweet, delicate child her parents caressed and petted like a little animal when, between parties and sleeping them off, they looked into the nursery. The little girl idolized her mother and, in her loneliness, cried herself to sleep night after night. She grew into a tall, skinny girl and, at the age of thirteen, was found to have tuberculosis. Her parents sent her to a Swiss sanatorium, where she remained for five years, visited once or twice a year by her mother or father. At the age of twenty she married a young doctor and emigrated with him to America. Her first pregnancy caused a flare-up of TB; she lost the child and had to wait years before she was allowed to try again. When her child was born she brought her widowed mother to America and installed her in a small apartment close by. She even bought her a tiny poodle so she would not feel lonely at home.

From the first moment, the widow relived her motherhood with the tiny dog as her child. But hating herself for the selfish mother she had been, and blaming herself for her daughter's illness and suffering, she acted this time as she felt she should have acted thirty years before. She slept with the little dog in her arms, combed it, brushed it, cleaned its teeth, eyes, and ears every morning, shared her breakfast with it, then took it for a walk. She bought the poodle collars and leashes to go with her dresses. The dog's coats were made of the same material as hers, and when she wore her fur coat, the poodle wore a similar one. When it was raining, she and the dog put on raincoats, rain hats, and rubber boots of the same color, and in winter both wore warm, lined boots. She would always put two pieces of Kleenex in her pocket to wipe the poodle's bottom after it had relieved itself on the curb. If there were visitors, the dog was always present, sitting in its special armchair. Everyone knew that the lady could not be invited without her dog, but they also learned that no invitations were accepted from people who had dogs, cats, or children of their own.

In spite of the extreme care—or, precisely, because of it—the poodle became ill at the age of five, and although the veterinarian did his best to save it, it died of pneumonia. The "mother" was inconsolable. Once again she had failed her "child." She had a nervous breakdown and has been under psychiatric treatment ever since.

An American executive, who lived in constant terror of someone discovering that his older brother, now dead, had once been a card-bearing member of the Communist party, resolved that his children would be model Americans with not a single intellectual or emotional hair out of place. His wife was the daughter of a self-made millionaire who, at the age of forty-five, became a strict Methodist in order to make himself and others forget the far from Christian methods that had made his fortune. She approved of her husband's ideas and helped put them into practice. The son and daughter, both attractive and intelligent, submitted to the parental brainwashing, and when she was sixteen and he fifteen, they were paragons of virtue whom their parents, their teachers, and their church were equally proud of.

No one, least of all their parents, could understand why, a year later, both young people ran away from home and joined a group of hippies. They refused to listen to entreaties or threats but told their parents that if force were used to bring them home, they would run away again and this time turn to drugs and crime. All they wanted, they said was to cleanse their minds of the "crap" they had been fed since birth, see the world as it really was, and learn to think for themselves. They hoped to grow into human beings, not just "Americans."

Unwilling to lose a valuable man, the father's "organization" came to his aid by transferring him to another state where no one knew him. Badly in need of a hobby, he bought two German shepherd puppies and began training them. He became so adept at this game that his dogs became famous throughout the state for their perfect manners, their absolute obedience, and the extraordinary feats they could perform. Both he and his wife were so proud of their dogs they took them wherever they went to show them off. The gratitude, love, and loyalty of their pets gave them great happiness, and if they mentioned their children to each other it was usually to express worry and fear of becoming involved should the children commit some illegal action.

A story of a mother, a son, and a dog that was published in *The People* in 1967, with the full names of the protagonists, deserves to be recorded here.

Mrs. Anne Brantschen-Marsh has spent more than 300 pounds in a nine-months legal battle against her 24 year old son Timothy over the ownership of Inky, a black Scottish terrier. She brought three court actions against her son after he gave the dog away and refused to disclose his whereabouts.

When, after becoming estranged from her second husband Mrs. Brantschen-Marsh went to Geneva to work she entrusted the 12 year old pedigree dog Inky, her cat and her birds to her son until she had settled down. Two months later she found out that Inky had been given away and when Timothy refused to disclose the name of its new owners, she advertised, unsuccessfully, offering a free vacation for two in Switzerland in exchange for the return of the dog.

First, Mrs. Brantschen-Marsh brought a private prosecution for theft against her son and his fiancee but when the case was dismissed by the magistrates she sued the young couple in another County. The action failed and when she took the case to the Court of Appeal the judge's decision that the dog belonged to her son and he was entitled to give it away, was upheld. In the meantime she found out that the dog had developed a tumor and had had to be put down.

"I started the court actions to try to frighten them into telling me where they had left Inky," Mrs. Brantschen-Marsh said. "When they refused to budge I had no choice but to go ahead with the actions as I was so desperate to find out that Inky was well. He was a delicate old dog, toothless, timid and nearly blind. He needed special attention. I desperately wanted him back. . . . There have been some terrible rows and scenes over this. . . ."

"This pretty sordid business has meant my mother and I cutting each other out of our respective lives," said the son. "It is very unfortunate mother developed such a fixation about this."

A large proportion of the people who, for one reason or other, have no children and yet consciously or unconsciously desire parenthood, and many people whose children have grown, leaving their parents with the memory of, and yearning for, small children in the house, adopt pet animals that they promote to the rank of children.

If one thinks of the millions of unwanted, poor, physically or mentally damaged, institution-raised children in the affluent West, or the children of the "expendables," or even the children reared in "normal" families who go to the dogs as a result of their upbringing, it is safe to say that the more potential parents go to the dogs or other pets for child substitutes, the better for the unborn children. Yet one often wonders why people who would probably make excellent parents and could afford to give children a decent home, a good education, care and happiness, adopt animals instead of adopting children. Who knows how many great artists, brilliant scientists and philosophers, with revolutionary ideas, are lost in the mass processing of socially useful, useless, or harmful adults only because people lacked the courage and determination to overcome their fear of other people's genes in the children they might adopt.

One does not quite know whether to laugh, cry, or get angry at adult persons calling themselves the "mummy" or "daddy" of a poodle, a Siamese cat, or a baby chimp. Mrs. W., who has a married son, is stared at every time she pushes the brand new perambulator, holding a young chimpanzee, along the street. The animal is being brought up like a child. He sleeps in his own bed, has a wardrobe full of clothes and a collection of toys no child in the neighborhood ever had.

He is regularly fed, has his teeth brushed and his hair combed in the morning, adores television, and often goes with his "mummy" to the local pub for a glass of orange juice. Mrs. W. is not an exception, even if a chimp as a child substitute is.

An East European refugee woman, working for the UNO in New York, had her terrier bitch brought out from her native land by the Red Cross. This animal was everything to her, fatherland, family, beloved child. When the dog fell ill and had to have an operation, she was in despair because, except on weekends, she could not visit it during visiting hours. She telephoned a friend and begged her to go to the hospital instead of her; it would break her poor darling's heart to be neglected when every other dog had a visitor.

The friend agreed reluctantly, saying she "hardly knew the dog," but when she finally went a fire had broken out in the hospital and the firemen would not allow anyone to enter. Not being a pet addict, she was fascinated by the hysterical scenes taking place outside the building. The women screamed, tore their hair, several fainted, and two tried to break through the cordon, crying that they wanted to die with their darlings. Fortunately the fire was put out and no pets were hurt.

This parent-child relationship between humans and their pets seems to be a generally accepted phenomenon in Western countries. Modern veterinary hospitals in America, in England, and several European countries have a "recovery room" for the "parents" of the pets brought in for treatment, for an operation, or to be put to sleep. The parents are offered coffee, tea, or tranquilizers and given first aid should they faint.

We should probably gain a great deal of information about the deepest layers of the human soul if psychoanalysts, veterinarians, and dog trainers—who also call themselves dog psychologists—pooled their experiences.

John Behan, head of a dog-training school called Canine College in Connecticut, has famous people like Joan Crawford, Irving Berlin, Raymond Massey, John D. Rockefeller, and Katharine Cornell among his clients. He tells of a woman who brought along her small, crippled dog and asked that he be taught not to bark so she could take him to the opera. When the ushers refused to allow even a nonbarking dog to attend the performance, the lady came back, asking that he be taught to lie quietly on her shoulder and imitate a fur collar.

Another training establishment, the American Training Academy, puts out a leaflet designed to attract the parents of dog children who wish to learn "The Secret of Communicating with Your Dog." The leaflet is "an invitation for the 1 dog owner in 3 whose concern for their dog extends beyond the physical necessities of life." The Message from the Director promises "a psychologically oriented system of dog development and training based on principles remarkably similar to child psychology. The key to this unique system lies in the concept of *psychological intensification*—a technique of teaching and communicating with your dog that harnesses your dog's innermost motivations and desires. A technique aimed at developing a level of communication between you and your dog so sophisticated it is almost human." Participation in the American Training Academy program is not recommended for the "average dog owner." But if you are not "average," but a good "mummy" or "daddy" ready and able to pay, for any sacrifice, "we can help you unlock new dimensions in your relationship with your dog. Dimensions so exciting and rewarding they will make your investment seem insignificant in comparison."

The investment, if it is a question of in-person training and consultation, "the finest expression of your love," is not to be sneered at. "Your counsellor conducts all consultation and training in your home . . . but between sessions he is available for telephone consultations on a 24 hour a day basis." The fees for this service, "commensurate with the intensity of the personal attention lavished on you and your dog," range from $40 to $950. However, if this service, which is available anywhere in the world, is conducted outside the New York area, transportation and living expenses will be added to the fees outlined.

When interviewed on the BBC, the British dog trainer and psychologist Frank Pettit said it is a good thing to "humanize" a dog. People fed up with humans often find happiness in their relationship with a pet. "A pet loves you for what you are, not for what you have." But a dog treated as a substitute child can become very demanding and may take the reins into his own paws. It frequently happens that a dog used to sleeping with his "parents" as a puppy eventually chases the husband from the bed because he wants to have his "mother" to himself. This clearly shows that the Oedipus complex is not a psychological disturbance confined to the human animal. It needs a smart dog-analyst to cure a dog smitten with it.

One of the places a parent can take his dog child in need of psychotherapy is the Canine Behavior Institute in Beverly Hills, specializing in the analysis of dogs suffering from mental traumata, depression, or suicidal neurosis. "It is not the dog's duty to understand man, but man's duty to understand the dog," say the dog analysts. The pet owner is required to participate in the six obligatory sessions—which will cost him something like $250 and, if successful, establish between owner and dog the same type of relationship that exists, or should ideally exist, between parent and child. One of the clients of this illustrious establishment is California's Governor, Ronald Reagan.

People who wish to understand their pet-child's character but cannot afford to take it to an animal psychiatrist can, if they know their pet's birth date, learn everything about it from Liz Tresilian's *Dog* or *Cat Horoscope Book*. A dog born under the sign of Gemini, for instance, is a very rewarding pet because it will remain a puppy, with a split personality, as long as it lives, and its behavior greatly resembles that of a highly intelligent, sensitive, exuberant child. There is, however, one significant difference that makes harmony between a Gemini dog and puritanical pet-parents impossible. He is the Don Juan of the dog world, as sex-hungry and as indiscriminating as the above-named gentleman.

If your dog was born under the sign of the Lion, you had better be a masochist, for he is domineering and authoritative. He will tolerate you only if you yield to all his rather exacting wishes. "The only person who stands a chance of gaining his affection will be someone who is weak-willed enough to kowtow and pay homage. Someone, who will be happy to sit beside him paring his nails and combing his coat . . ." If you have a sadistic streak in your nature, you will be best off with a dog born under the sign of Pisces, a passive, dreamy, comfort-loving animal who knows his place and, whatever you do to him, will not fight back.

"Libidinous attachments to animals are likely to escape detection as psychopathological manifestations unless carried to extreme degrees. Eulogies to beloved dogs, extravagances with reference to fine horses, panegyrics dedicated to cats and various other 'friends of man' are generally accepted as entirely understandable manifestations of human emotions. It is truly amazing to what degree popular taste permits the expression of such positive attachments without clear recognition of their essentially sexual nature," writes Karl A. Menninger in his essay "Contemporary Attitudes Towards Animals." *

Sexually frustrated people often show an inordinate interest in their children's sex life. They will spy on them and, if they catch them masturbating, tell the most hair-raising horror stories about what will happen unless they stop that "dirty" practice. They will bring up their daughters in the belief that intercourse is a revolting and painful duty a wife has to put up with in exchange for support and children, the *only* justification of sex, and they will teach their sons that sex is "filthy" and the woman they practice it with despicable.

The same educational methods are also applied to substitute sons and daughters. A great many people will have their pets neutered, not to prevent them from propagating, but in the belief that the operation will kill their desire for sex. They are sadly disappointed to discover their dog or cat daughters are just as pleased to accept the advances of the opposite sex as before. Others will pick up their pets

*Ibid.

in their arms or forcibly pull them away when they become interested in another member of their species in the street. It frequently happens that a pet owner suffering from a pathological revulsion to sex will develop such hatred for the cat or dog that has become pregnant in spite of the precautions taken that he will have the animal put to death.

On the other hand, those whose sexual frustration manifests itself in an unhealthy curiosity about it all will encourage their pets to masturbate, sometimes by deliberately exciting them, and watch with avid interest the preliminaries and the act of mating. Frustrated sadists will take pleasure in playing with their pets in ways that cause pain, but will be so careful that even an onlooker will not be able to construe these games as acts of cruelty.

Attachment to animals may also assume almost masochistic extremes. When the British had to be evacuated from Egypt, where mob violence threatened their lives, one of the women being interviewed in the Surrey refugee center told the newspapermen with tears in her eyes that she had had to leave behind her ten-year-old cat. Her sister had stayed in Egypt because she refused to be separated from her Doberman pinscher.

A couple ready to emigrate to Australia gave up their plan at the last minute when they were told they could not take their Alsatian because it had failed the medical exam. Canceling their passage and having their furniture sent back cost them £500, but they did not mind. "A new life would have been meaningless if we had sacrificed our dog for it," they said. Since they had sold their country pub and given up their home, they had to start a new life anyway. "She is part of our marriage," the young woman said. "I expected friends to criticize us for treating a dog like a member of the family, but they didn't. They realize that Kim is more than just a dog to us."

Another couple offered their £4,000 bungalow to anyone who found their vanished eleven-year-old Labrador. "This is our last desperate effort," they said. "If we get Lassie back we would be quite happy to sell up and move into a caravan."

In five years a British animal-lover has rescued 5,000 stray dogs from the pounds and gas chambers. His hobby costs him over £100 a week. He has spent thousands of his own and has mortgaged his ten-acre home at Ascot to be able to finance it. He usually has 140 to 170 dogs on his grounds and feeds them 280 pounds of meat and meal a day. The short article devoted to this eminently humane person contains no information on the reasons why he withholds his much needed help from his poverty-stricken compatriots and prefers to ruin himself for the sake of unwanted dogs.

A schoolteacher with no wife and children of his own had found happiness playing father to several dozen cats. When the neighbors complained, he was ordered by the local health inspector to get rid of his pets. Unable to give them away or have them put to sleep, he placed all but two of them in a private animal home, where he pays a dollar a day for each cat. After paying the monthly bill he has hardly enough left to eat on.

A similar case is that of the old charlady who retired nine years ago from her job in a large factory. As a parting favor she asked to be allowed to come back every day to feed the fifteen factory cats. Each morning she arrived with the milk, meat, and fish paid for out of her small pension. She had bought collars for the cats with their names engraved on them, and they are no less spoiled than her own ten cats at home. By the time she has taken care of twenty-five cats, there is not much left for herself, but she does not mind. "Sometimes, like anyone else, I'd like to lie in bed in the morning. But I know I've got to be up and about early to prepare and take the food to my little ones," she says.

The strongest taboo of all is the taboo on love between man and woman. When the Catholic Church invented the dogma of the original sin, the idea was to brand sexual pleasure as something shameful, filthy, abominable, so that anyone indulging in it should feel guilty and afraid of punishment and be compelled to turn to the church for absolution. The virulence of this dogma has remained almost unchanged for nearly two thousand years and has, by defiling bodily joy, contributed to the withering of the feeling of *love*. By poisoning the natural and the beautiful—man's healthy animal instincts—it has opened the floodgates of aggression, hypocrisy, and perversion. Protestantism has added insult to injury by persecuting even the sublimated expressions of love in art and the religious ritual, imposing a bleak austerity that crushes the imagination and replacing the mortification of the body with its complete negation.

"Thus, because of the cultural norms in Anglo-Saxon countries, people are deprived of the most basic way to experiencing their bodies—through human touch," writes Sidney Jourard, professor of psychology at the University of Florida, in his study, "Out of Touch: The Body Taboo." "I suspect that the dog patter, the cat stroker and child hugger, is seeking the contact that is conspicuously and poignantly lacking in his adult life. Why the touch taboo? I think it is part of the more general alienation process that characterizes our depersonalizing social system. I think it is related to the same source that underlies the dread of authentic self-disclosure."

The Protestant variety of the *Homo neuroticus* has been so effectively brainwashed by his religious reformers that in his efforts to neuter himself into virtue, he has become sex-obsessed. Every instinctive need of the body, from decent food, comfort, a warm room, to any physical manifestation of love or affection between human beings, even the handshake between friends, has become suspect. Convinced of the "purity" of his love for animals, he will often put more of himself into his relationship with a pet than into his relationship with human partners.

The love of pet animals may prevent people from marrying, may break up or hold marriages together, separate engaged couples, and sometimes bring together totally unsuited people. For instance, it was because of an Alsatian his mother had given him that Mrs. D. divorced the husband by whom she had had three children. He had become so fanatically fond of the dog that he preferred it to his wife and children. When the dog fell ill with cancer he ran up enormous veterinary bills they could not afford because he would not take it to the free clinic, paid for an expensive operation, and refused to get rid of the unfortunate animal even when it bit his small son. When, in spite of these desperate efforts, the dog had to be put down, the man was in such a state that he hardly noticed that his wife had moved out, taking the children with her.

Another woman divorced her husband because of his love for a five-foot boa constrictor. He insisted that his pet sleep in the bed with them, usually coiled round his body, and when his wife, who was afraid of the snake, protested, he abused her and sometimes even hit her. While he was at work, the boa rested in a large wicker basket with a closed top, but he would bring it with him to the dinner table, coiled around his neck and shoulders. When he began to feed the snake live mice while he and his wife were having dinner, she decided she had had enough. She was granted a divorce on the ground of mental cruelty, and his only comment was: "Good riddance." He acquired another boa and is now impatiently waiting for them to produce children.

In Germany a woman divorced her husband because he was so devoted to his two dogs that he refused to have children. He explained to her that since he wanted to give his dogs the best of everything, he could not afford to keep a child as well. Besides, he said, the dogs would be jealous: they were used to receiving all his attention and affection. This, the woman told the judge, was absolutely true. Once he had the dogs he had never shown her any affection or attention. He slept with the dogs, made them sit at the table for meals, and the only "marital duty" he demanded of her was to keep the house clean and cook the food for him and his dogs. He carefully checked the household accounts and would not give her a penny for her personal needs. She had had to take a part-time job to keep herself in clothes. "I shouldn't be surprised if he started barking instead of talking," she said.

However, it is not always the husband who prefers his pet to his spouse. In London a husband was granted a divorce on the ground of mental cruelty because his wife treated her dog like a husband and beat the husband, whom she treated like a dog. She insulted him, slapped him, humiliated him in front of their friends, shared her bed with her idolized pet, and made the husband sleep on the couch. In addition, she and her dog occupied the two easy chairs in front of the television set, and if the husband wanted to watch he had to sit on the floor at their feet.

Another man, whose wife kept half a dozen Siamese cats and would not get rid of them even though he had an allergy to cats and several times almost choked to death from severe attacks of asthma, divorced her though he was very much in love with her. This decision was all the more difficult because she was pregnant with their first child. When asked to choose between her husband and her cats, she said she could not live without the cats and only hoped her child would not inherit the father's allergy.

It also happens that a couple whose marriage is beyond salvation remain together because neither is willing to be separated from the family pet. Other couples fight it out in court over who should get custody of their beloved dog or cat. In one of the court cases involving pet animals reported in the newspapers, a husband was awarded custody but the wife was granted visiting rights provided she paid one-third of the cost of the animal's maintenance. In another the wife got custody of their pet Alsatian, but the husband was granted visiting rights if he agreed to pay veterinary and grooming bills and buy the dog its clothes.

One case, published in the Court of Appeal report of *The Times*, on February 21, 1968, is so fantastic that it deserves to be recorded here in full.

Glaister-Carlisle v. Glaister-Carlisle, Before the Master of the Rolls, Lord Justice Edmund Davies, and Mr. Justice Cairns.

When a husband vexed with his wife because he believed she had carelessly allowed his white miniature poodle bitch to mate with her black poodle, threw the bitch at her, saying "She is your responsibility now," the conduct and words were so equivocal that English law would not regard it as a perfect gift of the poodle by him to her.

The Court so held in allowing an appeal by Mr. Thomas Glaister-Carlisle of Sketty Road, Enfield, from the decision of Judge Granville-Smith last July at Edmonton County Court, declaring in proceedings under section 17 of the Married Women's Property Act, 1882, that the poodle was the property of his wife, Mrs. Phyllis May Glaister-Carlisle, of Mannock Road, Wood Green.

The Court declared that the bitch was the husband's property and ordered that it be handed over to him within seven days.

The Master of the Rolls said that the bitch had lived up to her name, Springtime Ballyhoo. She had had an illicit love affair with a black pedigree poodle, Alexis, who lived in the same house. One expected consequence of that was that she had puppies. Other unexpected consequences were that on one occasion the police were called in; lawyers had been consulted, the magistrates had heard all about it; the county court judge had decided it; and now the Court of Appeal had to consider it.

Her dam was owned by the husband and she was born in 1960. The husband registered her in his name with the Kennel Club. He was clearly her owner. He wanted her to have puppies and took her by arrangement to a Miss Evans, who owned Alexis. The dogs mated: the dog had puppies; and in 1962 her owner married Miss Evans. They set up house and had the dog and bitch with them.

In September, 1964, the wife had a broken leg. As they did not want the bitch to have puppies again, the wife had apparently asked the husband to take her to a Mrs. Boon to get her out of the way, but it was not done in time. One afternoon, when the wife was in a room unable to get out of her chair she heard skirmishing in the next room and a little squeak. She thought the dogs had probably mated and told her husband. There seemed to have been a row, each blaming the other.

Much of the case depended on what had happened. There were two versions. The husband's version was that he said: "I say they have mated. This time you can bear the responsibility and expense. . . . If there is a litter you win; if no litter you lose," and to that the wife seemed to agree.

The wife said that the husband had picked up the bitch, had thrown it at her, and he had said that, "She is your responsibility now"; that he had wanted to put the bitch down but instead had given it to her.

After the row the husband took the bitch to Mrs. Boon for three weeks and paid the bill. Later, when it was plain that she was going to have puppies, they both took her to Mrs. Boon and the wife paid. During that time the parties had been at arm's length and in February, 1965, the husband left the house.

About May, there was an uproar when he tried to claim the bitch and he was bound over. From that time he said he kept watch, trying to see the bitch. Lawyers' letters were exchanged; and eventually the husband began proceedings under section 17 of the Married Women's Property Act, 1882, to determine to whom the animal belonged. On Christmas Day, 1966, he kidnapped the bitch; and again there were proceedings. Eventually, the matter came before the county court judge on the one question: Did the bitch belong to wife or husband?

The judge found there had been a gift by the husband to the wife. The husband now appealed, saying there was no evidence on which he could so find and that he made the wrong inference from the facts he found. Accepting that the appeal from the county court in regard to property under 200 pounds in value, like the bitch, was only on points of law, was the judge justified in law in the inference he drew?

Under the common law, in order that there should be a gift, there must be a delivery of possession by the one to the other, an acceptance, and above all a manifest intention by words or conduct to transfer the property absolutely from one to the other.

As between husband and wife it was often very difficult, because, as was said in Bashall v. Bashall (1894, 11 T.L.R. 152), a husband might often deliver a thing to his wife not so that it should be her property but so that she should have its use and enjoyment. There, it was a pony and a trap, a saddle and a dog; and the Court held that she must show that the husband had done that which amounted to delivery and that if the facts proved were equivocal, the wife must fail. And in *In Re* Cole (1964 1. Ch. 175, at p. 192) Lord Justice Harman said that if the act in itself was equivocal it did not constitute delivery.

The same must apply to the conduct or words which manifested intention. They must be clear and unequivocal; if they were not, the gift was not established.

In the present case there was no suggestion that it was an ordinary kind of gift made out of natural love and affection. The conduct was equivocal. Therefore, the property remained where it started, in the husband. The appeal should be allowed.

Lord Justice Edmund Davies, concurring, said that the case sprang from the passions aroused by pedigree poodles. Why dogs should inspire strong emotions was not far to seek. Aldous Huxley said that, "To his dog, every man is a Napoleon—hence the popularity of dogs." Despite her amorous activities, so popular was Springtime Ballyhoo that the rival claimants had, doubtless at considerable expense, brought the dispute about her ownership right up to the Court.

The present case was direct converse of *In Re* Cole, in which Lord Justice Harman had observed that the English law had always been chary of the recognition of gifts. Here there had been a clear act of delivery of his poodle by the husband to the wife. The question was: What intention accompanied the act? In His Lordship's view, on the proved facts, no gift was intended or effected. It was most improbable that in the autumn 1964 the husband would be animated by any sort of generous impulse towards his wife. The dispute was symptomatic of deeper and graver issues; but the wife had not established the gift.

Mr. Justice Cairns, being of opinion that under the appellate section of the County Court Act, 1959, the husband could only succeed if he could show that in some way the judge went wrong in law, concurred in allowing the appeal.

Sometimes married couples are not even aware of the important role the pet animal plays in their lives. Mr. H., a gifted musician, believes he is a happy man. His wife is a beautiful, vivacious woman, and they have a charming and talented teen-age daughter. Since he has learned partly to suppress and partly to sublimate his powerful sexual urge to please his wife, who loves him but hates sex, they have lived in perfect harmony, and it never occurred to either of them that the frequent blinding headaches Mr. H. suffered had anything to do with his deprivation. Some years ago the family bought a pedigree poodle. For the first week or so, until the puppy settled down, Mr. H. sat up with it night after night and as a result it became very much *his* dog. When he is at home, the poodle never leaves his side. It lies at his feet, jumps into his lap, licks his hands and face, turns on its back to have its belly scratched, and constantly provokes physical contact. Mr. H. loves it. His wife and daughter laugh at him, saying that now at last he has the second child he always wanted, but they are mistaken. The warmth, the bodily contact he receives from the poodle, makes up, in a way, for the physical coldness of his wife. At least the fact that his headaches have completely ceased seems to point to this.

The same relationship existed between Mr. M. and his wife. After the birth of their two sons, the couple moved into separate bedrooms and, at her wish, gave up sex. When he was in his fifties Mr. M. bought a spaniel pup and they became inseparable. The dog slept with its master, and he spent every free minute he had with his pet. His wife must have been unconsciously jealous of the dog because when he asked her to take it to the vet for a distemper shot she

failed to do so but told him she had. Unfortunately, the dog
got distemper and died. Mr. M. was inconsolable. Although
he had been a commando in the war and was anything but
weak or soft, he could not get over his dog's death, cried
every time he talked about it, and finally had a nervous breakdown. He was ill for a long time, and when he was beginning to recover, a well-meaning friend surprised him with
a new spaniel pup. This brought on a relapse so severe that
he had to be taken to a mental hospital. In the course of his
treatment he came to realize that he had identified the dog
with his wife in his mind and the guilt he felt when it died
was caused by his having wished his wife's death.

Another obvious example of such substitution is the case
of Miss V., whose fiancé was killed in the war. Although
she was a pretty girl and had opportunities to marry, she
developed such a revulsion to men that she preferred to
remain a spinster. For years she worked in an uninterest-
ing job and went home in the evenings to her blind and ail-
ing mother. The third member of the household was Brutus, a boxer. He was the man in the house both women relied on for protection; he was the center of their lives, their
principal subject of conversation, and they considered his
physical well-being more important than their own. When
Miss V. took Brutus for a walk and he showed interest in
a lady boxer, she hit him with the dog whip she had acquired.
She also whipped him when, as dogs often do, he tried to
rub against her leg or stick his head under her skirt. But
when her mother suggested he be neutered, she became
rude and abusive, something she had never been before.
Brutus slept at her feet on the bed and would wake her in
the morning by pulling the covers off her, a habit she always
complained about but never tried to change. When her mother
died, Brutus became her only companion. Having inherited some money from her mother, she gave up her job to
be with the dog all the time, and when, rarely, she spoke
to a neighbor she always expressed her fear that he might
die before her. She was lucky. She died one night, not yet
fifty, of a heart attack. When, alerted by the neighbors,
the police entered the house three days later, they found

Miss V. dead in her bed and Brutus lying dead at her feet in his accustomed place.

A middle-aged, highly intelligent, and very sensitive man with a string of broken marriages behind him decided that he would not try again but would live out his remaining years with his beautiful Alsatian dog. As he drank more than was good for him or, rather, had a very low tolerance for alcohol, he probably owed his life several times over to the Alsatian, who got him home in one piece when he might have ended under a truck or frozen to death in a ditch. His many friends, male and female, often wondered who his next wife would be; they were convinced he could not live alone. He chose the least likely of all, a woman with whom he had absolutely nothing in common. When his friends asked him why he picked her, he replied very seriously: "Because our dogs got on so well together."

One would think that only middle-aged or old people with a real or imaginary reason to feel disappointed in their fellow humans developed quasi-pathological attachments to animals, but it is not so. We find the same, often inexplicable, misplacement of love in some apparently normal young people.

Before marrying her fiancé, a girl of twenty decided to make him sign a written agreement concerning the future of her two dogs, five cats, one dwarf donkey, and one pony. The agreement stipulated that the dogs would continue to sleep in her bed, the cats where they wished, in their own beds or with her, the dwarf donkey in a large dog bed in the bedroom, and the pony, though sleeping in his stable, would be allowed to enter the house when he pleased, as before. Very much in love, the unfortunate young man signed without demur, firmly convinced that, once married, his bride would change her mind. He was wrong. Except for the three-day honeymoon—she refused to stay away longer from her pets—he never again had his wife to himself.

In another case two young people could not marry because of a dog. Every time they tried to rent a flat with the intention of getting it ready before the wedding, they were told: "No pets allowed." They had agreed that her cocker spaniel would live with them and had to postpone the wedding again and again until, in desperation, the young man joined a building cooperative. Now they shall have to wait until the apartment building, not yet under construction, is ready. The girl does not mind waiting, but it bodes ill for the marriage that to keep her love the young man pretends to be as fond of the animal as she is. "We think the world of that dog," he says. "He is well worth the trouble. Neither of us would want to be without him."

"It is indeed repugnant to the average person," says Dr. Menninger in "Contemporary Attitudes Towards Animals," "to have his attention called to the fact that just as we see sublimations of the perversions in much that passes for normal human behavior, so the affection and hatred of man for animals has at its root unconscious elements which in their extreme forms are regarded as sexual perversions. . . ."

According to the Kinsey reports on the sexual behavior of the human male and female, approximately 3.6 per cent of the adult females questioned had had sexual contacts of some sort with animals after adolescence. Nearly all contacts occurred with household pets, in 74 per cent of the cases with dogs. Among the adult males asked, 8 per cent had had sexual contacts with animals after adolescence, the majority with farm animals, the minority with pets. The most interesting aspect of these statistics, which show that sexual contact with animals is relatively rare, especially among women, is that almost half of the people involved had been, or were, married, that is, people who, if it had not been for the prohibitions and compulsions molding them since birth, might have achieved sufficient sexual satisfaction with human mates.

The religious and social taboos ruling our culture have driven sexual fantasy underground and weighed it down with guilt. As a result, afraid of being accused of "deviation," most men and women do not act out their conscious or unconscious desires in their sexual relationships but behave as they think their partner expects them to behave. It often happens that two people whose desires coincide with or complement each other's live side by side, unhappy and frustrated because neither dares offend the taboos and reveal his fantasies to the other. Others, brainwashed in childhood into believing that *any* sexual fantasy is wicked, never overcome their fear and guilt and abstain from intercourse all their lives. But fantasy will out. The actions it triggers, of which sexual contact with animals is only one, provide abundant material for the yellow press and keep the judges busy.

When Professor Leach says, "Crimes are created by Parliament; it needs a policeman to make a criminal," he means the "new" crimes, the new outlets, or rather, escapes, for outlawed fantasy—marijuana, LSD, "purple heart" pills. The "old" crimes, privately committed but publicly denounced by Parliament, persecuted by the police, and prosecuted by the courts, were created two thousand years ago.

One exception, a not so new "created crime" gradually becoming accepted as a noncrime, is homosexuality. Ostracized by a stupid and hypocritical society, persecuted by the "law," and more often than not unhappy in their emotional relationships, many homosexuals find solace and the companionship denied them by society in their relationships with animals, primarily cats. While to the "others" any show of warmth or tenderness by a homosexual is "suspect" and, therefore, usually rejected, cats will accept but never demand affection. Independent and self-sufficient, they do not burden their homosexual masters with too much of the responsibility they are, because of their place in society, afraid of, and since cats are beautiful, they satisfy the aesthetic requirements of frequently artistic homosexuals.

It is not beyond the realm of possibility that if the Catholic Church and the Protestant churches suddenly declared that "lust" is a virtue, not a sin, there would be, after a while, a dramatic drop in the number of lust murders. If, to make a good job of it, they also lifted the taboo from sexual fantasy, then the yellow press, the members of the legal profession, the practitioners of the oldest profession, and the obscenity trade would all go bankrupt and some politicians would have to look for a new platform because there would no longer be any need for prostitution, for racial discrimination springing from sex envy, for pornographic literature and "art," for blackmail, mental cruelty as ground for divorce, and such substitute outlets as alcohol, drugs, and violence. We should, perhaps, see more smiling people in the streets and, who knows, produce a generation that loves and enjoys life and seeks better ways to preserve it, not better ways to destroy it. Professor Laing's judgment that "We live equally out of our bodies, and out of our minds" would, at last, lose its validity.

The religious and consequently social taboos on sexual pleasure extend, naturally, to sexual contact with the substitute object, and as we said before, this taboo is relatively rarely infringed. Psychoanalysts describe a few case histories, medical doctors and veterinarians probably come across a few, and so do pet dealers, some of whom tell of their experiences even unasked.

The most fantastic story, however, was told by an American couple with two children who spent a holiday in Vienna. Having little money, they decided to rent two rooms in a private home rather than go to a hotel. They found two large, well-furnished, and surprisingly cheap rooms in the apartment of a middle-aged couple. During the three weeks they spent in the flat, they met only their landlady, who told them her husband was a sick man, confined to his bed. When the children were noisy, the landlady knocked on their door and asked them, very politely, to be quiet because her husband was resting. Often the American lodgers would meet her in the corridor carrying a covered tray to her sick husband, and at times they heard strange sounds coming from behind the closed bedroom door.

One day, buying some bread in the bakery next door, the American woman got into conversation with the baker. She told him where they were staying and how sorry she felt for their nice landlady, who, as she said, had been looking after her sick husband for years. "Sick husband?" the baker laughed. "Miss G. has never had a husband in her life!" Then he told his American client that the creature in the bedroom, with whom Miss G. had been playing husband and wife for the last ten years, was a chimpanzee.

CHAPTER 7
THE JET—PET SET

It's time we realized that animals are *human!*

— A SPIRITUALIST

◉ ◉ IF THE *HOMO NEUROTICUS* KNEW WHAT IS good for him, his judgment of what is good for his pet could be trusted implicitly. As things are, it is not his knowledge but his ignorance of what is good for him that he shares with his pet. Living a pseudo-life in which, cut off from the proper outlets, every manifestation of his powerful and complex being escapes through substitute outlets, he *de-animalizes* his pets in exactly the same way he *de-humanizes* himself. Having been turned into a freak, he surrounds himself with freaks lest he be reminded of what he *could* but *cannot* be.

The Joneses, who can afford more numerous and more varied outlets for the prisoners within them, also make a more thorough job of alienating their pets from their animal selves than those who try, more or less successfully, to keep up with them. The difference, however, is only quantitative, not qualitative.

In Britain, from where *petishism* began to spread throughout the Western World, the cream of the Joneses and would-be Joneses meet each year at Cruft's Dog Show, in an atmosphere as festive and solemn as that of a coronation. It is here that the champions of the year are chosen from among the aristocracy of the British upper-class pedigree-dog population.

It is interesting to note that while in 1965 the cocker spaniel was the British top dog, in 1967 the top place has been awarded to the Alsatian while the miniature poodle that took ninth place in 1966 advanced to second place in 1967. One cannot but wonder about the psychological reasons for this change in taste. Can it be that the selection of such a large and fierce animal, *the* police dog of the world, at a time when the country's decline as a great power is gathering speed, is a *substitute show of strength.*

This is what the magazine *London Life* wrote about the 1966 Cruft's show:

> The cult of the Top Dog is close to the Loved Ones: that unhealthy, aberrated, obsessive love for an animal which, to an extent, is embodied in Cruft's. . . . The radical attacks this world, this concern for the well-being of dogs, be they aristocratic, bourgeois or proletarian: sees in this adulation much of the sickness of a world which

permits one third of its population to go hungry because it does not supply them with the basic daily calorie ration necessary for survival (2,300) while it gives a 1,950-calorie-a-day Alsatian 3,000 calories; gives a lowborn mongrel shins of beef at ls 8d a pound daily at the Dogs Home Battersea, while an East of Suez peasant is fortunate if he gets meat quarterly.

Why is it that whenever the "affluence" of the British animal world is compared with human misery, this anomaly is always illustrated with examples taken from Asian or African conditions? Do the "radicals" attacking the Anglo-Saxon obsession with animals ignore the obscene poverty existing in their own country, are they ashamed of it, or do they feel that the Asian and African poor are more deserving than their own? Do they share the view so often expressed by the far from radical, that the British poor could help themselves if they would only make the effort?

The National Cat Club's annual show where, in 1967, 1661 cat aristocrats competed for championship, is second in importance to Cruft's but no less popular. One of the exhibits, a Persian valued at two thousand guineas, was protected from possible thieves by a bodyguard of its own. The stud fees of this playboy are immense, and kittens sired by him sell at fifty guineas apiece.

Although they probably love animals, pedigree dog and cat breeders are in the business for the considerable profit they can make. They give their "merchandise" every possible care to keep them healthy and happy, but they know that overpampering is detrimental to animals. It is not they but the private owners who go to the ridiculous, and often revolting, extremes that deprive their pets of all their animal dignity and benefit no one except a set of smart businessmen who grow rich on their lunacy.

Needless to say, Americans would feel humiliated if they could not outdo the British in the adulation of champion pets. This is easy for them to achieve, since their animal aristocracy does not have to share idolhood with a people aristocracy as the British pets do. If Cruft's can be compared in festive solemnity with a coronation, the great American dog shows, like the Westminister Kennel Club's show at Madison Square Garden, New York City, can be compared, in their importance and excitement, with Presidential elections.

For the last seventeen years the poodle has been America's top dog. One possible explanation is that this immense, rich, and powerful country requires no strength symbol but can afford to pamper small and weak creatures without loss of face. But there, too, the critics of pet humanization forget to point out that while over three billion dollars are spent annually on pet animals, 40 per cent of the nation's 22 million Negroes—to mention only one group of "expendables"— are officially classed as poor, meaning that they have family incomes below the level that will sustain life. Of those 9.6 million people, only one-third receive help of any kind.*

Pedigree pets, especially if they are champions, are more severely guarded than were young virgins in Catholic countries during the Middle Ages. While some progressive people *would* let their sister marry a Negro and even royal princesses are sometimes allowed to marry a commoner, class and racial differences must never be bridged in the animal aristocracy and if, in spite of every precaution, it does occur, the scandal shakes the entire Kennel Club world. It frequently happens that those responsible for the unpardonable crime are sued for damages, reported to the police, beaten up, or even shot at by the enraged owner.

In Aachen, Germany, a man's beloved pedigree German shepherd bitch gave birth to a litter of half-poodle, half-shepherd puppies. Beside himself with fury, he sought and found the father of the puppies and sued the owner of the dog for damages amounting to thirteen hundred deutsche marks. He was unable to prove that the poodle's master had failed to exercise proper control over his dog, but determined to wreak vengeance, he bribed a married couple to give false

*Newsweek, Nov. 20, 1967.

testimony before the court. Afraid to lie under oath, the couple told the truth, causing legal proceedings to be taken against the owner of the shepherd bitch. The court found him guilty of incitement to perjury and sentenced him to six months in jail plus a fine of five hundred deutsche marks.

In England the owner of a pedigree Labrador expecting a third litter by a frowned-upon mongrel reported the owner of the mongrel to the magistrate's court. The Bench made an order against the mongrel's owner that the dog be kept under proper control and fined him two pounds. "She is a lovely pedigree animal and it would not be so bad if a handsome pedigree Labrador came courting her, although we did not intend to use her for breeding purposes," the Labrador's mistress said. "I think the trouble with my dog is that he just doesn't realize that he isn't eligible," said the mongrel's master.

The owner of the aristocratic Labrador has tried chain-link fencing and a kennel with boarded-up sides to keep out the passionate suitor. She was probably unaware of the effective methods of birth control in existence—the Pill, or ovary surgery—that would have prevented pregnancy without depriving the lovers of their pleasure, and the mini-panty, called Petnix, that allows petting but says "nix" to mating.

In America the different manifestations of race-consciousness—rabid discrimination, liberalism until it has to be put into practice, honest progressivism, neurotic guilt that does more harm than good—are all reflected in human-animal relationships. The owner of a very expensive imported champion bulldog bitch in the Midwest became so enraged when he caught a mongrel in the process of mating with his bulldog that he went into the house for his rifle and shot the mongrel dead. To the edification of the crowd that assembled outside the fence, a veterinarian had to separate the dead animal from the living one.

An intelligent and liberal professional couple in New York who have a champion Alsatian and a pedigree spaniel allow the Alsatian to run around loose in Central Park and never interfere with its sex life. On the contrary, they are much amused by their dog's preference for commoners, either much larger or much smaller than himself. Their spaniel, however—would you let your daughter marry a Jew?—is an entirely different proposition. She has to wear panties when she is in heat!

Young people usually allow their pets the same freedom they enjoy themselves. They may have them operated on to prevent pregnancy, but not because they object to breed mixing. They wouldn't know what to do with the puppies. Yet the no-longer-young, but all the more neurotic, daughter of a psychoanalyst, given a pedigree poodle by a friend, became so hysterical when he advised her about its mating and delivered such an impassioned tirade against extending racial discrimination to animals, that he took back the gift for fear she might mate it, for ideological reasons, not merely with a different breed but with a different species.

The wealthy American girl who dressed her Great Dane in tailcoat and top hat for her wedding, and the eccentric English lady who dresses her bulldog in morning coat and pearl gray top hat when she takes him to the Ascot races, may be exceptions, but the difference between them and most pet-lovers is less significant than one would think. Although men will treat their anthropomorphized canine friends as well, or better, than themselves, and even more frequently better than they treat humans, women support the pet trade and pet industry and create the new professions that have sprung up in the pet world.

One day, after a lower-middle-class family moved into an upper-middle-class London suburb, the postman brought them two letters. One was addressed to the mistress of the house and the other to her corgi. Both were invitations to tea, one signed by a lady living in the same street, the other by her poodle. Much amused, the woman accepted both invitations and arrived with her dog on the appointed day. She was less amused, however, when, upon joining the other guests in the garden, she saw that the other

ladies and dogs wore identical, flowered summer hats and
the dogs light coats of the same material as their mistresses'
dresses. When tea was brought out, the dogs were served
theirs in cups and saucers placed on the lawn and, with the
tea, plates heaped with biscuits and little cakes. Immediately after tea the new—bareheaded—neighbor took her
bareheaded and bare-bottomed dog and hurried home to
her normal, human-loving family.

Invitation cards are only one of a series of greeting cards
available from pet to pet, from pet to human, from human
to pet, and from pet owner to pet owner. Pets can send Christmas cards to their friends; birthday cards to "wonderful you,"
to their husbands, wives, boy or girl friends; valentines
to their "sweethearts" and "darlings"; congratulation cards
to young pet mothers and even fathers, "get well quickly!"
cards to sick fellow pets, and so on. Most of these cards are
for dogs and cats, but some are now available for pet birds
and aquarium fish and for wild animals, reptiles, and amphibians kept as pets. Should the pet wish to thank the sender,
human or animal, for the good wishes, it can do so on special stationery with its own portrait, or just the portrait
of its breed, on the letterhead.

In Italy a dog is so much a part of a well-dressed woman's
outfit that at certain fashion shows each mannequin walks
in with a dog on a leash. When the mannequin shows a polka-
dot dress, the dog, usually a white poodle, has polka dots
painted on its fur. When the dress is checked or flowered,
the dog is painted in the same pattern. A pink, blue, or green
dress is accompanied by a pink-, blue-, or green-dyed dog,
and spring or autumn outfits are matched to the color of
Labrador, spaniel, or other dark-coated dogs led by the mannequin. The collar and leash match, in color and material, the
shoes and handbag worn with the outfit.

The French, the world's most food-conscious nation, show
their affection for their seven and a half million dogs by paying as much attention to canine "cuisine" as to their own.
Although the sale of tinned dog and cat foods increased by
300 per cent between 1963 and 1966, the pet aristocracy

and wealthy bourgeoisie enjoy meals suggested by Christiane Ripault in her three-hundred page cookbook for sophisticated pets.

Sample weekly menus facilitate the task of the dog's mistress by allowing her to kill two birds with one stone and serve the same meal to her husband and her pet. *Lunches*: Monday, boned rabbit boiled with vegetables, with grated parmesan cheese; Tuesday, grilled barbecued steak, boiled rice with a cube of butter, salad; Wednesday, ham, macaroni, yogurt with honey or jam; Thursday, chicken soup, boiled chicken, string beans; Friday, steamed fish, mashed potatoes, cheese, stewed apples and peaches; Saturday, breaded veal chop, coeur d'artichauts, fruit. On Sundays a pet dog should be allowed to sleep late and share three meals with its masters: breakfast, a cup of sweet cocoa and buttered toast; lunch, leg of lamb, potato salad, vanilla ice cream; dinner, two boiled eggs in a glass, grated carrots, caramel pudding, biscuits. The cookbook makes no mention of aperitifs or wine, though it is difficult to imagine a self-respecting French dog surviving on water. It seems probable that they too get the small quantities of alcoholic beverages French parents give their children.

Known for their excellent taste in clothes, French women are very particular about dressing their pets. Several dressmakers specialize in mistress-and-dog outfits for every occasion, but there are also many specialty shops where pet owners can buy every little thing their pampered darlings may require, from woolen dressing gowns to silk or velvet evening coats, from patent-leather booties to snow boots, from inflatable swimming pools to sunglasses, from nylon cushions to electric blankets, from gold-studded collars and leashes to fur coats.

The kitchen is the only domain where the British cannot complete with the French, and as a result British dogs consume exactly *one half as much tinned dog food as all six countries of the Common Market together*. However, when it comes to clothes, health care, and luxuries, they are not one step behind France. There are jeweled nylon-velvet collars with leads to match in every imaginable size; Glamour Wear House collars in pearl and crystal with jeweled clasp for dogs and cats; tartan, lambs wool, and kinky coat "for the dog who is really with it"; lace-trimmed panties, nightgowns and pajamas, after-swim suits and trouser-coats; for cocktail parties elegant, bikini-shape panties in brocade, gold and silver lamé, and lined nylon lace or made-to-order from the same material the mistress is wearing, from real silk to mink; raincoats and hoods, booties for every occasion, and lately, jewelry to match the owner's.

The Jewelry Trade Centre, which opened in London in 1967, advertised for dogs and cats to take part in a series of fashion parades and model real-diamond studded and heavily jeweled collars and leads. Soon afterwards a cat owner put an ad in the personal column of *The Times* offering a substantial reward for the return of a pearl necklace lost in S. W. London and the black female cat wearing it.

Even the cradle-to-grave health-care system Great Britain is justly proud of remains behind the health care offered to pets, most of it given free of charge by the animal clinics mentioned, some of it for huge fees by private veterinarians. There are hormones for the termination of unwanted pregnancies; antibiotic injections for abscessed dogs; special nursing for orphaned sick dogs; blood transfusions, anesthetics, all the various mycins for bacteria-infected dogs; X rays, antihistamines, saline for dehydration, codeine, calamine, splints, tranquilizers, calcium and vitamin preparations, and on and on. There are artificial eyes for blind dogs, contact lenses for dogs with cataract of glaucoma, resection for ear infection, false teeth, caesarian section for dogs incapable of normal delivery, ovary surgery for nymphomaniac dogs, and artificial insemination. There are slimming cures for fat dogs and special, fattening diets for thin ones; and extensive research into cancer in dogs has been undertaken.

There is a big demand in America, where artificial insemination is also practiced, for the sperm of British champion dogs. Some owners have offered as much as five hundred dollars for this service, but unfortunately veterinarians have so far been unable to keep dog's sperm fertile for longer than twenty-four hours. American pet owners very particular about the background and character of their dog's suitor can, of course, go to a dog and cat marriage bureau to find Mr. Right.

Naturally, hygiene and beauty are as important as health. There are charcoal tablets for halitosis and sprays for body odor, ordinary and dry shampoos, toilet waters and perfumes, tear-stain removers, and a series of other preparations that make a dog a more agreeable companion than many a human. A smart London hair-stylist with a select clientele of ladies and poodles is selling hairpieces for poodles at prices ranging from eight guineas to twenty-one guineas and has begun to create modern hair styles requiring additional hair for other breeds. Each time the pet's hairpiece has to be shampooed and set, it costs the owner two guineas.

Artists of every kind offer their services to pet owners that wish to immortalize their Loved One. Photographers specializing in pet animals will provide studio portraits in black and white or color, painters will paint them from life or, should they have passed away, from photographs, in oil or pastel chalk, on canvas or on velvet. If the owner wants something unusual, he can have a portrait in silk embroidery, framed and under glass. Sculptors are called in, usually only after the pet has died, to prepare its likeness for the tombstone.

Whatever the British can do for their pets, Americans can do better. It was they who invented tinned and dry foods for dogs and cats, and although the emotional attachment to animals and their substitution for humans is an Anglo-Saxon trait, it is they who began the anthropomorphization of pet animals in externals, that is in housing, clothing, health care, cosmetics, and all the luxuries that 90 per cent of the world's population never had and may never have.

The foods to tempt pampered pet dogs and cats are becoming more and more sophisticated. There are turkey dinners for Thanksgiving and Christmas, country dinners for holidays, TV dinners in tins or on sectioned trays like those used on airplanes, Doggie Do-Nuts for dessert, and, for a treat, beautifully appointed boxes of candy for pets or, for the more ferocious type of dog snack, designed perhaps with bloodhounds and police dogs in mind, People Crackers!

Naturally pets have to be at least as well dressed as their owners, and the growing number of canine clothiers are kept busy satisfying the demands of their fashionable animal clientele. A "with it" pet can choose from a selection of mod coats, polo coats, chesterfield coats, vinyl Go-Go coats, and Secret Agent K-9 trenchcoats, cable-knit sweaters, houndstooth jackets, mink stoles, TV lounging robes, gold lamé stretch pants, aprés ski suits, slickers, and terry-cloth pajamas. Pets wear leather slippers at home, but when they go out, gold and silver boots, sequined evening clothes, and matching diamond earring and necklace sets. Upper-class dogs would not be seen dead in ordinary collars and leads when they go walking. For day wear they have to be made of alligator, ostrich, or lizard skin, and for evening nothing less than a rhinestone collar and leash set will do, though diamonds are preferable. A sport-loving owner can buy his pet a pair or rather, two pairs, of ice or roller skates for a paltry seventy five dollars.

If health care for pets in Britain is as good, or better, than it is for people, in the United States it is incomparably better. Seventy-five hundred small-animal hospitals and approximately 10,000 of the 22,000 veterinarians look after the well-being of the nation's pets. The number of animal hospitals increases nine times as fast as the number of human hospitals, and as a result the life span of dogs and cats has doubled in the last two or three decades. As an American veterinarian said: "Ninety per cent of American dogs enjoy better medical care than half the people in the world." But veterinarians looking after the *elite* of the pet world run certain risks, of course. In San Francisco four of them were sued for $266,100 in connection with the demise of a three-month-old poodle owing to alleged negligence and carelessness. It would be interesting to know how that figure was reached.

The American pet has joined the pill-swallowing millions. It gets its daily vitamin pill, its tranquilizer, air- and sea-sickness pills, antibiotics and aspirins, its cod-liver oil and cough syrup, digestive aids and calcium. Aggressive, violent pets are given female hormones to improve their disposition; shy, nervous pets male hormones, and those who gain or lose weight are given metabolism tests to determine the causes. Aging pets can have false teeth, even entire dentures, and those hard of hearing, hearing aids. Pets from all over the world are brought to the animal hospital in Idaho that specializes in eye operations to have their cataracts removed. In Poolesville, Maryland, Dr. Raymond Zinn has started to build up a blood bank for dogs, and up to seven major canine blood groups and two minor ones have been found. The project, it is hoped, may be instrumental in saving the lives of more than two thousand dogs a year.

In addition to the various dog shampoos, deodorants, toilet waters, and "His" and "Her" perfumes, the pet-cosmetic industry produces cream rinses, hair coloring "that will give a graying pet a young look," tints in different shades, silver or gold hair sprays for the evening, a dozen shades of nail polish for day and evening wear, mascara and false eyelashes for poodles, a spray dentifrice called Happy Breath, battery-powered vibrating hair- and toothbrushes, and many other cosmetic products used by people. Syndicated columnist Sylvia Porter reports that the latest in pet beautification procedures includes *face-lifting*.

Pet housing is another area where the ingenuity of the trade knows no bounds. Aquariums covering an entire wall are used in interior decoration, and you can buy a cage in the shape of the Taj Mahal for your favorite bird. For pampered cats there is a two-story house called Kitty Duplex, with the ground floor serving as a cushioned living room and the upper floor as bedroom. When they have had enough of their owner's company, dogs can retire into an air-conditioned doghouse with piped-in music, an electrically heated wall-to-wall carpet, running water, and a $600 built-in dog toilet, but if they prefer they can sleep in a Louis XV bed or their own special armchair with a washable Swiss velveteen cover. A New York firm offers a poodle-sized Italian silk tent for $75, but there are also chinchilla tents for $560, with an additional charge of over $800 for a chinchilla bed.

A banker in New Jersey spent over $1700 on a green and gold stucco home, complete with gold drinking fountain and red velvet cushions, for his Alsatian, and a college professor in New York saw so little difference between his "best friend" and himself that he put the dog's name under his own in the New York telephone directory "in case his friends wanted to telephone him."

Although the Great American Hoax, Alan Able's "Society for Indecency to Naked Animals," launched to "protect our children from the sight of naked horses, cows, dogs and cats," seems to have won over dog lovers alone, the other members of the pet world also enjoy a standard of living much higher than the overwhelming majority of people. A British manufacturer puts out tiny mattresses for pet mice, Americans produce phonograph records that help teach parrots to speak, and to be not merely forewarned but forearmed, pessimistic pet-owners in both countries can buy fall-out shelters for pets. A British firm developed a small underground shelter for animals, complete with food supplies, that would be buried away from the family shelter and give pets an equal chance of survival. But pets are not dismissed entirely from the family shelter either. It is suggested that a "small fish tank fitted therein would be a welcome reminder of happier days and an immense psychological asset and attraction during the emergency which might test to breaking point our physical and mental endurance."

Pet owners who wish to travel can, if they give Great Britain, the USSR, and Australia a wide berth, take their pets with them wherever they go. Airlines and shipping lines, no longer surprised at anything passengers will do, are well prepared to cater to the needs of their customers, whatever species they belong to. A leaflet issued by Trans-

World Airlines, for instance, assures the animal Knicker-
bockers that "sophisticated dogs, itinerant cats (and any
other travel-minded pet) will truly love fine flying aboard
a luxurious TWA Super Jet." A small dog, a cat, or a bird
is usually allowed to travel next to its owner in the same
compartment, but large pets will travel in the cargo compartment in a Bed Rock VIP Kennel "made for pure pet
pleasure" that the owner can purchase from the company
for ten to forty dollars, depending on the pet's size. Naturally, pet traveling requires a great deal of preparation. When
going abroad it needs four copies of the Shipper's Export
Declaration available at any TWA office, a health certificate,
a rabies inoculation certificate, and other papers required
by some countries. It is advisable to take the pet for a romp
in the park before departure time, give it a light meal six
hours before takeoff and, if it is of a nervous disposition,
a tranquilizer. If the pet travels in the cargo compartment,
accompanying its owner on a long trip, it can enjoy its favorite dish *en route*, if you put the food in a cloth or mesh bag,
not forgetting an inexpensive can opener for canned food,
and attach it to the kennel. "TWA makes it easy to take
this very important member of your family with you!"

Easy, certainly, but not cheap. Small animals traveling
in the passenger compartment pay an excess bagage rate
of 1 per cent of the first-class fare. Thus, $19.66 from New
York to Bermuda, $17.32 from New York to San Juan, and
$38.64 from New York to Mexico City. If they travel in the
cargo compartment, add the cost of the kennel which, in
the case of a forty-five pound pet, amounts to $40.50. And
you had better make your reservation well in advance or you
might have to put off your trip for lack of room for your pet.

Britons who really love their dogs will take them abroad
only if they intend to stay there. Otherwise, coming back,
they would have to give them up for six months of quarantine at a cost of about £50. The total cost of the London-
New York flight for a dog is only very slightly less than his
owner's fare.

The American magazine *Pet Fair* tells all about the services provided by the shipping lines should a doting pet-

owner wish to take along his or her darling on a cruise. In
the past, when the furred, feathered, and scaly creatures
were still animals and not people, they traveled in the ship's
kennels, well away from the passenger decks. Today many
lines allow them in the cabins, at least in the day time. Since
the major lines standardized the price of pets' tickets—and
shifted cutthroat competition to the domain of catering for
them—the transatlantic tariff for a dog is $50 flat one-way,
for a cat $10, for a bird $5. It is necessarily higher for large
exotic pets like adolescent lions or middle-aged crocodiles.

The Cunard Line "Queens" have carried ten of thousands
of pets in their time, famous pets like the corgis of the Duke
and Duchess of Windsor, Elizabeth Taylor's poodles, Rex
Harrison's basset, Vivien Leigh's Siamese cat, Salvador
Dali's ocelot. On board ship the pets live like kings. They
are served the choicest quality joints, prepared specially
for them and never, but never, leftovers from the *table d'hôte*.
Naturally, if the owner asks for special food for his pet—corn
flakes for breakfast, breast of chicken for dinner—his wishes
are a command. Some ships, like the *United States*, have
printed menus for the pets; on the *France* it is even printed
in English and French, and tinned foods, unless specially
asked for, are out! To while away the boredom of traveling, the pets do as their owners do and between meals enjoy
snacks of biscuits in all shapes and sizes. If the pet stays
in the kennels during the trip, the owner is advised to give
it some toy to play with or, even better, a slipper, cardigan,
or cushion with the owner's scent on it. That will calm down
even the most nervous little dog.

But the British and Americans don't really know what
service is. They do their utmost to satisfy their pet passenger's bodily needs, but only the French take into account
that a dog doesn't live by filet mignon alone. To relieve the
heartache of homesick dogs the *SS France* has installed
a New York fire hydrant and a Paris lamppost on one of
its decks.

Some people, however, are never satisfied. In New York
a lady passenger sued a steamship line for giving her toy
poodle an inferiority complex. In the ship's kennels, where

the little animal had to spend the nights, his specially built private traveling kennel had been placed between one containing a fierce police dog and one housing a Great Dane. While it was not possible to find out whether the lady has lost or won her case, it is more than probable that she has had her little darling psychoanalyzed and cured of its terrible ailment. It also seems probable that for fear of developing a similar complex, she has taken good care to marry a husband half her size.

Animal welfare organizations, pet industries, publishers, and pet columnists each year publish lists of hotels, boarding houses, motels, holiday camps, and so on that receive pets with open arms for the many animal lovers who take their pets on holidays by train, coach, car, yacht, or leash, at home or abroad. They also provide lists of "pet hotels" for owners who can bring themselves to leave their pets for a weekend or even a few weeks and go on holiday without them.

While most of these lists and guidebooks are good and contain a great deal of up-to-the-minute information, first prize goes to the *Guide Mi Chien*, dog version of the *Guide Michelin*, written by Jacques Lanzmann and Monique Gilbert and published by Denoel in Paris. This 380-page, beautifully appointed book is printed on paper of three different colors:— white, blue, and yellow. Part One, on white, is a dictionary of dogs that provides solutions to every problem a dog owner may come up against. It deals, from A to Z, with every facet of dog life, from adoption through hygiene to *wagons-lits*, and has numerous entries on feeding, elegance, dog psychology, and sex.

One recommended daily menu for a large pet consists of breakfast 1.7 pints of milk, two eggs, several slices of toast; lunch 2 pounds of minced beef; dinner 2 or 3 pounds of minced beef, boiled vegatables, bread, and dessert. Under "Pill" it tells you where you can buy birth-control pills for your dog and how to make it take the pill. Under "Day Nurseries" it tells you where you can leave your pet if you have business to attend to during the day, the service offered depending on the amount you are able or willing to pay. Under "Celibacy" it informs you that the practice of it is physically as well as psychologically harmful because a dog has the same sexual problems man has. Therefore, as shown in the entry on "Mating," the best thing to do about celibacy is to put an end to it. Under "Postcard" the book tells you that if you have your pet at home while you go on holiday (which is absolutely immoral!) you should at least send him a special postcard invented for pets and masters in love with each other. Wear the postcard near your skin for a few hours before mailing it so that when he sniffs it, your pet will again feel secure in your love and in the knowledge that you think of him and will return.

Part Two, printed on blue paper, lists all the hotels and restaurants in French towns with more than ten thousand inhabitants where pets are welcome, gives prices of rooms and meals and the amount to be paid for the pet's meals. In good hotels and restaurants the price of a dog dinner can be as high as fifteen new francs, but in really first-class establishments the supplement "varies," which probably means that your dog's dinner, like your own, has to be ordered "a la carte."

Part Three, on yellow paper, is the Who's Who, and What's Where, of the dog world. It lists the addresses of dog clubs and animal welfare organizations at home and abroad and the documents needed to take your dog abroad and tells you how to proceed if you wish to register your pet with the Kennel Club. It also gives the addresses of dog hotels and the best dog-furnishing shops in France.

What the *Guide Mi Chien* forgets to mention is that to promote dog tourism, the famous French spa Evian has opened a source of water that serves exclusively the health of dogs. It is believed that the water can cure numerous dog illnesses.

When summer approaches, the animal welfare organizations and pet columns erupt in hysterical activity, letting loose a volley of good advice onto the hapless pet owner, who usually just ducks his head and does what he would have done anyway. "Traveling with Your Pet" leaflets tell him how to feed his pet on the way, what tranquilizers to give it to keep it smiling and ensure that it makes a good impression on the hotel or motel keeper, what to do if it gets train sick or car sick, how to make it comfortable. . . .

It is obvious that to travel comfortably the pet, be it a budgerigar or an Alsatian, requires room to move about. A wealthy English couple who like to have their two 200-pound St. Bernard dogs with them wherever they go solved the problem by buying them a £1000 station wagon of their own. Now wherever they go, their pets can follow in their comfortable, chauffeur-driven automobile.

Hotel keepers are, at times, difficult, particularly if they have an obsessive dislike for certain species of pets. Some will admit dogs, ponies, horses, but refuse to put up cats or birds. Others admit small dogs but will not take in large ones. But on the whole they are more willing to admit pets of any kind than children, especially in Great Britain, where parents had better buy the *Children Welcome* guidebook before setting off with their offspring for an English holiday. In America two tourist guidebooks that list establishments where Negroes can get overnight accommodation give the address of one hotel in Montgomery, Alabama, and none in Danville, Virginia. Dogs traveling with white owners are welcome in five Montgomery hotels and four in Danville.

Throughout the Western World, boarding establishments for cats, dogs, birds, small mammals, and every other type of pet animal have become a booming business. Usually the animals are called for in specially constructed vans or station wagons and taken back home when required, and while at the boarding establishment, they are given the same, or greater, individual care than children receive in camps. Owners, reluctant to leave their pets in the hands of strangers, arrive with long lists of instructions concerning the feeding and treatment of their pets and are willing to pay through the nose if assured that their instructions will be obeyed to the letter.

One lady, going abroad with her husband, an architect, for two months, left her beloved poodle with "foster parents," a couple who make an excellent living by looking after the Top People's Top Pets while the owners travel. The poodle arrived in a station wagon, the back of which was crammed full of "absolute necessities." There was the poodle's red-velvet-upholstered TV armchair, its bright-blue-satin-lined basket with a pink mohair blanket and an extra electric blanket for cold days, its bathtub with a built-in thermometer to make sure the water was neither too hot nor too cool, its toothbrush, brushes, combs, hair dryer, and grooming utensils, its shampoo, toilet water, eyedrops, tranquilizers, vitamin pills, its stainless-steel dishes, its innumerable toys, and its fantastic wardrobe, consisting of complete outfits for every kind of weather. The *piece de resistance*, however, was a gold traveling clock in a red morocco case. When the "foster-mother" asked what the poodle was supposed to do with the clock, the lady instructed her to place it each night next to her pet in its bed. "He is used to sleeping with me," the lady said. "The ticking of the clock will create the illusion that he is listening to the beating of my heart, and he will sleep much more peacefully if he doesn't feel lonely."

After paying one month's fee, eighty pounds, in advance, and clasping the poodle for a last time to her bosom, the lady departed. Ten minutes later, having investigated its new surroundings, the poodle was sleeping happily under an ordinary iron and plastic kitchen chair on the bright linoleum floor of its foster-parents' kitchen.

A dogs' holiday home in Munich, Germany, never accepts more than twenty-four boarders at a time. Although they have a long waiting list, the couple who run the home could not possibly cater properly to more. The standard fee for small and medium dogs is five dollars a day, for large dogs eight dollars, but this does not include such extras as grooming, the weekly veterinary visit, and special food requirements. The holiday home tells owners in its advertisements that whatever the dog is used to at home, he will get in this "home away from home." This promise is not always easy to fulfill. The boarders that just "have to have" their daily spinach, daily banana, apple, chocolate bar, biscuits, breakfast cereal, or half a cup of coffee or tea with milk and sugar, present no problem, but it is sometimes hard to find the time to take a spoiled Alsatian to the pub for his glass of beer every night. If the foster-parents forget to give the pampered old bulldog the exactly twenty drops of brandy he always gets before breakfast—eye-dropper provided by the owner—he reminds them by overturning his bowl of milk and the dachshund, used to having its paws wiped clean after a walk, will, if the ritual is forgotten, bring a towel and place it at its foster-parents' feet. There are only two boarders that cause the couple a real headache every time they are brought back: a cocker spaniel that will not go to sleep until someone rocks it in his arms singing one particular lullaby, and a poodle that can sleep only in bed, between man and wife, and gets hysterical when they give each other as much as a good-night kiss.

The Animal Hostel at London's Heathrow Airport, run by the RSPCA, has witnessed many a strange thing, but was jolted out if its complacency when a poodle was handed in with a note saying that it ate only Chinese food. The note said that its favorite dish was prawn chow mein, but it had to be served on a dinner plate and consumed in human company. After trying, in vain, to tempt the sophisticated little animal with chicken liver and beef broth, they gave up and did as they were bid to do. They served the poodle a dinner plate heaped with prawn chow mein and plenty of noodles, and one of the kennel maids sat with it until it had finished the meal. Then she put the satisfied guest on a plane for Canada, where its owner was impatiently waiting.

A rich American woman who moved into a sanatorium to be at the bedside of her incurably ill husband during his last days put her three pedigree pets, two snow white cats and a snow white poodle, into an exclusive pet-boarding establishment because she did not trust her servants to look after them properly. When she went to fetch them after her husband's death she took with her two lengths of black moire ribbon for the cats' necks, and a black fur-lined, velvet coat and cap, black leather boots, and black collar and leash for the poodle so they should all be correctly dressed for the funeral. She had telephoned the day before to ask the owner of the establishment *not* to give her pets anything to eat or drink for twenty-four hours, hoping hunger and thirst would reduce them to such misery that they would make the appropriate noises at the grave.

When she sent out black-bordered invitations to her friends, asking them to the last reception her husband was giving at the funeral parlor—where he awaited them properly dressed for the occasion, his eyes sparkling (with belladonna), his face smoothly shaven and pink, his lips stretched in a smile —her three pets also sent black-bordered, printed invitations to *their* friends. The funeral relieved the lady of thirty-thousand dollars—and a husband she never really liked. Her aggression satisfied by the illusion that she had buried him alive, she set out, at sixty, to enjoy her many remaining years, and the millions he left her, in the company of numerous animal-loving widowed girl friends—and her pets.

People who believe that there is more to life than meets the eye and go to astrologers to be foretold their future on this earth, to church to pray for their future beyond it, and to spiritualists to ask their departed loved ones about life after death will also share their spiritual hopes and fears with their pets. Pet owners from all over England take their dogs and cats to palmist and clairvoyant Margaret Kilner in Brighton, who reads their paws and prepares doggie and kitty horoscopes. She predicts the future of hundreds of pets, tells prospective owners what star their future pet should be born under, and advises on the proper sign of the Zodiac for the mate of a nubile bitch. "Animal personalities are affected in the same way as people," Margaret Kilner says. "I find that I am able to foretell a dog's future by studying its paw and feeling the vibrations that come through it."

A small ad in the personal column of *The Times* reads: "Animal faith healer, help badly needed for doomed Alsatian. Please write Box BB890." The advertiser obviously did not know of Miss Hazel Ward, who, it it true, protests against being called a "faith healer." "Animals and babies haven't faith," she says. "They are too young." Her gift is "spiritual healing," and she accomplishes it by the laying-on of hands or, in the case of absent human and animal patients, through her Indian time-guide, Silver Star. She once cured a sixteen-year-old dog in Queensland, thirteen thousand miles away, and after a month the dog was running about, to the amazement of the neighbors. Miss Ward's service is free, but she is saving up for a sanctuary to be open permanently for treatment and welcomes donations. She knows nothing about anatomy and does not need to because her guide calls on veterinarians in the spirit world who were authorities on the illnesses she is treating, and they tell her where to put her hand. Miss Ward has a card-index drawer for absent healing and gives each animal at least ten minutes concentrated thought every night.

Throughout the Western world the first Sunday in October is declared Animal Sunday in honor of St. Francis of Assisi. Animal welfare organizations have asked the clergy and ministers of all denominations to preach kindness to "man's lower fellow creatures" on that day. In a booklet entitled "Service of Prayer for Animals," the RSPCA suggests subjects for sermons, prayers, and hymns to be sung. Although the theme is animals, these services are held for people.

There are, however, special services for animals as well. In Vienna, for example, people bring their pet animals to the Animal Sunday service at the Votiv-Kirche, where, last year, they were blessed by Bishop Pichler. In April, 1967, at the occasion of the British Pet Trade Fair at Harrogate, one budgerigar, a guinea pig, hamsters, rabbits, three ponies, six poodles, and a large number of dogs and cats attended an open-air pets' service conducted by the Reverend W. H. Hewitson.

A most memorable service for animals took place five years ago in St. Paul's, Covent Garden, where Canon Clarence May blessed thirty animals, among them a black dog named Satan. The star soloist, who had himself composed the hymn he sang, was Lady Violet Munnings' dog Toby. According to his mistress, he would have done better but for a sore throat. Also, she felt an Alsatian sitting in the front pew put him off a bit. "You see, when he sings for the BBC, he sits in an armchair in a room all by himself," she said.

Last summer the Duchess of Norfolk organized the first interdenominational service for seven hundred pet animals on the grounds of Arundel Castle, Sussex. The service was by "invitation only" and restricted to the members of the Friends of Clymping animal sanctuary, of which the Duchess is president. The invitations were sent to the pets, asking them to bring their owners with them, and the service was conducted by a Church of England minister and a Roman Catholic priest. It would be interesting to know in what way it was ascertained that the seven hundred pets attending were all definitely C. of E. or Catholic.

Some pet owners do not wait for special animal services to take their pets to church. A deeply religious lady in Halberton, England, took her terrier, Pip, with her every single Sunday, and after the dog had listened patiently to the service, she shared Communion with him. The vicar did not mind the presence of the dog in church, but he definitely objected to its taking Communion. However, when the lady declared that unless Pip could share Communion with her, she would never again put her foot in his church, the vicar consulted his superior, the Bishop of Exeter. The Bishop ruled that dogs could not take Holy Communion, and since then the lady has given up going to church. Why the Bishop objected to a dog's partaking of the Holy Communion is hard to imagine. If God, in his infinite patience, puts up with people why should he feel offended by the devotion of a creature as honest and harmless as a dog?

CHAPTER 8
PETS AS STATUS SYMBOLS

Some follies are as catching as disease.

— LA ROCHEFOUCAULD:
Maxims

◉ ◉ THE *HOMO NEUROTICUS* EITHER HAS TO FIND his own identity or assume one. Finding one's own is a full-time job. It begins with breaking up all existing distorting mirrors and seeking a true one, and it continues with the

168

rejection of all the "products," intellectual, material, and spiritual, that modern society offers and that serve to create surrogate identities accepted by most people as their own. Maybe it is just as well. To some of us it could be a rather painful experience to come face to face with the Thing lurking under layer upon layer of falsehood. On the whole, people are liable to confuse *status* with identity, even though the rating they give themselves may not coincide with the rating others give them.

"Most of us surround ourselves, wittingly or unwittingly, with status symbols we hope will influence the raters appraising us, and which we hope will help establish some social distance between ourselves and those we consider below us. The vigorous merchandising of goods as status symbols by advertisers is playing a major role in intensifying status consciousness," says Vance Packard in *The Status Seekers*. "One-time upper class symbols such as limousines, power boats, and mink coats are available to a variety of people. Coincidentally, there has been a scrambling to find new ways to draw lines that will separate the elect from the non-elect."

In America class is not always identical with status. The *top class* is the American aristocracy, the Mayflower crowd; the *top status*, on the other hand, is the "meritocracy," the people who got there through their high IQs, education, hard work, ambition, the firm belief that in America everyone can become president, and by now, of course, inherited wealth as well.

In England, class differences are still rigid, even though a very mixed crowd is invited to the Queen's garden parties and anyone who has done something important for the country can obtain a knighthood. Still, to many people an "impoverished gentlewoman" living on charity remains superior to a middle-class financial wizard, even if he was educated at Eton and Oxford. The reason for this may be that the British "meritocracy" has not been able to do as much for Great Britain as the American meritocracy has done for America.

In France, Germany, Italy, and the other European countries, republics, or kingdoms, aristocracy and meritocracy have merged in a rich and educated upper bourgeoisie. And yet, except for the top class in every country — which overestimates itself because it is overestimated by the others — everyone tries to keep up with the Joneses.

The individual has an infinite variety of ways to keep up with the Joneses. The snobs are, on the whole, modest because they try to keep up only with those one grade above them. The *inverted* snobs, however, are more ambitious because no matter how low their stratum, they try to keep up — and believe they achieve their goal by a superior indifference to all visible symbols of topdom — with the most exalted Joneses of their respective countries. Most ambitious, of course, are the eccentrics, who put themselves not merely outside but *above* the entire class structure and status scale and thus create a parallel set of Joneses with their own admiring and ambitious followers.

While in the past pet keeping was an accepted upper-class symbol, the mere fact of having pets no longer raises the owner above his stratum. Nor does one get a higher rating by owning a pedigree dog or cat; there are too many of them. Belonging to the Kennel Club or Cat Fanciers' Club in Britain, one of the national cat or dog clubs in the United States or in Europe, does lend a little prestige, though it costs quite a bit of money. By entering one's dog for Cruft's, most important of the 3500 annual dog shows in Britain, or for the top dog-show in other countries, one is almost there. But the real, died-in-the-wool class and status Joneses possess, or are possessed by, national champions or pets sired by them, and the parallel, eccentric Joneses keep unusual or exotic pets, the larger and more expensive, or the smaller and less expensive, the better.

To the latter group belong the California college professor and his wife who own, and dearly love, a 4½-foot, thirty-five-pound alligator they bought as a baby. This not-so-cuddlesome pet lives with them in their apartment, sleeps in a large dog-bed, and splashes around happily each morning

in the bathtub. Dried with a bath towel of its own, it then
proceeds to the living room, where it spends the day listening
to music. Since it adores riding in a car, its devoted owners
take it along with them wherever they go.

"Love is sought when pets are bought," says R. L. Mac-
Lean, Ph.D., Sc.D., in an article published in the American
trade magazine *Pet Shop Management*. "In the pet field we
see the pathos of love—gifts for incurably ill children—blind
parents—estranged lovers—and it is indeed a privilege
to help them all." Dr. MacLean is so right—and he so over-
simplifies the question. Love bought in pet shops indeed
includes the love given to, and received from, animals, but
it also includes, among many other kinds of love, some of
which ought to be discouraged, the love of *status*, the love
of being better than others, of showing off, of climbing, with
the help of a pet, onto a pedestal to look down with contempt
on those less wealthy or less fortunate or simply less vain
and less arrogant.

There is no difference between the love you get from a
mongrel or a champion German shepherd, and you don't
get more love from a pedigree Siamese than from a stray
kitten picked up in the street. And although you may get
love from a chimpanzee, you certainly don't get any at all
from an alligator. Yet throughout the Western world, more
and more people buy pet animals that are neither loving
nor beautiful and often not even interesting to observe,
because they are relatively rare, expensive to buy and to
keep, and because they lend their owners a *pseudo-status*
to glory in.

In London, if you wish to improve your status or enhance
your standing as an eccentric, you walk into Harrods and
buy or order any animal you have read about, seen on television, or know is owned by the Joneses you wish to emu-
late. If on top of being a status seeker you are a bad sleeper,
you can buy a bush baby, a nocturnal animal that will keep
you amused during the night. If you want intelligent conversation you can buy a parrot, but if you cannot afford it, a
mynah bird or budgerigar will perform the same service

at a considerably lower cost. If your hobby is tracing your family tree, you can get a monkey or, even better, a chimpanzee, and there are, at the moment, some five thousand people in Britain eager to trace back their ancestry that far. If you have an inferiority complex, you might buy an elephant, a tiger, a puma, an ocelot, cheetah, lion cub, or bear. If your status depends on being "quaint," you can get a boa constrictor or a python or rattlesnake or, if you are really eccentric, a tarantula. To impress the one-grade-above-you neighborhood you have chosen to live in, you would do well to purchase a pair of peacocks, cranes, black swans, black storks, or a few flamingos.

People not satisfied by the selection offered by Harrods can go the the zoo, choose the animal that appeals to them most as a pet, and order it. A white-faced scops owl will make a wonderful pet, and so will a vulture, a mongoose, a hedgehog, a Gambian pouched rat, a genet kitten, a flying fox, a manatee, or an otter. If you have joined the Buy British movement, partly out of patriotism, partly because the devaluation of the pound has caused the price of imported pets to soar sky-high, or if you wish to be really "with it," you might acquire a dwarf donkey, called a "mini-moke." One you can pop into a suitcase and take on a trip will cost only two hundred guineas. But if you wish to create the impression that you are so high up on the social ladder you couldn't care less about the opinion of the Yahoos, you can keep a goat as a pet. If you get them young enough, they can be trained like dogs, taken out on a lead, and taught to obey and love you.

A British family belonging to the eccentric Joneses have turned their house into a veritable zoo and live happily with their pets amid torn, chewed up, completely wrecked furniture. Their three lions used to sleep with them in their bed, until they grew too big and pushed their owners out of it. They had to be exiled to the living room which they share with a leopard, three dogs, and a black lamb. A friend of theirs, a dog breeder, mother of two, has a puma sleeping on the settee in her living room. After the pint of beer he is offered by his mistress each evening at the village pub, he undoubtedly enjoys sweet dreams.

Horrified at the way Harrods kept a young otter, a lady bought it for fifty five guineas and took it home to her private zoo to be saved. Before doing so, however, she stirred up such a row that the whole animal-loving world resounded with it. "Many animals like this are just bought by wealthy people as a gimmick," said the director general of the Wild Life Fund supporting the belligerent lady. "When they are no longer the hit of the cocktail party they are foisted off on a zoo, or, worse, killed off." Harrods' animal buyer disagrees. "It is a growing trend," he says. "People sometimes find that pumas, leopards, etc., are easier to keep than cats and dogs." To do justice to Harrods it has to be recorded that whenever they sell an exotic animal, they first make certain that the buyer is able to look after it properly.

A proof of this "growing trend" is that when a bird farmer advertised wild animals for sale, he was flooded with inquiries from all over the country and his telephone never stopped ringing. Although the prices were pretty steep, he obtained an order for a baby elephant, several for tame tiger cubs and full-grown leopards, a large number for bear cubs, and three for his twelve-foot-long king cobra. When the RSPCA advertised for a loving home for a monkey, they received, within days, four thousand offers. But the most unusual pet in Britain is Achmad, the camel owned by an innkeeper in Dorset. By the time it arrived here from Tibet, and spent a whole year in quarantine, it had cost its owners five hundred pounds. They intend to have it carry empty bottles from the pub to the shed, give customers' children rides, and the wife wants to use it herself as transportation into town or to the beach.

Exotic pets are becoming so popular in all Western countries that they will soon lose their status as status symbols. Since pets are not, as yet, included in the population census and their number is generally calculated on the basis of licenses issued, the sale of pet foods, animal health products, cosmetics and accessories, the number of exotic pets, living usually on fresh foods and live animals, is difficult to determine.

But people who feel that owning a chimpanzee, for instance, no longer raises them above their fellow men can acquire a new type of status symbol—a picture painted by a chimp-Picasso! The paintings of two chimpanzees, exhibited at Dudley Castle, Worcestershire, were snapped up within half an hour by an appreciative public. The best of the abstracts was bought for £15.10 by a biologist and zoologist at the request of his wife, a former Slade Art School student who liked the painting very much indeed. Even Sotheby's, the world famous auctioneers of art works and antiques, included a finger painting by a gifted American chimpanzee at a sale of impressionists, modern drawings, and watercolors. It was a lovely picture in red, white, yellow, and green that, according to *The Times*, "can bear comparison with the work of many human bashers and smashers of today." It was bought for £20.

The prices paid for the chimpanzee paintings were, admittedly, not very high, but many a great artist, whose paintings fetched hundreds of thousands after he was dead, would have been only too happy to receive such sums while he was alive and starving.

In our era, when everything is impermanent and change is like a runaway locomotive that has long since left its tracks headed for an unknown destination, public figures, whatever their public, have to have an "image." They must become identified with a symbol to retain public attention for at least a while.

In the not so distant past, public figures like royalty, politicians, four-star generals and commanders of armies of occupation, whose status was halfway between men and gods, often appeared in newsreels and picture papers in the act of performing the child-kissing ritual. Roosevelt kissed children and Churchill kissed children, Hitler kissed children and Stalin kissed children, kings and queens kissed children, and even General de Gaulle would sometimes, for a moment, forget his divine calling and kiss a child — in front of the camera. Today, when it is becoming increasingly obvious that people have lost all faith in their elected or self-appointed leaders and anachronistic royalties, and nobody could care less whether or not they kissed children, public relations men have turned to animals to raise, if not the prestige, at least the appeal of the "great."

Whenever possible, Queen Elizabeth II is shown with her pet corgis or with her race horses. In her particular case this is probably an excellent idea. A shy person and by no means an accomplished actress, she is rarely as relaxed and her smile rarely as genuine and charming as when she is with creatures for whom she is not the Queen but merely a warmhearted, lovable human being. The popularity of Prime Minister Harold Wilson, however, cannot be saved, no matter how often he is seen and photographed with his yellow Labrador, Paddy. Nor can dogs do anything, but anything at all, for President Lyndon Johnson, although his PRO has worked harder at it than any PRO that ever lived. When his two beagles, Him and Her, died, the nation's press shed crocodile tears over LBJ, America's most bereaved pet-owner. Then a little girl gave him a white collie — "I think he will cheer up your loneley job a bit" — and Blanco became First Dog of the Nation. Lately, he has been photographed with another dog, Yuki, standing on its hind legs and watching the President sign important papers, going visiting with him, and comforting him when his "loneley job" gets him down. It was even reported that the dog could not accompany his master to Lynda Bird's wedding for reasons of protocol.

Learning from his Anglo-Saxon colleagues, Chancellor Kiesinger's PR man is also trying to build up his employer's image as a dog lover. However, he made a tremendous *faux pas* by allowing the publication of a picture of the Chancellor and his dog with the caption: "When alone, Waldi pursues birds, field-mice and rabbits." The indignant animal-lovers calmed down only when assured that although Waldi adores the excitement of the hunt, he has never yet caught either a bird or a mouse.

The world's No. 1 diplomat, UN Secretary General U Thant, won many hearts when the magazine *Pet Fair* published a short article and a large picture of him with his beautiful shepherd dog Bala. Each night when the Secretary General returns home the dog rushes to meet him "in greeting of unmistakable devotion and love. U Thant pauses, strokes the sleek head, scratches the deep chest and flattened ears, bends to speak to Bala in Burmese. . . . The moment is brief, but the little ritual seems to content them both."

Throughout the world, show people compete to imprint unforgettable images of themselves on a fickle and sophisticated public, and in our day of the animal craze, nothing seems more effective than the possession of an unusual pet. The world's foremost showman is, of course, Salvador Dali. Even those who do not appreciate art in general, or his art in particular, enjoy the sight of him walking his ocelot on a lead through the streets of Paris and New York. Adamo, the singer and movie star adored by the French public, takes his leopard, Damo, with him wherever he goes, but at home, in his garden, he has an entire collection of exotic pets — monkeys, penguins, and parrots.

Michel Simon, perhaps France's greatest actor, is also an animal fanatic. When his adored mother died, he asked for a sign assuring him that she was still with him in spirit. As he did so, a wild bird entered through the window and allowed itself to be caught and caged. Michel Simon believes that animals are reincarnations of departed humans. He owns several cats, two monkeys, a dog and a parrot.

Brigitte Bardot is an active member of the French animal welfare organizations. Once, when she visited a shelter and saw fifteen unclaimed dogs awaiting execution, she put all fifteen into her car and took them home to her farm, where they have been living happily ever since. When she married Gunther Sachs, he gave her a cheetah as a wedding present.

Poor Jayne Mansfield had a hard press when she appeared in England in 1967. Yet the British public could not reject a woman who, afraid of being separated from her two Chihuahuas, tried to smuggle them into the country under her furcoat to avoid quarantine. All animal-loving hearts were won when a picture of her, clutching the two tiny dogs to her famous bosom, appeared in the papers with the caption: "I am animal crackers! I have had Chihuahuas ever since I was a little girl. They are so dependent . . . they appeal to my mother instinct!" Kim Novak also retained the affection of her fans when, after the breakup of her marriage, she was presented to them as a shy, melancholy girl happy only in the company of her three adored pets, a Great Dane, a West Highland Terrier, and a Siamese cat.

Elizabeth Taylor, whose devotion to her four Pekingese has added to her popularity in Britain, marred her image by a very "Hollywoodish" publicity stunt that the British found in poor taste. To keep her dogs out of quarantine while she and her husband made films in Britain, she and Richard Burton hired a 191-ton, extremely luxurious diesel yacht, the *Beatriz of Bolivia,* as a "kennel." The yacht was tied up at the Tower Pier and the dogs were watched over by the famous couple's secretary, George Davis.

Since regular checks were made to make sure that Miss Taylor's dogs remained on board, Dr. Reginald Bennett, Conservative M.P. for Gosport and Fareham, asked the Home Secretary what police manpower had been allocated for the surveillance of the dogs and what it cost to public funds. A letter to *The Times* also asked whether "in these days of crimes of violence, burglaries, and so forth, we can really spare police to keep an eye on Miss Taylor's dogs? Or is it because it is Miss Taylor, and not an insignificant person who is keeping the dogs?"

Many French actors and actresses, singers and comedians, enhance their appeal by having themselves photographed with their pets. Jean Marais, George Brassens, Mylene Demongeot, Juliette Greco, Charles Aznavour, Fernandel, and a number of lesser stars resort to this gimmick, not, perhaps, because they need it, but because in the eyes of Western audiences a person without an animal is only half a person.

If this is true for France, how much more true it is for England! One of Britain's most popular pop groups, the Manfred Mann group, became still more popular when its lead singer, Mike d'Abo, had himself photographed with his cat, Alfie, and newspaper readers were told that his four Siamese are almost as dear to his heart as his pretty wife, Maggie.

One pop group calls itself "Animals," another "Monkees" and a third "Family Dog," but even the greatest and most famous of all, the Beatles—animals that had gone out of fashion since the adored Egyptian scarab—seem to require this publicity gimmick. When recording their song "A Day in the Life," they ended it with an ultra-sonic whistle, "a loud and clear call to all dogs" but inaudible to humans. "The Beatles are very fond of dogs, and it seemed a novel way to round off a record," said their recording manager. Paul McCartney, owner of a Shetland sheep dog called Martha, said: "I planned it as a message for Martha and for all other dogs in the world. I wanted them to have something completely to themselves."

Another group of people who have to have an "image," not to impress the public at large, but to maintain their status in their own circles, are the "great" of the underworld. A journalist, interviewing one of America's foremost animal-importers in his office, saw a flashily dressed, dark-haired, stern-faced man of about forty enter without greeting, followed by a young fellow who remained at the door with both hands in his pockets. The man told the animal dealer he had come to buy two young tigers. The journalist, female and therefore unashamedly curious, pulled the man's sleeve and when, obviously indignant at such impertinence, he gave her a withering look, she asked him why tigers of all possible pets? "Because I've had everything else," he said. "But don't you think they're dangerous beasts to have a-round?" she asked. "Dangerous?" The man shrugged contemptuously. "The animal I can't tame hasn't been created yet!" When told there were no tigers in stock but he could have them in two weeks, the man signed the order and departed with the young man in his wake.

"What do you think of him?" the animal dealer asked the journalist. "He's a gangster," she replied without hesitation. "He looks as if he'd just stepped off the cinema screen." "Cosa Nostra," the animal dealer said. "He needs tigers as a status symbol, but also as bodyguards. He's shed much blood, that one, but the less you know about it the safer you'll be."

It is not easy for people at the top, no matter what they're at the top of, to offer their pets more than those below them, but if they try hard they can still find ways and means. The king of all eccentric pet-owners in England is probably the Marquess of Bath, a Peer of the Realm, who keeps about thirty lions on the grounds of his stately home at Longleat. The fact that for a modest fee coach loads of tourists from all over Britain and abroad may view the Longleat lion park does not detract from the lions' status as pets, for when not otherwise occupied, some of them enjoy the company of their owner, reclining, relaxed, on the settees in his lounge. Tired of always seeing the same animal faces, the Marquess has now imported a family of hippos and allowed himself to be photographed wearing a cowboy outfit and riding the first of the hippos to arrive in Britain—family-father Manfred.

The Earl of Cranbrook likes them smaller. He exercises bats in his bathroom. "I keep them for about three months, feed them well, then let them go," he says. His recipe for an ideal bat-meal is: the yolk of a hard-boiled egg, cream cheese and banana in equal portions.*

In America, too, top people like small pets. The prize goes to Lynda Bird Johnson, who started a fashion by wearing two tiny bird cages with live birds in them as earrings. She is outdone in her taste for jewelry-*cum*-pet only by the South

*Christian Science Monitor, Jan. 27, 1967.

American *dolce far niente* crowd. They wear large, hairy spiders encrusted with precious stones on the shoulders of their evening dresses instead of orchids. The spider, frightened of light, clings motionless to the folds of the dress. At home it is placed in a box and fed flies until its next public appearance. Another jewel-*cum*-pet is the gilded and stone-encrusted beetle, attached to a pin by a thin gold chain, that walks over the wearer's shoulder and neck as far as the chain allows it to move. This, too, is housed and fed with care when not worn. Some French ladies of fashion wear tiny, live South American snakes attached to golden clips as earrings.

However, a pet does not have to be exotic to live like a king. The owner of a three-year-old poodle in America, explaining that a dog's third birthday is equivalent to a human's twenty-first, threw a coming-of-age party for her pet to which twenty-nine dogs were invited. Dinner consisted of an aperitif (sherry diluted in water), an assiette Anglaise for hors d'oeuvres, steak and vegetables, and ice cream for dessert. With their meal the guests drank strawberry-flavored milk poured from champagne bottles. Naturally all wore their best party clothes; the boys collar-and-bow-tie dog collars, white fronted black jackets, and lace-up patent leather boots, the girls brocade, velvet, or sequined evening jackets with matching panties and booties, flowers or ribbons in their hair, and a great deal of expensive jewelry—earrings, necklaces, and ankle chains. Their sailor-boy mackintoshes and furcoats, their caps, hats, or turbans had been taken off in the cloakroom. The birthday presents, laid out on a separate table, included a musical box playing "Happy Birthday to You," a collection of squeaky toys, among them a rubber mailman and policeman, several large boxes of mint bonbons called Doggy Breath, a leather-bound appointment book with the season's invitations already marked in it, and several fancy costumes the birthday poodle was to wear to other similar parties—a harlequin costume, a cowboy outfit, and a fireman costume.

In Germany top pet-owners like to wine and dine their pets in restaurants. Many first-class restaurants have a special dining room for pets, but most owners prefer to have them at their table. Clothes for pregnant bitches are bought at the Maternity Shop for Dogs, that also has a "delivery-room," where top pets can have their puppies in comfort, surrounded by every imaginable luxury and attended by first-class veterinarians.

Determined to give their pets everything an honorary human should have, the French have started a new-for-them type of holiday scheme called Pet-Exchange. Large dogs, like Alsatians, German shepherds, and Great Danes that never get enough fresh air and exercise in Paris, are sent to the Bretange or to the mountains for the summer holi-days. They are cared for by people who own small dogs — poodles, spaniels, dachshunds—that are, in exchange, taken in by the Paris families. Since the scheme is new, it has not been possible to establish whether the little country bump-kins enjoy the nightclubs or the museums most.

Americans, of course, are the most ingenious at think-ing up new ways to show off their anthropomorphized pets' status in the world. The January 7, 1968, issue of *The New York Times Magazine*, carrying a long article on top poo-dles, published the following social note:

Along with its dinner parties and lawn parties the Palm Beach pet set recently attended a fashionable wedding of its own when two well-connected toy poodles were joined in matrimony at the Poodle Boutique. Miss Petite Brabham, the bride, wore a dual-length ivory satin gown trimmed with Alencon lace, and a long veil of French illu-sion hanging from a crown of seed pearls. The groom was Muggins Carvey, son of Signature's Silver Pride and Su-zette Al'Kahira. He was conservatively attired in a white top hat and a black bow tie. Among the notable guests — all poodles—were the Smith brothers. Beau Smith wore a sunlight-yellow double-faced wool coat with collar and martingale in jonquil velvet, while his brother Michael appeared in a pink felt coat with fuchsia-colored yarn fringe. Gigi and Mouton Kimberley were also there, Gigi in a pink sequined evening coat with white mink collar, and Mouton in a royal-blue sequined day jacket bowed at the back. After the wedding party posed for pictures, everyone retired to the patio for a short reception.

Another poodle-bride was given a four-poster bed as a wedding present, with a built-in combination safe inscribed "My Personal Treasures." Her groom, somewhat hard of hearing, got a five-thousand-dollar hearing aid.

As all pet owners realize, a top pet should be not only properly dressed but properly groomed. In addition to patronizing the poodle salons that multiply by leaps and bounds all over America, Great Britain, and the Continent (though dog owners in Scotland, for instance, still complain bitterly about the shortage of facilities in certain areas), top poodles are, if their top salon cannot give them an appointment, served by free-lance groomers who come to the house. The most sought-after of these arrive with their equipment and, for fifteen dollars, not counting the extras, give their clients a full beauty treatment. Before a party, the bath, trim, nail clipping, etc., is followed by evening makeup: a gold or silver spray, a special hair style, artificial eye lashes, and nail polish in one of more than a dozen available colors.

Large dogs that cannot be bathed at home are taken to one of the many petshops with grooming facilities. These charge a minimum fee of twelve dollars for an Alsatian, though the grooming of an exotic pet, let us say a puma or tiger cub, costs considerably more, depending on the size and disposition of the client.

A well-paid occupation for elderly people or, in the school holidays, for students, is dog walking or pet-sitting. Many large apartment houses in American cities have a built-in dog-walker who will take out the residents' pets for a modest fee, two dollars for a walk. Finding sitters for the various usual and unusual pets their owners hate to leave at home alone when they go out is a more difficult proposition. Some of the animal welfare organizations and clubs have their own dog-and-cat-sitting service and a telephone call will bring a reliable pet-sitter for a fee of five dollars an hour, but in America, as well as in England and elsewhere, most baby-sitters will do the job if asked.

The problem with pets, as with people, is that they do not remain young forever. Owners who learn to grow old with dignity after a few face-lifts do not mind having their aged pets with them until one or the other, pet or owner, dies. If the owner goes first, the top pet is left well provided for; if the pet goes first it is laid to rest in a manner befitting its status.

British pets have nothing to worry about, even if they are not included in their owners' wills. There is always a place for them in one or another of the old-age homes for pets run by the animal charities.

German pet-owners, worried about the fate of their elderly pets should they be left alone, can now buy them annuities. An animal protection society will act as guardian, and the pension will be paid to the person looking after the orphaned pet. An adequate yearly payment, fifteen hundred to two thousand deutsche marks for a poodle, ensures that the pet, dog, parrot, cat, monkey, or alligator will be given the same care, if not, perhaps, the same love, it was used to.

In America the Bide-A-Wee Home Association, Inc., has launched a Pension Plan for Aged Dogs and Cats, acclaimed by pet owners who do not particularly enjoy being reminded of passing time or who do not have the time to look after their aged pets properly. This "home away from home" offers spacious landscaped grounds in Westhampton, Long Island; attractive new buildings for cats and kennels for dogs; modern heating to maintain even temperature; individual outdoor runs with plenty of sunshine and shaded areas; medical treatment when necessary; nourishing foods and special diets; trained attendants to care for the pets; a visitor's room. Elderly cats and dogs over five years old will be accepted subject to: physical examination by a veterinarian, the signing of the Pension Plan Agreement, donation. The fee is three hundred dollars a year. All pensioned pets remain the property of the owner and may be taken home at any time, on a visit or for good.

Pets also die. While the death of "expendable" humans is acknowledged with a resigned shrug and the moving parting words, "It's best for him/her, too . . . ," and the death of someone really loved is hidden away in a secret drawer of one's conscious mind, the death of a top pet, a Loved One, is made into a memorable occasion. The display of emotion toward animals not being taboo, the owner of a departed pet can give free rein to his sorrow and, not obliged to relate its death to his own mortality, can arrange for, as Evelyn Waugh says, "a ritualistic, almost orgiastic" funeral with all the trimming and regardless of the cost.

In Essex, England, in a cemetery dedicated by the Bishop of Chichester, two thousand top dogs lie in "final contentment." Some were buried with full Christian ceremony conducted by a clergyman, the mourners weeping unrestrainedly while their pet's oak-lined casket was lowered into the ground. In spring and summer hundreds of people arrive to lay flowers on the graves, plant bushes, and spend an hour remembering the days when their beloved pets were still with them.

If so desired, the funerals include embalming and the recreation of a lifelike aspect by morticians. A coffin costs between £35 and £60, a headstone between £15 and £150. One imported Italian marble memorial, that was made for the dog of a Lloyd's broker and cost £200, is surrounded by a grave of marble grated paving with curbs and posts. Inscriptions on the headstones read: "Toppie waits here" or "Your love is with us evermore, darling" or "At the going down of the sun each day, dear one, we remember you," or, appropriately, "For the loved one." At one ceremony, when a dog's tombstone was uncovered by his weeping mistress, the covering was the Union Jack.

Many of the pet cemeteries in England are full, and new ones have to be opened. A Garden of Rest for Pets on a two-acre plot donated by an animal lover in Norfolk provides resting places for dogs, cats, birds, and other small animals. The decision to open this new cemetery was taken when it was found out that the animals humanely destroyed by the RSPCA were buried by bulldozers on a refuse heap.

In the affluent parts of the Americas, of course, pet lovers would consider the British pet's way of death painfully poor and "understated." In Rio de Janeiro, for instance, where 22,480 dogs have graves in a cemetery more luxurious than those of the majority of humans, some of the graves are worth more than £820. Several dogs a day are buried there, with candles, flowers, tears, and prayers; some mourners faint, and at several funerals hysterical women tried to throw themselves into the open graves. According to the watchman, heart attacks are not a rare occurrence. The epitaphs bear witness to the owners' great love for their pets, and some even explain it. "Chiquita—my daughter denied me but you, my companion, loved me!" "To the unforgettable Rumba, nostalgia from your little father." "Sheika—the more I know of humanity, the more I come close to animals."

In the United States the Humane Association and *Pet Shop Magazine* know of ninety one animal cemeteries, though there may be others run by persons "whose consideration of pets and their masters' peace of mind surpasses their love of money." At the Hartsdale Canine Cemetery in Westchester, the forty thousand pets interred are not all dogs. There are monkeys among them, goldfish, parrots, cats, salamanders, and a lion. One lady, who has so far buried fifty eight pets there, has a piglet and a bantam rooster among them. But most of the more than three hundred pets brought annually from all over America, South America, and Europe are dogs of all kinds, seeing-eye dogs and even war heroes. One of the latter was buried in a major's uniform. There lie the pets of many famous people, including Fritz Kreisler, Gene Krupa, and Elizabeth Arden.

A plot costs $40 to $60, a plain pine casket $17, and a mahogany one $150. However, with Cadillac transportation to the cemetery and other services, the bill for a funeral tends to rise to $400 or more. When the weather is good, at least a hundred people spend their Sundays visiting the graves of their departed pets, but even on a freezing weekend there are never less than twenty five. A former Navy man has been coming for fifteen years to place flowers on the grave of his dog, and a woman, who comes twice a week, takes off her shoes before entering the cemetery in tribute to her dog. She walks in barefoot even in snow and rain.

The Pet Memorial Park run by the Bide-a-Wee Home Association Inc. charges $40 to $150 for a plot, $15 to $26 for the container, $8 for the interment, and $3 for the maintenance. One payment of $100 assures perpetual maintenance. Christmas decoration of the grave costs $3, special care, including flowers, $9 annually, and perpetual special care $300. Headstones are optional—except in the more costly sections, where they are obligatory.

The Hinsdale pet cemetery near Chicago, where several war dogs have been laid to rest, has room for another twenty thousand pets. Granite headstones start at $35, but people rarely buy the cheapest. A five-foot casket for a large dog costs $85, embalming $50. The bill for a funeral will often run up to $600 to $1000. One man bought a medium-size headstone for his pet, than decided it was not adequate and exchanged it for a large one. A woman who had installed a memorial for her dog set aside $2000 in her will for a new monument. Two skunks, several horses, and a turtle that was killed at the age of forty by a dog, are buried there.

The most exclusive Garden of Rest, however, is run by the Animal Funeral Home, Inc. Its brochure describes the services offered as "a new, desirable elevation in animal service," at astronomical prices, of course. The dead pet is picked up in a white station wagon whose driver is instructed to handle the corpse with due reverence. At the funeral parlor it is groomed and placed on a bier in the position it was wont to lie in when alive, until the owner and the human and animal friends have paid their last respects. People for whom only the best is good enough can get the "preferred service," conducted from one of the "slumber rooms" opening out of the softly lit lounge and with piped-in music. There are special "slumber rooms" for each pet species—poodles, Siamese cats, Irish terriers—the color and furnishings harmonizing with the breed and character of the dear departed.

Anglo-Saxon pet-lovers expect their friends and acquaintances to share their sorrow and will often put announcements of their pets' deaths in the newspapers and animal magazines. One, in *The Times*, reads: "JAKE, bull terrier, beloved friend of Cynthia, Cedric and Christopher Masterman, died February 6, aged 12 years, three months. Buried Nettlebed, Oxfordshire." Another, in *Tail-Waggers Magazine*, reads: "Sweetest memories and love our darling Sealyham PATSY gave during 12½ years she was with us. We shall never forget you, Patsy-Girl!"

More moving still is the In Memoriam in the American magazine *Dog World*: "In loving memory of Lainesand's Red Cloud, 15 July 1963-16 January 1966, after caesarian operation. God wanted one more angel to grace his heavenly throne, and so he took our Mandy, and bid us not to mourn. We wanted so to keep her, for she was to us given, but Jesus said it could not be, he wanted her in heaven. From your brokenhearted mum and all at Lainesand's Boxers."

And lastly, also from *Dog's World*: "In the shocked silence that followed the death of Abraham Lincoln, one of the generals at his bedside uttered the unforgettable phrase: 'Now he belongs to the ages.' We can only paraphrase this utterance at the news of the death of Ch Phidgity Snow Dream!"

Part III

◎ ◎ THE PROFIT MAKERS
AND NEED CREATORS

CHAPTER 9
PET POWER

> The myopic preoccupation with production and material investment has diverted attention from the more urgent question of how we are employing our resources and, in particular, from the greater need and opportunity for investing in persons.
>
> — J. K. GALBRAITH:
> *The Affluent Society*

◉ ◉ THEY DID NOT HAVE TO FIGHT FOR IT. THEY do not even want it. Yet in the last decade or so, the petishist millions, too powerless to wrest power from the hands of those leading them to perdition and too confused to "invest in persons" who could lead them away from it, have thrust immense power upon the only creatures they still trust, those symbols of unselfish love, loyalty, and innocence, their pets.

A quarter of a century ago the power wielded by pet animals was only emotional. They gave love where love was needed, loyalty where loyalty was needed, companionship where companionship was needed. In return, they were allowed to share the creature comforts of their masters; they were brought in from the cold, they ate what remained from their masters' meals, they slept on the rug near the fire or, in exceptional cases, at the end of their masters' beds. Their metamorphosis from animal to substitute human was, at first, so slow that it was hardly noticeable. People smiled at the elderly lady who knitted a warm coat for her elderly dog, and at the little girl who dressed up her puppy and played with it as if it were a doll. The three factors that speeded up this metamorphosis of the urban domestic animal were growing alienation, affluence, and leisure.

Alienation, and the resulting neuroses that produced a rapid deterioration in human relationships, put an added value on human-animal relationships. Affluence gave fuel to snobbism and established the cult of the pedigree; and leisure, dropped into the lap of people intellectually and educationally unprepared for it, caused domestic animals to be used as an antidote to boredom.

The day Big Business woke to the realization that its market, the human community, could be extended to embrace the parallel community of domestic animals became the birthday of the anthropomorphized animal. Ever since, the entire artillery of open and "hidden" persuasion, employed to relieve the human consumer of his money and make him buy first what he needs, second what he thinks he needs, and third what he can be made to believe he needs has been geared to create a set of even more synthetic needs—those of the *new consumer*, the pet.

Thanks to the highly developed brainwashing techniques of the American advertising industry and the affluence of the victims whose subconscious minds they manipulate,

American pet-lovers own the largest number of pets and
spend the most on them. As consumers America's twenty-
six million dogs rate first, representing 40 per cent of the
pet field, meaning the pet trade and pet industry. Fish rate
second, representing 25 per cent of the pet field; birds third,
with 16.5 per cent; small animals and exotic pets fourth,
with 10-20 per cent, and cats fifth with 8 per cent.

The dog population in the United States is growing twice
as fast as the human population, and if the trend continues,
dogs may, in the next century, outnumber people. They
produce a million new customers a year, and as the demand
for pedigree dogs increases—in 1967 the American Kennel
Club recorded 804,000 new registrations—the needs of these
pampered animals, created and satisfied by Big Business,
become more and more sophisticated.

At the Chicago Convention of the Pet Food Institute in
October, 1967, it was stated that a recent study compar-
ing the 1957 and 1967 status of pet foods showed that in
that decade the dollar value of pet foods had increased 85
per cent, the number of new items increased 61 per cent,
the weekly dollar margin went up 99 per cent, and the linear
shelf-feet devoted to pet foods increased 56 per cent. This
fantastic growth of the pet industry was attributed partly
to the suburbanization of the youthful population, partly
to a change in the sociological attitude to pets. Pet animals,
dogs in particular, occupy the roles of adolescent children
in the family. One example of proof that most dog owners
endow their pets with human needs, and reward them accordingly, is that one-half of all special *treat* foods given them
are human foods and one of the most prevalent is ice cream.

Dr. Lester Fisher, director of the Lincoln Park Zoo, Chicago, told the delegates that in the next ten years pet medical care is expected to advance to a level close, if not equal,
to human medical care. Veterinary medicine is becoming
more specialized, animal hospitals will be staffed by surgeons, orthopedists, ophthalmologists, and radiologists,
as well as licensed and more highly trained technical per-
sonnel. The advances in pet medical care include injectible
and oral drugs, replacing surgical procedures to neuter ani-

mals, and both the size and sex of the litter may be controlled by related hormonal products. B. S. Hambleton, vice president of Jewel Companies, Inc., said that pet foods is the fifth largest item handled by the company. The public is clamoring for more variety, more quality, better nutrition value, and better taste in food for pets than it did for children ten years ago.

Universities, shaping the parents of the future, seem to be aware of this "away from children" trend and are, therefore, helping the pet owners of the future to go out into the world fully prepared to face their responsibilities. Pennsylvania State University has added a course on the care and training of dogs to its noncredit courses. Instruction on feeding, shelters, disease, and parasite controls make up the major part of the dog course, but breeding, whelping, and puppy care are also discussed in detail. The course stresses the responsibilities of dog owners and, to ensure good human-animal relationships, gives hints on the selection of the most suitable dog.

Fifty-seven per cent of American dogs are owned by people with an annual income of $7000 and over, 34 per cent by people in the $3000-$7000 income group, and 9 per cent by people earning $3000 or less. Forty-five per cent of all single-dog homes and 41 per cent of all multidog homes have incomes of over $7000.

According to a 1966 compilation by the Chase Manhattan Bank, New York, Americans spend over $3 billion annually on their dogs: food, $550 million; clothes and accessories, $450 million; purchase of dogs, $700 million; licensing fee, $150 million; shots, $150 million; veterinary fees, $600 million; miscellaneous, $400 million.

Most of these figures are already dated. In 1967 the money spent on commercially prepared dog foods was $590 million and the nationwide sales gain by pet shops was over 11 per cent. The figure for "miscellaneous" is also way off. Grooming alone accounts for $150 million annually, and according to Dr. Schroeder, president of the American Veterinary Medical Association, the sale of health aids comes to more than $270 million, most of it for dogs. If we add other forgotten items, such as poodle cosmetics, traveling expenses, kennel fees, AKC registration fees, pet club membership fees, toys, photographs, pensions, funeral expenses, the grand total is probably nearer $4 billion than $3 billion.

Nor has it been taken into consideration that the top layer of dog owners who prefer fresh food to tinned food for themselves will give fresh food to their pets as well, and that the lowest income group of dog owners will feed theirs on table scraps and the cheapest meats available. It would require a large-scale investigation among butchers to obtain the real figure on spending for dog foods.

Although only 16.5 per cent of America's twenty million cats are pure bred and only 20 per cent eat commercially prepared foods, cat food sales, in 1967, reached $220 million. Here again the total spent on cat foods could be established only through extensive research among the butchers and fishmongers that supply the food for the remaining 80 per cent. Other expenditures on cats, such as litter, health aids, and articles of hygiene, the purchase of pedigree cats from pet shops, the quarter of a million pedigree cats bought from 5500 catteries in 1966, cat club registration and membership fees, veterinary fees, traveling expenses, boarding fees, cat furniture and toys, pension and funeral expenses, and so on, have not been added up, but it would be safe to assume that the nation's cats cost their owners at least half a billion dollars a year.

Tropical fish are also becoming increasingly fashionable, though very few figures are available on them. It is estimated that in addition to goldfish, 50 million to 100 million tropical fish are sold annually. One fish wholesaler sells more than 25 million fish to variety stores. One dealer states that salt-water-fish sales have increased 100 per cent in three years and collectors will pay as much as $300 for one fish. The fashionable fish, like sharks and piranhas, cost less.

There are approximately 20 million aquarium owners in the United States. Each year more than 3.5 million aquaria are produced and sold, and one manufacturer, the Metaframe Corporation, increased its sales by 25 per cent in the second half of 1966 to reach a record level of $3,321,000 for the six months ending December 1. During that time profits increased from $65,000 to $90,000. The wholesale price of a five-gallon aquarium is $14.99, of a fifty-gallon one $71.98. The smallest stand costs approximately $8, the largest $16. If, however, you want a really superb aquarium stand, you will have to pay $39.95 to $49.95 in the stores.

Owners who like to watch their fish against colorful backgrounds can obtain them in sizes to fit their tanks. One ready-made background called "Atlantis" shows decorative ruins amid lush vegetation, another called "Shipwreck," the battered remains of a ship among the boulders of the sea bottom. Another shows a diver attacked by a man-eating shark, another, called "Oriental", displays Japanese gardens and behind them a snow-capped Fujiyama.

In 1967 the nation's fish consumed fish food valued at $15 million. In the same year the aquarium industry produced eighty-one new items for them, against twenty-six in 1965.

More than 7.5 million families in the United States own one or several pet birds: parakeets, canaries, parrots, pigeons, and others, plus a large number of exotic birds. Each year some 100,000 psittacine birds are smuggled into the country and add to the number of feathered consumers. Prices vary greatly, but in general, pet shops mark up the wholesale prices about 100 per cent.

A few examples from the price list of the Justamere Bird Ranch, which supplies pet shops, will illustrate the wholesale price of birds: canaries, from $6.50 to $12.50 each; new-strain canaries, white, cinnamon, ivory, and ivory rose, $20 to $50; parakeets, from $1.75 to $10; love birds, from $10.50 to $35; cockatiels, from $8.50 to $250; baby parrots, from $16.50 to $350; macaws, $250 to $500; Lutino ring-neck parakeets, $300; Humboldt penguin, $150. A sulphur-crested cockatoo smuggled out of Australia will cost as much as $1600.

If one adds to the price of the pet bird the price of the cage, the feed, the health aids, the toys, and the various novelties, of which forty-seven new ones were produced in 1967, one comes to the conclusion that even a pet bird can put a considerable strain on the family budget. But if birds were not a good business, pet suppliers would not go all out to "Sell Sympathy for the Birds," that is, wild birds, and their winter feeding. Hanging feeders, to be attached to trees and holding suet and bird seed, cost $1.80 to $5 wholesale and yield a profit of 70 per cent. There are also electric water-warmers, for cold days when the water containers in the garden freeze and the wild birds cannot drink. And a bird lover used to luxury and wishing to offer it to wild birds can put up a bird house in his garden for about $38.

Today there are also commercially prepared foods, health aids and equipment produced for the small pets, such as mice, rats, hamsters, and guinea pigs. Their numbers, and the money spent on them annually, have not yet been calculated, but their popularity is still on the increase. Gerbils, a kind of furrowing rodent that just a few years ago could be bought for $2.50 apiece in Texas, now cost between $5.95 and $10. In 1967, sixty-two novelty items were produced for small animals.

It is difficult to decide whether spiders, tarantulas, millipedes, ants, and bees should be listed among the small or the exotic pets. Pet shops keep them because they sell well and at a very high profit. An Executive Ant Farm, goldplated, with walnut base, sells for $10. The first style manufactured had the New York skyline as a background, but at popular request they are now also made with the skyline of your choice.

The amount spent on exotic and "extremely exotic" pets is a mystery, partly because most of these pets do not live on commercially prepared foods, partly because there has not yet been a pet-population census.

In an article published in *The Pet Dealer* in 1966, the well-known New York animal importer Henry Trefflich says that movies like *Born Free* and the nature films shown on television have quickened people's interest in unusual pets. The "relatively small but extremely significant segment of the population" that first went in for "extremely exotic type pets" started a trend that has been on the upswing ever since. Some people buy lion cubs, or ocelots, or even a baby tiger, as "attention getters," or status builders, but, says

Henry Trefflich, the rising crime rate in some areas has also contributed to the popularity of pets believed to be "ferocious," even though they are the tamest and most harmless creatures when properly handled. While a relatively small number of consumers will buy lions, tigers, ocelots, cheetahs and the like, countless others buy exotic pets of other types, especially monkeys and, strangely enough, snakes. The woman to whom Mr. Trefflich sold a six-foot yellow rat-snake told him that "it made the very best of pets," and the demand for kangaroo rats exceeds the supply.

Decorative animals are also on the upswing. The Joneses who wish to outdo the other Joneses are now going in for peacocks, antelopes, deer, flamingos, and emus. Snakes as status symbols are on the way out, since one single pet-dealer sold 12,000 boa constrictors in 1967.

A selection of wholesale prices will give you some idea of what people are ready to pay for "attention-getting" pets: gorilla, $4500; chimpanzee, $700; female elephant, $2500-$3500; leopard, $400; orangutan, $2000; Diana monkey, $250 a pair; wanderoos, $500 a pair; black-neck swans, $400 a pair; Chilean flamingo, $125 each; demoiselle crane, $225 each; light-phase rock python, $150; pigmy hippopotamus, $5000. Any animal not listed can be ordered and obtained within a reasonable time.

The Grove Otter and Pet Ranch in Oklahoma offers a wide variety of pets to pet shops. The pet shop may mark up the price from 50 to 150 per cent, depending on its overhead and the rarity and quality of the animal. Some Grove prices are as follows. Thailand otters, babies, $225 each, half-grown, $195 each, adult, $150 each; ringtail cat, $25; lesser anteater, $55; capybara, $45; two-toed sloth, $35; hog-nose skunk, $65; ocelot, $195; kinkajou, $65; young raccoon, $20; woolly monkey, $65; Capuchin, $27; weeper, $28.50, etc.

Other unusual pets for the discerning buyer include armadillos, badgers, Goliath beetles, boa constrictors, bobcats, cheetahs, chinchillas, chipmunks, civet cats, coatamundis, coyotes, crows, dingos, ferrets, foxes, hedgehogs, jaguars, jumping beans, kangaroo rats, llamas, manatees, ostriches, pelicans, penguins, prairie dogs, rabbits, seals, sharks, tapirs, tarantulas, timber wolves, vipers, vultures, wallabies, waltzing mice, and wild cats. Not mentioned are the fashionable dwarf donkeys that can be bought directly from the stud farm for $225.

The *Pet Shop Management Directory* shows 5856 pet shops in the United States and lists 3472 chain retail outlets selling pet supplies. The number of grooming establishments selling, at least, poodle cosmetics has not been determined. The number of veterinarians dealing with pet animals exclusively is 2619. Fifty per cent or more of the animals handled by another 3885 veterinarians are also pets.

One may not be far off in saying that in 1967 Americans spent a total of $5 billion to $6 billion on pet animals and that, in spite of the Vietnam War and the resulting squeeze, the pet business continues to thrive.

According to *Pet Shop Management*, California, the richest state in America, has approximately 1240 pet shops. Since Hollywood rules the world of the cinema and San Francisco rules the world of the hippies and wealthy people retire to California to enjoy its beauty and climate, there is perhaps no other state where more money is spent on pets, conservative and kinky.

Mrs. E., wealthy widow of a paper manufacturer, lives in Santa Monica in a three-room apartment. When her husband died in 1966, friends talked her into acquiring a Sealyham terrier, imported from England, for $250. She grew very fond of the dog but, having many other interests, did not treat it as a child or go to the extremes of pampering some of her friends indulged in. When the dog was one year old, Mrs. E. decided, out of mere curiosity, to find out how much she had spent on it.

As she herself never ate tinned food, she fed her Sealyham on fresh food, following the advice given by Richard de Rochemont in his *Pets' Cookbook*. For breakfast she gave it cereal or dog biscuits soaked in warm milk, and twice a week a lightly boiled egg. For lunch it had raw beef or lamb cut into tiny pieces and mixed with rice and boiled vegetables. For tea the little dog had cereal again, soaked in soup stock or broth instead of milk. For supper she gave it diced beef or lamb, lightly cooked in a little fat, and fresh vegetables, and before putting it to bed a cup of warm broth, milk, or cocoa. These simple meals, plus between-meal snacks such as biscuits, pet turnovers, and chock-drops cost her $1.50 a day, that is, *$547.50 in one year.*

During the year she had taken the Sealyham to the veterinarian three times, once for its shot, once for an upset stomach, once for a sore ear. The three visits, plus medicines and the dog's daily vitamin pills, cost her *$50.*

Grooming, once a month, plus the deodorant, antihalitosis spray, and the little cosmetic items the groomer talked her into, cost her *$120 in one year.*

She bought the following accessories for her dog: two dishes, one for food, one for water, $2; two collars, one for $8 and one for $15; two leashes, one for $3 and one for $5; one brush for $3; one bed for $15; one blanket for $5, and an electric blanket for $10; two sweaters for $10; two coats for $30; one raincoat with hood and rubber boots for $15; one dog-tent, where the Sealyham liked to retire when the sun was too hot in the garden, for $25; toys, Christmas gifts, $25. *Total: $151.*

When Mrs. E. flew to New York to visit her sister, she took the dog with her. She bought a traveling kennel for $35 and a cushion for it for $9. The return fare for the dog was something like $40. *Total: $85.* In the spring she flew to England to visit another sister but could not take the dog with her because of the British quarantine regulations. She put it in a boarding kennel at $2 a day. *Total, for three weeks: $42.*

When Mrs. E. found that *she had spent, in one year, $994.50 on her dog, a sum equivalent to the annual income of a migrant worker in California,* she decided there was something basically wrong about treating animals, however much one loved them, better than people. She conceived the idea of starting a small-scale Human Rights movement among her friends and acquaintances but decided first to investigate how much *they* spent on their pets. The outcome of her investigation—in the course of which she quarreled with a good many of her friends—was worse than she expected. Several of her female friends, especially those with poodles, spent twice, or three times as much, on their pets as she had, and couples with several pet dogs, large and small, or exotic pets, spent enough for a middle-class family to live on in relative comfort.

One woman, whose snow-white toy poodle, Beauty, had a room of her own, felt that the little animal was like a daughter to her and treated it accordingly. The room had white wallpaper with different color poodles on it, and a wall-to-wall white nylon carpet. The furniture consisted of a white bed with nylon sheets, changed every second day, and white woolen blankets, washed each week. For cool nights Beauty had a white electric blanket. A white wardrobe and a chest of drawers held Beauty's clothes, and shelves, running the whole length of one wall, were loaded with her toys. After lunch the little dog had a snooze on a white washable leather divan with a selection of washable velvet cushions in various colors. A white toilet table with drawers held Beauty's health aids and cosmetics and her silver-backed brushes and combs.

The lady had bought Beauty, an imported English toy poodle, for $350. The decorating of the room and the furniture had cost her $800. Every time she bought new clothes for herself, she bought a complete matching outfit for Beauty. Since these outfits were made for her specially, collar leash, coat, panties or trousers, and boots never cost less than $100. In addition, Beauty owned six pairs of pajamas (at $10 each), two bathrobes (at $10 each), two winter and two summer dressing gowns, ($15 - $20 each) and a selection of slippers. Like her mistress, she had three fur coats, one mink, one leopard, and one white ermine. The three had cost $500. Her jewel box contained diamond earrings, for which her ears had been pierced, a diamond necklace and four diamond-studded gold arm, or rather ankle, bands, and various other, less expensive pieces. For parties she also had two hairpieces, one white and one black, made of human hair (at $45 each). Every three weeks a specialist came to the house to groom her at $25 a visit, but whenever Beauty was invited to a really elegant party, he came to make her up with false eyelashes, nail polish in the required colors, and so on.

Every two months, whether she needed it or not, Beauty was taken to the veterinarian for a checkup, but his advice was never followed. The dog took all the health aids and vitamin pills he gave her but never had the prescribed diet. Eating human food with her mistress, Beauty was always overfed.

Like Americans in general, Beauty got very little exercise. At home she played with her toys, life-size stuffed animals, such as a black poodle, a red setter, a tiger, and a monkey ($30 - $40 each), a selection of rubber dolls, most of them squeaky or musical, and rawhide chew articles.

When she went out with her mistress, it was always in the car. For short trips she was placed in a canvas holder attached to the passenger seat, for long trips in a special wire-mesh station-wagon kennel with a cushioned floor ($45).

When her mistress had to go abroad with her husband and could not take Beauty along, she was placed not in a boarding kennel but with her groomer, who put up "special" pets, never more than two at a time, for a fee of $5 a day. The first time she was left alone this way for three weeks, Beauty had a nervous breakdown and had to be treated by a dog psychiatrist. The treatment cost $250, but it was worth it because the following year she survived the separation without tragic consquences.

This, naturally, was one friend Mrs. E. could not win for her Human Rights campaign. Some of the others were more understanding. Although they refused to deprive their pets of any of the comforts they were used to, they donated modest sums of money to various social organizations looking after destitute humans.

It would be a mistake, however, to believe that only wealthy people pamper their pets and surround them with unneces-

sary and unwanted (by the pet) luxuries. A waitress in a
Brooklyn cafeteria patronized by the shopkeepers and employees of the neighborhood spends no less than $500 a year
on her faithful Alsatian bitch. Although the owner of the
cafeteria has repeatedly offered to let her take home leftovers, raw and cooked, she feels these would be below her
dog's canine dignity.

She figured out that on the average she spent 50 cents
a day on the dog's food, *$182.50 a year.* Once a month she
took it to a neighborhood petshop to be bathed and groomed,
which cost her, with tips, $12 each time, *$144 annually.* The
yearly shot, having its teeth attended to, vitamins and other
health aids, came to *$35.* One bed, two blankets, two dishes,
one brush, one comb, dry shampoo, flea powder, deodorant,
cost *$40.* Every time she bought new clothes for herself,
she bought her dog a new collar and leash. In 1967 she had
bought him five sets, adding up to *$25.* She felt that to dress
up a large dog in all sorts of clothes was ridiculous, but since
she took him with her practically everywhere, he had to
have a warm coat with snow boots for the New York winter,
and a raincoat with rubber boots for rainy days. She spent
a modest *$10* on the two sets. Once, when she was in the hospi-
tal for ten days, and then again for two weeks when she
went on holiday with a friend who had no extra room in his
car, she put the dog in a boarding establishment for $2 a
day, *$48 total.* Another *$30* or so were spent on his toys, Christmas gifts, and odds and ends she could not remember. This
woman, who had been abandoned by her husband and lived
alone with the dog, earned about $80 a week before taxes, plus
two meals a day at the cafeteria.

Many pet-owners are unaware that for a modest annual
premium of about $40 they can obtain a combined medical-
hospital-surgical, and accidental-natural-death insurance
policy from the Pet Insurance Agency, Inc., in Philadelphia.

The medical insurance entitles the policy-holder (subject
to $10 deductible from each claim) to: office calls, up to $5
for each call; hospital calls when the veterinarian is not a
surgeon, $3 for each visit with a limit of one visit a day, maxi-

mum of seven days; hospital room and board, $3 per day with a maximum of seven days for each confinement due to sickness or injury; miscellaneous expenses up to $25 for each sickness or injury, expenses such as X rays, electro-cardiogram, fluoroscopy, anesthesia, oxygen, drugs, medi-cation, antibiotics, vaccines and boosters, casts, splints, trusses and surgical dressings, laboratory and microscope services, physiotherapy, dental work; surgery, up to $100 for caeserian section, obstetrical services, spaying and castra-tion and, in addition, more than 190 other surgical opera-tions; private nursing care, $5 for each eight-hour period, with maximum allowance $15; private ambulance service, maximum $5.

Should the pet die of illness or accident, the owner is paid a $100 death benefit. However, special policies of up to $500 are available for pedigree dogs and dogs over five years of age. The premium in these cases is 10 per cent of the owner's own valuation of his pet, and "really good" dogs will often cost $5000 and over.

Cats, though less expensive to keep, can also cost their owners quite a bit of money. One special pet shop in Chi-cago sells pedigree kittens before they are even born, at prices starting at $150. The shop, called Feline Inn, charges a 25-cent entrance fee deductible from the purchases made. In addition to selling "Everything for the Cat," from food to beds, collars to toys, dishes to blankets, and litter to cos-metics, the shop maintains on its premises a "Luxury Hotel for Cats" with air-conditioning in summer, plenty of warmth in winter, flea lamps and hi-fi system that plays music to keep the residents calm and happy. Each cat has ample accom-modation, with bed, potty box, and a fresh blanket every day, at a moderate daily fee of $2. There is a tiled garden called "Catio," with a kitten house and a catnip bar for the feline guests and chairs and tables for the visiting owners. There are also "mating cages" and large rooms with double-bed accommodation for the cat owners who came in pairs. People wishing to buy a pedigree kitten put down a deposit and are notified when the kitten is ready to leave the store. Burmese kittens start at $100, the rarer Russian blues at $150. Any cat can be hired as a model for a fee of $25 a half-day.

Another pet shop employing one groomer makes $9000 a year from grooming and $400 a month from boarding pets, except during vacation time, when the income from boarding rises to $2000 a month. The New York shop Everything for Everybody will board a cat for $8 a week and walk pets for $2 an hour.

Pet shops all over the United States are doing very well indeed. Henry Trefflich sold $500,000 worth of livestock in 1966. (In the early postwar years, before European dealers began to compete, the figure was $1,500,000.) Another pet shop in Long Beach, California, sold dogs and dog supplies for $75,000, fish and fish supplies for $36,000, birds and bird supplies for $20,000, and miscellaneous items for $15,000. A small pet shop in New York, on the corner of Second Avenue and 100th Street, a relatively poor area, sold $75,000 worth of pets and supplies in 1966.

The markup on livestock sold by pet shops can be anywhere from 75 to 300 per cent. The overhead for pet shops with an annual turnover of $100,000 is approximately 35 per cent. Aquarium fish will sell for double or three times the invoice price, aquarium plants are marked up 50 to 400 per cent. The markup on canaries is usually 100 per cent, on cockatiels 125 per cent, on mynah birds 100 to 150 per cent, on parakeets 100 per cent, on hamsters and other small animals 100 per cent, on monkeys 100 per cent, on ocelots 50 per cent, on leopards 75 to 100 per cent, on raccoons 75 per cent, on pedigree puppies and kittens 100 per cent.

A nationwide investigation by *Pet Shop Management* established that people in large towns spend 1.4 per cent of their total grocery bill on pet foods, in small towns 2 per cent. High-income blue-collar workers spend 1.8 per cent on pet foods, low-income blue-collar workers 1.6 per cent, young people and Negroes 1 per cent. This, naturally, applies only to commercially prepared foods.

The 1968 *Directory of Pet Store Management* lists 55 new pet-supply manufacturers, 30 new pet-supply wholesalers, 231 new livestock-dealers, 8 new live- and frozen-food dealers, and 4 new animal-importers.

One example will indicate why so many new firms consider it worthwhile to join the pet field. Sternco Industries, one of the giants in the field, increased its sales by 330 per cent in the seven years between 1958 and 1965. For the nine months ending September, 1967, sales were $19,252,192 against $16,994,898 during the same period in 1966. This company specializes in tropical fish and pet supplies.

The human-food manufacturers moved in long ago on this very profitable market. General Foods, the Ralston Purina Company, Quaker Oats, the Carnation Company, Kellogg, are doing very well indeed with their dog and cat foods. It is not surprising, therefore, that they should have been followed by the cigarette companies. Liggett & Myers, P. Lorillard, and United States Tobacco have all taken over pet-product manufacturers. The cat food sales of Usen Products Co., bought up by United States Tobacco, rose considerably faster than the industry's average increase of about 20 per cent in each of the past five years.

Drug chains throughout the United States are going into a broader variety of pet items, some increasing the space given to them by 30 per cent. Even so, they find it hard to keep pace with the growing number of pet health aids. The June, 1967, issue of *Drug Trade News* states that Pet'M Products spent $861,000 on TV ads for the Daily Food Supplement and pet care products, plus $730,000 in general magazines and $350,000 in newspapers. During the same time Hartz Mountain spent $270,000 on TV ads, Sergeants $825,000 and Pulvex $100,000.

In case someone should think that petishism is confined to civilians, let us state here that Army post exchanges are authorized to carry pet supplies, with the exception of dog and cat foods, which are sold in commissaries. Bird, turtle, fish, and other pet foods are sold in exchanges.

Not content with the vast sums spent on pet animals in America, a California company has come out with a revolving charge card enabling dog and cat owners to obtain a variety of services and supplies on credit. The scheme, called *"Protecta-Pet,* covers veterinary fees, including hospitalization, grooming, training, foods and supplies, accessories, boarding and kennel services, and even the purchase of a pet. The company is planning five Protecta-Pet divisions across the country to provide everything a pet owner could want, including the nation's largest pet cemetery on fourteen acres and a pet museum with 350 wax likenesses of famous race horses and famous dogs of history.

The pet owner pays $5 annually for the credit card, and since people are always tempted to spend more than they originally planned when buying on the cuff, the pet credit-card system will certainly help the pet field to climb from tenth place in the order of retail trades to ninth, eighth, or even seventh. One item not mentioned so far, although the owners of female pedigree dogs and cats who do not wish to deprive their pets of the pleasures of motherhood spend quite a bit of money on it, is stud fees. Let us quote here only one advertisement that gives some idea of the sums involved and contains an amusing *double entendre:*

> Les Mew Cattery proudly presents Montpellier La Creme Victor
> At Stud to Approved Queens: Fee $150.00

While the bulk of the pet trade and industry caters to the bodily needs of America's pet population, there are two special industries, one catering to the psychological and the other to the intellectual needs of the animals and their devoted owners—the pet-toy industry and publishing.

VO-TOYS Inc., perhaps the largest producer of pet specialties, has on its price list 121 different toys for cats, from catnip-filled felt Santa Claus to deluxe multifaceted Snap Apart Collar, from Squeaky Mouse to Catnip Candy Cane, from Musical Man Cat Toy to Felt Catnip Sombrero with squeaker inside and feather attached "for your cat's enjoyment." There are 192 different toys for dogs, from Large Leather Slippers, with crackle inside, to Rawhide Frankfurter, from Vinyl Ice Cream Pop to Vinyl Fire Plug, from Jumbo Leather Crackle Bone to Vinyl Pussy Cat, Large Nylon Rat, Whole Vinyl Chicken and Ham, or Large Vinyl Poodle for company.

Pet books, as distinct from books about animals, are so profitable a business that more and more general publishers are competing with the specialized pet-book publishers. These books also provide an extra income for the pet shops.

To turn animals into *conscious* consumers, America's Big Brother, the advertising industry, has invented a new gimmick, the synthetizing and electrical reproduction of the essential tones and harmonies of the dog whistle to be used at the beginning of dog-food commercials on TV. The sound will be inaudible to most adults, although children under nine will be able to hear it. Tests have shown that urban middle-class dogs and alert country dogs react to it with tail wagging, barking, sometimes even savage growls, but the upper-class dog riding in a Cadillac and wearing a diamond collar considers himself above responding to a whistle. Different types of commercials will be designed to appeal to different types of dogs, according to breed, size, and geographical area.

Now that it has been ascertained that the overwhelming majority of dogs react happily and noisily to this new and wonderful invention, it remains only to be seen how the owners of the wooed four-legged consumers will react to the only too painfully audible reaction of their pets. It may well be that the result will be a sudden increase in the sale of television sets to replace the ones kicked to pieces by irate dog-owners. But really to appreciate the meaning of the $5 to $6 billion Americans spend annually on pet animals, one should remember that in 1966 the average family income of Americans was $6957, though families whose head was between fourteen and twenty-four years of age averaged only $5611. With increasing age the average family income increased to a maximum of $8861 up to fifty-four years of age. After that it dropped sharply, with families whose head was sixty-five or over having an average income of $3645.

While the possession of a "ferocious" pet may discourage criminals from breaking into the homes of individuals, the conspicuous affluence of American pets has encouraged a new type of crime—*pet*napping. In Greater New York alone some fifty thousand dogs disappear annually. The majority are sold to laboratories, or to dealers, privately or at auction, adding up to a $20-million-to-$50-million-a-year racket. Some of the petnappers, however, have found that they can do even better by returning the pets for ransom money.

An obviously opulent couple in Florida left their toy poodle in their car while they went to a restaurant for a meal. They had reached the main course when they were called to the telephone and informed by a "gruff" voice that their pet had been kidnaped. If they wished to get it back alive, they were told, they should leave a parcel containing $1000 in used one-dollar notes at a certain place on the beach. Without a moment's hesitation, the couple obeyed, and an hour later were reunited with their beloved pet.

A rich woman in New York had to repeat the payment of $1000 five times before her pedigree Alsatian was returned to her, and a man whose purchase of a champion Chihuahua for $7000 had been reported in the newspapers had to pay the same amount again after dognapers had spirited away the little animal. He was lucky because in several cases the dognapers have taken the ransom money but never returned the pet.

In each case the owners were warned not to call in the police, and just like the parents of kidnaped children, they religiously obeyed the orders received. "Petnapers," says an American authority on pet animals, Ria Niccoli, "deserve not only fines and prison but *hanging!*"

The British artist Ronald Searle, well known throughout the Western World for his bitingly sarcastic cartoons as well as for his nightmarish drawings, is disgusted with his native country because all they care about is his "ruddy cats." While his serious work elicits but little enthusiasm in Britain, his cats and dogs sell in tens of thousands of copies. Just how much the British public spends on two-dimensional animals, portraits, oil paintings, photographs, embroidery, and so on, nobody knows. Nor is it a simple matter to find out how much is spent on the three-dimensional, live ones either, since the British like to keep not only themselves, but also all relevant information, to themselves.

In America you get a straight answer to a straight question. If it is not necessarily a true answer, in most cases when you have been told a lie, your interlocutor will change his mind and tell you the truth after all. When asked for his annual turnover figure, one pet dealer said it was $65,000, then, with a smile and a shrug, added: "O.K., you can round it up to $100,000." But Britain, as Cecil King, chairman of the International Publishing Corporation, has said, is a "secretive society" in politics as well as in everything else.

Questions relating to the economics of pet keeping elicited the following replies:

1. "Are you working for the Americans?" (Meaning industrial espionage.)
2. "I am awfully sorry, but I just couldn't tell you!" (Whether "couldn't" means indeed couldn't, or wouldn't, is another question to which no answer is available.)
3. "We can't tell you but perhaps if you got in touch with . . ." (Passing the buck. The next letter or telephone call, and the next and the next, achieved the same result.)
4. "We spent a great deal of money on research to obtain answers to exactly the same questions you have put to us. Thus, you cannot expect us to let you have the information and allow our competitors to find out." (As the same reply was received from several of the pet industrialists approached, the market research firm responsible for the investigation must have done a very good business selling the same information several times over.)

One of the pet-trade periodicals, told that the author wished to subscribe in order to obtain reliable data for a book on pets and people, refused to accept the subscription, with the excuse that some private persons have tried, in this way, to obtain merchandise at wholesale prices.

According to the magazine section of the September 9, 1967, issue of the London Sunday *Times*, Britain spent £95,555,304 on pet foods in 1965, to feed well over 5 million dogs, aproximately 4.5 million cats, 3.5 million budgerigars and other cage birds, aquarium fish, and small animals.

An investigation carried out by Spillers, the largest British pet-food manufacturers, in 1965-66, to establish whether pet ownership is related to socioeconomic class and to children (or the absence of children) in the family, and whether owners of one pet are likely to become owners of other pets as well, showed the following results. Only in the case of birds is there a significant difference between owners of different social classes. Thirty-nine per cent of households owning cage birds are in C2 social class, and only 5 per cent in A and B. Ownership of dogs varies only slightly according to the age of the housewife, and a person's social class has even less influence on whether one becomes a dog or cat owner. Households with children are more likely to have pets than those without children. (On the other hand, a Quaker Oats survey found higher pet ownership among widowed and divorced housewives. Households without children are more likely to have two or more pets if they have them.)

A study of the psychology of pet ownership by Petfoods Ltd. concludes that domestic animals are an outlet for feelings not acceptable in human society. Nothing people can do will embarrass their pets, and therefore people need not feel embarrassed themselves. Nor is there any need for pretense.

Dog owners are more likely to anthropomorphize their pet than cat owners. Perhaps this is the reason why almost half the dogs and only about 6 per cent of the cats are pure bred.

A survey by an English market research firm in the last two months of 1966, to discover if the present difficult economic situation was affecting personal spending and on what items people intended to reduce spending, produced some very interesting results. In London and the South West area only 3 per cent of the people between sixteen and sixty-four who were interviewed thought of reducing spending on pet foods. For the rest of the country the figure was 5 per cent. By comparison 28 per cent intended to save on household cleaners, 24 per cent on soaps and detergents, and 26 per cent "did not know."

The consumer magazine *Which* published in early 1967 a report on dogs and dog feeding. The results showed that the cost of keeping a small dog for a year (including food, license, inoculation, and a boarding kennel for two weeks) comes to £31.7.6. A medium-sized dog, such as a cocker spaniel, will cost £39.5 a year, while a large dog, such as a boxer, can cost as much as £60. If we round down the number of dogs to five million, and take an average of £40 for one year's expenses, this would add up to £200 million, a figure easy to accept if we again consider that pet-food manufacturers base their own figures only on the consumption of commercially prepared foods, and though the market for canned dog foods has doubled in the last five years, the majority of dogs still live on fresh foods and table scraps.

A 1966 investigation by the London Sunday *Mirror* shows that Britain spends six times as much on pet foods as on baby foods, and roughly sixteen times as much as on cancer research. Most of the large pet-food manufacturers are controlled or owned by U.S. firms to whom Britain is a "marketing man's dream," partly because there is still plenty of opportunity for expansion but also because in Britain, unlike the United States, the law does not require the contents of a tin to be marked on the label.

Spillers estimates that there are 140,000 grocery outlets in Britain, and since the profit margin on pet foods is, on the whole, higher than on the goods traditionally sold by them, an increasing number sell canned and dry pet foods.

Some chains, like Sainsbury's, find it more profitable to make their own brands, and drug chains, like Boots, are also going in not only for pet health-aids but also for pet foods.

According to Spillers, British housewives spent £19 million on canned cat foods in 1967. This, again, is only a fraction of what is really being spent on cats. Bird foods cost Britain approximately £1.5 million in 1967, and thanks to the Budgerigar Information Bureau, set up and financed by Petfoods Ltd., and the £25,000 company spent on press and TV advertising to popularize the budgie, bird-food sales may keep pace with the 15 per cent annual increase of other pet-food sales.

When calculating the annual spending on a dog, *Which* included only food, license, inoculation, and boarding fees for two weeks. However, keeping a dog can involve a number of other expenses as well. The 1968 supreme champion at Cruft's was Fanhill Faune, a white Dalmatian with black polka dots, the value of which is now £4000. Cruft's always being a trendsetter, there will now be a rush to buy—and breed—Dalmatians, which since they are large dogs, may cost their owners more than they are ready, and in many cases able, to pay. The actual spending of a London couple on their one-year-old Dalmatian in 1967 was the following: Purchase of puppy *£25*; food, partly tinned, partly fresh, *£52*; treats and snacks, *£15*; veterinary fees: inoculation, removal of a cyst, medicines, *£18;* grooming, six times a year, *£12;* health aids: vitamin pills, flea powder, deodorant, etc., *£3*; folding bed with mattress, *£7.10*; brushes (two), dishes (two), *£1.15*; collar and lead sets (two), *£1.5*; toys, *£0.15.6*; galvanized mesh "dog compartment" to fit in back of shooting break for traveling, *£4*; comprehensive insurance, *£17.10*; boarding, two weeks, *£8.1. Total: £165.15.6.*

Naturally, in Britain as in America, fanatic dog, especially poodle, lovers can spend considerably more on their pets. There is nothing a pampered poodle lady needs that Ellson of Nantwich does not produce, or rather, everything Ellson of Nantwich produces, a pampered poodle lady will, sooner or later, believe she needs. There are pajamas and berets, coats in every color and shape, and trouser suits, raincoats and boots, collars and leads for every occasion, perfumes and dentifrices, travel cages and toys. As the company says, "What you want, we have, and what you don't want, we'll make you want."

In Britain, dogs are not only man's, but also the government's, best friend. In 1967, $1.4 million worth of pedigree and champion dogs were exported to the United States alone, an increase of 18.6 per cent over 1964. The total export in 1966 was $3 million. Prices range from £50 and up for an ordinary pedigree puppy to £1000 for a champion, but offers of £7000 to £10,000 for supreme champions have been refused.

One man who "Backs Britain" by doing his bit for British exports is the Reverend John Eddy, Rector of Bluntisham, Hunts. This excellent Christian gentleman breeds and exports fighting cocks for up to £100 each. He sends them in batches of twenty—in separate compartments so they don't kill one another on the way—to Peru, Malta, Kenya, Cyprus, and India. Whether or not he sells them in Great Britain as well is unknown, although, despite the 1849 Act of Parliament banning this extremely educational sport, cockfighting still goes on in the West Country, the Midlands, and the North Country.

English pet-food manufacturers spend something like £350,000 annually on research. In 1966 they spent £3,982,224 on TV commercials and a further £267,794 on press advertising. None of that money is wasted in a country that is so dog conscious that the sight of a pretty little dog will blind them to what goes on in front of their eyes.

A few months ago the police in Devon were looking high and low for a pair of striking-looking and smart shoplifters who had invented a novel and highly effective method. An attractive, red-haired, mini-skirted woman and a tall, long-haired man visited a number of shops and got away with considerable loot. The woman carried a tiny Chihuahua tucked in the top of her jumper with just its head peeping out. While the shoppers crowded around the woman, admiring and petting the little dog, and the sales staff watched to see what was happening, the man went to work without being spotted.

Britain's approximately 3.5 million budgies and other pet birds consume £1.5 million worth of bird food per year. Wholesale prices for budgerigars vary from £1 to £5 a pair, but in a pet shop one pays £1.5 to £1.10s. for an ordinary budgie. The wholesale price of parrots varies between £7 and £22 each. If we add the price of the cage, £2 to £3 each, the birdcage stand, cost about the same, cage appliances like feeder, drinker, landing platform, swing, bath, and the growing number of bird toys, plus veterinary fees and health aids, we would underestimate the real figure by saying that the birds of Britain cost their owners £4 million to £5 million annually.

Not content with their sales, bird-food manufacturers have launched a large-scale campaign in favor of wild birds. Bread crumbs or a lump of suet suspended from a tree is no longer enough. The softhearted British are now encouraged to buy wild-bird feeding stations for their gardens and stock them with bird feed, fruit and nut treats, and water. While wild birds are thus properly taken care of and get their meals without having to ask for them, only about half of the half million children in England and Wales who, due to their parents' low income, are entitled to free school meals actually take advantage of this benefit. Rather than suffer the humiliation of having to raise their hands for their food, they prefer to do without.

Going still further, the days are past when Britain's more than two thousand pet shops sold nothing but dogs, cats, birds, and small animals like white mice, guinea pigs, and hamsters. More and more of them stock aquaria, complete with tropical fish and plants, gravel, tonic, cleaning and heating appliances, pump, light, and filter, rock and pottery ornaments, so that by the time you have set up your first medium-sized aquarium you can congratulate yourself if your bill does not exceed £40. But to keep up with the American pet-dealer Joneses, they also keep an increasing number of unusual or exotic pets: monkeys and flying foxes, snakes and rats, mongooses and skunks, alligators and terrarium animals.

It would take a long and costly investigation to figure out what the British public spends on its beloved animals' in one year, including legacies and donations to animal charities, membership fees in the various pet clubs, subscription fees to the more than thirty animal magazines, the purchase of pet-care booklets, the purchase of the various pets, the equipment they require and the luxuries they receive in the form of food, accessories, veterinary fees, boarding fees, travel, health aides, cosmetics, grooming, toys and on and on. It would not be surprising if the total amounted to *several hundred million pounds.*

In France, the sale of pet foods increased by *300 per cent* in the brief *three-year* period between the beginning of 1963 and the end of 1966, thanks to the efforts of the American pet-food manufacturers.

One in four French families owns a dog, 6 per cent two dogs, 2 per cent three dogs, 0.5 per cent four dogs, and 0.5 per cent five or more. Seventeen per cent of French families own one cat, 7 per cent two cats, 3.5 per cent three cats, 2 per cent four cats, and 2 per cent five or more. There are 16.5 million dogs and cats in France, more cats than dogs, and 10 to 15 per cent of the families own cage birds.

In 1963, pet owners spent *28 million new francs* on pet food, 86 per cent of which was produced by a French company pioneering in the field. By 1966, spending rose to *125 million new francs,* with 92 per cent of the market divided between three companies, one French, two foreign. It is hoped that by 1970, pet-food sales will reach *300 million new francs,* meaning an annual increase of 35-40 per cent.

There seem to be no significant differences in pet ownership between social and income groups. Thirty per cent of industrialists, merchants, and professional people own one or several dogs and one or several cats; 24 per cent of the blue-collar class own dogs and 20 per cent cats; and 27 per cent of the industrial workers own dogs, 27 per cent cats. Only one in two thrifty French pet-owners spends money on food for their pets, the others feeding them on table scraps. And even within the first half, only 20 per cent buy commercially prepared pet foods. Thus, of course, total spending on dog and cat food cannot be calculated.

Whether General de Gaulle likes it or not, by ending the Algerian war and putting France back on its economic feet, he has opened the door not only to the Anglo-Saxon pet-food manufacturers but also to Anglo-Saxon "petishism," which soon caught on among the snobs. So far only 7-8 per cent of France's dogs are purebred, but soon the upper classes, intent on maintaining their superiority, will not even want to be found dead with a mongrel mourning them.

For the time being, however, they can prove their "differentness" only by owning exotic pets, such as reptiles (there are now more than 5000), giant, so-called "vampire" bats (there are 200), and monkeys, of which there are 20,000 in France, considerably more than in England. Naturally the "image merchants" have succeeded in persuading those in the limelight to acquire extremely exotic pets, from lion cubs and tigers to ocelots and crocodiles.

Because the use of pet animals as status symbols is still a very new trend in France, there are no figures available of the spending on veterinarians, health aids, cosmetics, accessories, clothes, boarding fees, travel, etc., but beauty parlors, pet hotels, training establishments, fashion shops, pet shops and clubs are springing up all over the country. There is no doubt that the growth of the entire pet trade and industry, as well as the various professions connnected with them, will keep pace with the fabulous increase in pet-food sales.

The German Federal Republic, a country as status-conscious, but considerably more class-conscious, than America has begun to extend its increasingly high standard of living to its pet animals. If the Neo-Nazis continue to win ground, there will be a rapid growth in the percentage of purebred animals among West Germany's 3 - 4 million canine and feline pets, but in any case within the last ten years there has been a 200 per cent increase in the pet field. The annual spending on pet foods reached *385 million deutsche marks* in 1967, and the market is far from saturated. According to the *Zoologischer Zentral Anzeiger*, journal of the pet trade and industry, the total spending on pet animals is *600 millon deutsche marks annually, two-thirds of the amount spent on cigarettes*. In West Germany, there are more than 2500 shops dealing exclusively, or partly, with pet animals, though pet foods, accessories, health aids, can be found in most department stores and drugstores.

Judging by the number of birds — 20 to 30 million, among these 5 million budgerigars and parrots — and the 100 to 150 million cold-water and tropical fish, which are, on the whole, less expensive to keep than four-legged pets, there are still certain differences in the social class and income group of pet owners.

The annual import of exotic animals consists of approximately half a million birds, some 100,000 tropical fish, an estimated 50,000 reptiles and amphibians, and more than 20,000 mammals, mostly monkeys. And the fashion of possessing unusual pets has only recently begun to spread.

The purchase price of the various pets is not included in the estimated 600 million deutsche marks spent on them annually, and since prices are pretty steep, the total would be nearer 900 million deutsche marks. Pedigree puppies cost the buyer 170 deutsche marks for a black poodle, 250 for a brown poodle, 250 to 380 for a toy poodle, depending on the color; 195 for a pekingese, 155 for a cocker spaniel, 160 for a fox terrier, 210 for a boxer, 280 for a Dalmatian, 160 for a German shepherd, 200 for a collie, 300 for a St. Bernard. Budgerigars cost 39 deutsche marks and up, African birds up to 56, South American birds up to 70, Asian birds up to 90 each, cockatoos 195, and parrots up to 300.

Monkeys are priced from 190 to 320 deutsche marks, reptiles from 20 for a baby alligator to 110 for a boa constrictor, 170 for a python and 200 for a Pytas Korros. A full-grown alligator, however, costs 1000 deutsche marks, a young brown bear 1000, a guepard 3000, a gorilla 15,000 to 20,000, a jaguar 3000, a leopard 2000, a chimpanzee 3000, a tiger cub 8000 to 10,000; and should someone wish to purchase an elephant for his garden, an African elephant costs 15,000 and an Indian elephant 10,000 to 13,000 deutsche marks.

To keep a dog in style seems to be considerably more expensive in West Germany than in England or America. An ordinary collar plus lead costs up to 29 deutsche marks, and the same in a more elegant edition 42. Coats cost from 10 to 28, a trouser suit 40, dog jeans up to 55.5, knitted pullovers up to 43.6, shoes and rubber boots up to 12, pajamas up to 15.5, panties up to 13.2, sunglasses 13. An ordinary dog basket costs from 24.5 to 64 deutsche marks, and the mattress to go with it from 11.8 to 24.5. A somewhat more luxurious dog bed is priced at 98.

But the West German pet trade is extraordinarily ingenious in thinking up new ways to improve business. An investigation carried out in 1967 among consumers to find out whether they were content with what they already had, or were open to persuasion to acquire more, showed that 14 per cent were satisfied, 30 per cent had acquired most of the things they wished to possess, 14 per cent were planning to acquire a number of things they thought desirable, and 4 per cent were still dissatisfied with what they had. This means that there are still more than 9 million consumers who, if properly handled, can be made to acquire pet animals or, if they already have them, more and better pets. It can be explained to them that just as one's house or the style and quality of one's furniture denote social status, the sort of pet one keeps or the way one keeps it can also add to one's prestige.

One idea—to advertise bird cages, aquaria and terraria as interior decoration—has caught on quickly, and lately shop windows have displayed aquarium stands in various styles, modern and antique, to fit the furniture, and aviaries built in the shape of glass-fronted cabinets or wardrobes. Another very successful idea was to combine women's fashion shows with dog fashion shows.

However, German businessmen realize that their compatriots, like the members of any other nation, can be seduced into buying pets most easily by demonstrating to them that the public figures they love and respect also own pets. The influence of personalities on public opinion has always been considerable. If consumers can be convinced that unless they own pet animals they are no longer "with it," it won't be long before families without at least one pet will be treated with contempt by their neighbors.

But needless to say, the trade has not entirely forgotten those consumers whose homes are truly unsuitable for pet keeping, either because they are too small or because animals are prohibited or because a spouse objects to their "messing up the house." The problem of the aquarists is already solved. In one German town they have formed, with the help of the pet trade, an aquarium club where each member has his own tank and tends and feeds his own fish. The club is open twenty-four hours a day, and whenever a member feels like playing with his fish, or simply like getting away from his wife, he can spend as much time as he wishes indulging his hobby. During holiday time an expert hired by the club looks after the tanks.

One cannot but praise the German pet trade for trying in every possible way to solve the problem of leisure.

CHAPTER 10
PET POWER BY PROXY

> ... a good many of the people-manipulating activities
> of the persuaders raise profoundly disturbing ques-
> tions about the kind of society they are seeking to
> build for us.
>
> — VANCE PACKARD:
> *The Hidden Persuaders*

◉ ◉ IN THE NOT SO DISTANT PAST, WHEN ANIMALS
were still animals, they were associated in an adult person's
mind with children. Little children were given rubber ducks to
play with in the bath, teddy bears to cuddle, chocolate bunnies

at Easter, picture books with animals in them and, a little later, story books about animals, though these, like *Winnie the Pooh*, were often enjoyed more by the parents than by the children. Still later, children were taken to the zoo on Sunday mornings and, in the afternoon, to Walt Disney cartoons. Parents were glad when their sons and daughters showed an interest in natural history in school, gave them books like the big Brehm animal encyclopaedia and if the children asked, bought them pets. In brief, the world of animals, real and imaginary, was the world in which the child could exercise and develop his budding intelligence and imagination.

Then came the day when the *Homo neuroticus*, alienated from the world of adults, joined his children in their child-animal world. While for the child this world is but a station on the road to adulthood, for the adult it became a refuge, a reversion to the childhood he conveniently remembered only for its simplicity and freedom from responsibility. It was then that Hollywood, sensing the new need, scrapped the animal heroes so dear to children — Rin Tin Tin, Lassie — and began to address the animal message to adults.

The popularity of nature films is still growing, partly because people living in overcrowded cities find nothing more refreshing than the sight of wide open spaces, partly because those same people feel reassured by the knowledge that the law of the jungle — the struggle for survival, the indiscriminate use of any means at the individual's disposal, from conformism to murder, from cunning to cannibalism, to remain alive, still his hunger, and obtain his sexual gratification — prevails not only in the human community but in the jungle as well.

In addition to producing nature films, the film industry began to go in for two other types of animal feature films: those like *Born Free*, that allow people to identify themselves with animals that, living in captivity, become alienated from themselves and their kind, and horror films about monstrous animals that bring to mind the man-devouring animal gods of the early civilization, and the dragon that survived far into the Middle Ages. While the former appeal to a more intelligent public, more or less aware of its situation and more or less resigned to it, the latter attract those who, unable to understand their uneasiness in our culture, react to it by a suppressed or indulged need for violence.

The trend, started by the film industry, was adopted and carried through *ad absurdum* by television. The proliferation of animal programs has reached fantastic proportions though it must be admitted that they are usually far superior to the majority of other programs and considerably less harmful.

It would be difficult to decide whether the publishing industry or the film industry was the first to discover the very profitable market for its products focused on animals. It is certain, however, that the two types of books that every publisher knows will sell are textbooks and animal books.

In America the 1968 *Directory of Pet Shop Management* lists among its book sources eight publishing houses publishing *only* pet books, and twenty-two general publishers publishing pet books *also*. In print today are 66 books on aquaria, prices varying from 35 cents to $20; 70 books on birds, priced from 35 cents to $8.95; 22 books on cats, from 85 cents to $6.75; 407 books on dogs, from $1 to $12.50; and 36 books on other pets—ants, hamsters, iguanas, monkeys, ocelots, raccoons, snakes—from 35 cents to $12.50.

All these are *pet books*, as distinct from the animal books we shall discuss later. They can be obtained in pet shops, book shops, and from a number of American distributors specializing in them, such as The Cat Book Centre, which has them all, in or out of print, and the C&B Book House. These books and booklets bear titles like *Enjoy Your Chameleon, Know Your Monkey, Poodles in Particular, Fabulous Feline.*

Several of the American pet-book publishers have, in the last few years, invaded the British market where, so far, they successfully compete with the British publishers who were a bit slow to wake up to the almost unlimited possibilities of the pet field. Today, Foyle's catalogue on dog books lists some 500 titles, partly English, partly American, priced from 6 shillings to 6 guineas, and some publishers, the Wolfe

Publishing Company Ltd. for instance, have started series on exotic pets with titles like *How to Keep a Man-eating Shark* and *How to Keep an Elephant*. Naturally the "How to care . . ." handbooks, books on breeding, training, grooming, also belong to the pet books.

The "useful" books are the second line of attack on the pet-keeping public, books like the *Pets' Cookbook*, the *Dog and Cat Horoscope Book*, the *Guide Mi Chien*. The third consists of the humorous books, like *Yours for Decency* by Alan Able, *How to Live with a Pampered Pet*, and *How to Live with a Calculating Cat* by Eric Gurney, *Dog People Are Crazy* by Max Riddle and many others.

Other types of books that have contributed a great deal to the prosperity of the pet trade and industry are the enchanting, moving, and amusing works of various pet-lovers: Gavin Maxwell's books about otters as pets, Jacqueline Susann's *Every night, Josephine!*, about her poodle, Buster Lloyd Jones's *The Animals Came in One by One*, and books written by naturalists about wild animals, such as *Born Free*, David Attenborough's fascinating travel and animal stories and, last but not least, the absolutely irresistible writings of Gerald Durrell. And then there are the natural history books proper, usually beautifully published and very expensive, like *The Wonderful World of Horses* by Beth Brown, *Birds of the Antarctic* by Edward Wilson, and an endless succession of attractively illustrated, large books and encyclopedias on virtually every animal species under the sun.

With the last few years animal lovers have discovered another type of animal book, to the great joy of the publishing business and the pet field. In this category are the learned books on animal psychology, like those of the German zoologist Konrad Lorenz and his disciples, and books taking us down a peg or two by demonstrating that whatever we may think of ourselves, the difference between the animals and the crown of creating, man, is almost negligible. Robert Ardrey's illuminating work, *The Territorial Imperative*, should be made obligatory reading in all secondary schools throughout the world as an antidote to arrogance.

All the above-mentioned types of animal books are also gaining ground rapidly in France and Germany, half a dozen or so are reviewed in every issue of *Bêtes et Nature*, and although natural-history books have always been widely read in Germany, it is only in the last ten years or so, since the healthy interest in animals has degenerated into pet craze, that the demand for pet books has begun to grow rapidly.

In addition to the pet books, there are forty-five American and more than thirty British magazines devoted to pet animals. The Dog Writers Association of America ensures an uninterrupted flow of dog books and magazine articles, and just as in Great Britain, where pet writers have not, so far, felt the need to organize, they are always at hand when an empty space in the columns of the daily papers has to be filled at a moment's notice. No matter what happens in the world, no matter how many people are killed in war, how many starve to death, how many perish in floods and earthquakes, nothing equals the indignation aroused by a brief article describing the beating of a dog or the eager popular response elicited by an appeal to the readers to offer a home to a kitten whose "mummy" has died.

Publishers, however, are not the only people to benefit from the scope and neurotic overtones of Western's man's relationship to animals. The advertising industry, which catches on immediately to trends it has not itself created, has found an inexhaustible store of gimmicks in the animal world and uses them for all they are worth.

How should TWA advertise the quality of its cargo service if not by showing a contented sea lion and declaring that no one in the world except a TWA hand would have thought of telephoning the Los Angeles Zoo and asking the curator what to do with the quaint passenger? And who but a TWA hand, they say, would go to the trouble not only to give the sea lion a nice shower at every stop but to make sure the water is not colder than sixty degrees? Not to be outdone by TWA, Eastern Airlines—which had a booth at the International Pet Show at the New York Coliseum in 1967—shows the full-page portrait of a Yorkshire terrier, sitting on a cushion, wearing a pair of modern sunglasses and a bow in its hair, and saying: "But darling, I always fly Eastern!"

The General Motors Acceptance Corporation advertises its Time Payment Plan by flanking the text with the photograph of a well-dressed, bespectacled, middle-aged lady with a tired, middle-aged poodle sitting at her feet. There is not a word about the dog in the text, but looking at the picture one feels that this poor, tired little animal with its beseeching eyes simply *cannot* be expected to walk. It *must* have a car to go about in.

There must also be a good reason why the automobile industry names many of the new cars after animals, like the Buick Wildcat, the Chevrolet Impala and Camaro, the Dodge Charger, the Ford Falcon, Mustang, and Thunderbird, the Mercury Cougar, the Plymouth Barracuda, the Shelby Cobra, the Alfa Romeo Duetto Spider, the Corvette Stingray, the British Jaguar and Sunbeam Tiger and on forever. What strikes one about these "aggressive" names is that although almost as many women as men own and drive cars, the industry still seems to have only the male buyer in mind. Why not call the station wagon the housewife takes her kids to school and does her shopping in "Donkey" or "Underdog," and the independent, professional girl's small car "Kitten," "Chick," or "Teddybear?"

One would think that the Bell Telephone System in America had no need to advertise its services, but advertise it does. In a full-page ad it tells eight little stories to illustrate the usefulness of a telephone. Of the eight, three are connected with animals and a fourth with an "in-between," a mermaid.

1. "A West Coast woman phoned several dog pounds in search of her lost pet. One animal fitted the description. 'Put her on the phone,' she asked the attendant. A few words

from the owner and the dog went wild with joy. (Your voice is *you* by telephone.)

2. "The Cincinnati Zoo once had a chimpanzee who suffered from fits of depression. So a phone was installed in his cage and when he felt low a call from his former trainer cheered the chimp immensely. (Humans respond the same way to a friendly call.)

3. "An Ohio man, pursued by a persistent billy goat, dashed into a public phone booth, braced the door and called the police to the rescue! (We try to place our public phones so that you'll find one handy when you need it—almost everywhere.)

4. "Finally, down in Florida, one of our men put in an underwater telephone for the use of a live mermaid at a tourist attraction. (Our installers go anywhere to give service . . . glub . . . glub.)

If America's "expendables" are not convinced, after reading this advertisement, that the possession of a telephone will completely change their lives, they are, indeed, hopeless.

Electricity is another service that, one would think, no longer needs to be advertised. But a full-page ad extolling the virtues of a modern electric water heater proves that "You live better electrically" by showing a huge bloodhound sitting in a tub of warm water and being scrubbed by three children. Do they mean to say that although some people might not, dogs *can* afford a modern electric water heater?

The Beneficial Insurance Group, insisting that a "thoughtful" man will go to *them* and no one else for his life insurance policy, supports its contention by a full-page picture of a smiling, self-assured man leading a basset hound on a leash and, as proof of his "thoughtfulness," carrying a large fire hydrant under his arm. The Dreyfus mutual investment fund contends that it takes what it considers *sensible* risks to make its clients' investments grow. To show just how sensible that risk is the client, looking at the ad, is faced with a huge lion coming toward him in a New York street.

Synthetic-fiber manufacturers also use animals to prove their excellence. Chemstrand shows a pretty girl in stretch pants and jumper feeding a huge goat from a milk bottle. Kodel advertises children's winter wear by placing a huge polar bear between a little boy and a girl. Acrilan coats—"28 degrees warmer inside"—ride a dogsled in the Arctic. And if you don't believe that a man is not a man without a stylish Panther coat, made of cotton and synthetic fiber poplin, just look at the tiger tamer with a tiger on his back, and wearing a Panther coat, smiling broadly while the animal is busy chewing up his wrist. Mauled, pawed, clawed, the coat remains clean and unwrinkled.

Kellogg's not only implies but shouts from the housetops that unless you start the day with their "famous Special K breakfast" you will never Feel like a Healthy Animal, charged up, sleeked down, loaded with sheer animal spirits. Be big and powerful as a polar bear, they say, or strong and graceful as a horse. If the mental effort of being a healthy human is too much for you, forget it and make it your life's aim to be a healthy animal.

When night falls, the Animal Kingdom comes alive in the young American's bedroom "with a jungle beat that is irresistible!" If Kellogg's breakfast food and the large amount of alcohol consumed during the day have failed to turn you into a "healthy animal" ready to perform your marital duties, the giraffe, zebra, jungle-cat, or peacock-patterned cotton percale sheets sold by Macy's are sure to inspire fantasies that will turn a mouse into a bull. But if even that is not enough, use a little of the Mark II Cologne, Mark of a Man, a woman's Great Gift for the Male Animal, and you will pounce like the flashing-eyed, bristling-mustached, sleek black panther depicted in the advertisement.

Having made the little woman happy, a proud husband's first thought will be to show her his appreciation (of himself) by buying her a present. Why not get her a golden crocodile with ruby eyes shedding diamond tears for $130? Or a shaggy dog of diamond-glittered eighteen-carat gold with sapphire eyes, a real pedigree pet, for $315? Or a few new charms for her bracelet: a cocker spaniel, a German shepherd, a poodle in gold, for about $25 each? or what about an animal skin for a bedside rug? Wouldn't she love to step out of her jungle bed straight onto a blue-black or gray wolf skin, a polar, black, or brown bear, or a zebra, for a mere $395?

As even American purses are not inexhaustible, there is a good selection of more modest gifts for the Male Animal to choose from. If you wish to give her a Pet She Can Wear, choose a wildcat, bird, peke, or dachshund brooch in gold or silver finish for only $1.50. Buy an Arctic owl, handmade by Eskimos, for $4.25; a papier-mache animal, donkey, elephant, bull, for $10.95; or an "exact replica of a world famous animal sculpture," a crouching cat for $18.50, a frog for $26.50, a baby bear for $18.50 or an owl for $16.50. If you want something a bit more original and in excellent taste, what could be better than a radio set dressed up as a pekingese or a poodle?

But the gift to end all gifts, a heaven-sent present for animal lovers, is Chappie, the Robot Dog in "Soft, Cuddly Finish" that barks, wags its tail, walks at your command, with the help of three transistor-operated remote relays that convert a sound wave into an electrical impulse. It costs only $12.95 and is infinitely better than the real thing. But its inestimable value for both the giver and the recipient lies in the unexpressed promise that, perhaps in a not too distant future, you will be able to purchase, for a modest sum a transistor-operated robot spouse as obedient and undemanding as Chappie.

Nor is the British advertising industry less ingenious than the American in inventing ways and means to make use of the legendary Anglo-Saxon love of animals. To prove that "Martins go to extremes to be helpful," the full-page ads for Martins Bank Ltd. show smiling employees remaining unflustered even when their clients walk in with a kangaroo, a hippo, a seal, an elephant, or a camel on a lead. And why not? Martins do not discriminate. As long as he does not ask for a loan or an overdraft, one client is as good as another.

Hambros Bank sports an old-fashioned lion over the text of their advertisement reminding the reader that they will "help you get the lion's share of equity growth." The smartest, however, is the Midland Bank, which calls attention to itself by displaying, in color, the Vanishing Wild Animals of the World, and underneath, a short biography of the animal shown. At the bottom of the page, we read: "Presented by Midland Bank which, with more than 2,650 branches in England and Wales, is a good deal easier to find than [for instance] an Atlantic Walrus."

British Oxygen uses a snow field with an army of contented penguins to illustrate the level of cold produced by its refrigerators. The Gas Company displays a bathtub with five grinning dogs in it to prove the excellence of its Ascot water heater. Happy dogs and cats lie in front of various electric fires in large advertisements telling people to buy that particular make, and even paraffin is sold by a green-eyed cat "photographed from a warm mousehole."

England's best-dressed women, from the Countess of Coventry and the Duchess of Rutland to pretty models who help sell British-made clothes, are, for some mysterious reason always photographed in the advertisements stroking or clutching a dog, feeding a horse, or being in physical contact with some other animal. Armstrong's vinyl parquet floor is shown with a wooden elephant standing on it because "The elephant! He's a tough long lasting character too!," and the same company's texture flooring has an armadillo on it. Why? Because "He's beautiful too (to another armadillo)."

BOAC advertises its continent-hopping with the help of an extremely ugly large kangaroo photographed *en face*, and White Horse Whiskey with a real white horse standing among the clients at the counter of an elegant pub.

One of the most successful advertisements is for Player's Gold Leaf cigarettes. Successful at least, for the pet trade, since it has greatly increased the popularity of the English setter, one of which gazes with such adoring eyes at its Gold Leaf-smoking master. Since the setter began appearing in the ads, dog breeders have noticed a marked increase in the demand for pedigree English setter pups, and a great many visitors at Cruft's compared the exhibited members of this breed with Yankee, descendant of an international champion and shown in the advertisement.

Naturally, TV commercials are even more effective than posters. People who would never have bought a large dog to keep in their small flats have been seduced to do just that by the huge, hairy, Old English sheep dog used by Dulux Paint to advertise its products. As a result of these ads, the Old English sheep dog has risen dramatically in the Kennel Club registration chart, from 310 to 951 in three years. The basset hound, advertising Hush Puppy shoes, has also become a favorite with the public, and a Dalmatian, like the one advertising Pal dog food, became supreme champion at Cruft's in 1968.

It throws an interesting light on the dog-buying public that according to the breeders, poorer people who cannot really afford it will give a large dog a really good home. Yet a Great Dane, for example, made popular by TV commercials, will grow almost as big as a pony and consume five pounds of meat a day!

TV cats can sometimes make a lot of trouble by doing too good a job at selling the merchandise they advertise and becoming too important to the company that hired them. This is the case with Arthur, the white cat that persuades cat owners to buy Spillers' cat food. Mr. Toneye Manning, the actor, who owns the cat, issued a writ against Spillers claiming return of "one white cat, Arthur," a £2000 damages, and an injunction over the television commercial. On February 6, 1968, he obtained judgment because Spillers did not enter a defense. He picked up the cat at the kennels where Spillers kept it, brought it to London, and, on February 10, took it to the Russian Embassy. An official was just coming out, and Mr. Manning stopped him and asked him if he was a diplomat. Upon receiving a positive answer, he asked for "political asylum" for his cat and explained the situation. The official, according to Mr. Manning, took the cat and walked off with it.

A few days later Mr. Manning was served with an *ex parte* injunction over Arthur by Spillers' legal representatives, to be followed by application for a court order for the return of the cat. The next step was a hearing in private at the High Court, where Mr. Justice Cusack ordered Mr. Manning not to take Arthur "out of the jurisdiction of the Court or harm him." At the next hearing he was ordered to return the cat to Spillers within five hours.

The press attaché at the Russian Embassy declared that the cat was not with them, nor had anyone approached them with the request to give it asylum, although Mr. Manning maintained that not only did he hand Arthur over to the Russians but that he had visited the cat three times through a "third man" who acted as a go-between with the Embassy. It then turned out that the "third man" was a Hungarian friend of the actor who brought the animal back to him the day he was ordered by the court to produce it. On February 21, Mr. Manning decided to appeal against the order to return the cat to Spillers.

The birth of a polar bear cub called Pipaluk, Eskimo for "little one," has provided British industry with a new sales gimmick, and pet power with a new symbol. Stepping out into the sunshine in the London Zoo for the first time, Pipaluk set off a million-pound sales campaign as the first of the Zoo's animals to be registered as a trademark. He will be turned out in the thousands as a soft doll, on badges for schoolboys, in a range of ten books, as a jigsaw puzzle and a strip cartoon. Soon there will be mints and bubble gum with Pipaluk wrappers, Pipaluk wallpaper for the nursery, and the public may rest assured that animal lovers of all ages and all income groups will be offered a large selection of products, from everyday necessities to the most sophisticated luxuries that have been given a face-lift by the application of the Pipaluk image.

In England, too, jewelers are doing pretty well with "Pets You Can Wear." Garrard, the Crown Jewellers, sell animal brooches like an eighteen-carat gold elephant, encrusted with diamonds and ruby and sitting on a Vespa, for £257.10; a gold duck wearing a bonnet and decorated with pearls, diamonds, and ruby for £185; a gold mouse dressed in dinner jacket, cape, and top hat, with a cane in one hand and a clarinet in the other, his shirtfront made of diamonds, for £162.10; or a gold tiger for £150. Less expensive, but also in atrociously bad taste, are the crabs and lobsters stuffed with plastic and costing 12 and 15 guineas respectively that Fortnum and Mason sell very successfully for table decoration. Their toy department offers a basket of electric dogs for 98 guineas.

If the amounts spent in the West on pet animals were added up, the total could probably be matched by one single line of business making use of animals and, in the last decade or so, of pet animals in particular. That business is *the stamp business.*

A great many varieties of animal series have been, and are being, put out by many countries of the world, but it is the less affluent and underdeveloped countries, to which stamps are an excellent source of hard currency, that are the most ingenious. At first each country featured its own fauna on its stamps, but when philatelists were no longer able to cope with the number of animal stamps available and began to specialize in one animal species—horses, dogs, cats, birds, fish or groups of wild animals, many regarded as pets—today like big cats, reptiles, amphibians—the poor countries, eager to sell, went into every imaginable kind of animal series.

The Iron Curtain countries, especially, do an excellent job of satisfying the demands of the world's estimated seventy million stamp collectors. In 1963, Poland issued a series of nine large postage stamps featuring nine fashionable dog breeds in natural colors. This series was followed by ten stamps representing cats, European, Persian, and Siamese. Other series picture horses, wild animals, birds, and fishes. The Rumanian post office is also becoming more and more pet-conscious, and so are the Hungarians, who, along with Israel and a score of other nations, have gone in for the so-called "silent pets," tropical fish, executed in natural colors and with great attention to detail. Yugoslavia has issued greatly sought-after series of terrarium animals and snakes.

Another industry that owes its new prosperity to petishism is the toy industry. There have always been animal toys, but in the last decade the selection has broadened to include every kind of pet animal kept by adults, from bugs to penguins, from otters to snakes, from scary gorillas to nonsmelly skunks, from caterpillars to dolphins and billy goats to crocodiles. In addition, while in the past, animal toys were at the most child-size, today they can be bought lifesize at astronomical prices.

However, the most unlikely industry to climb on the bandwagon and make a thumping profit from the Anglo-Saxon animal craze and lack of taste is the furniture industry. It will not be surprising to anyone that here again America is in the lead. Although flies cannot exactly be called pets, nor are they beautiful, they serve, in the United States, as a model for—lavatory pans. The body is made of gleaming bronze, the wings of leaded glass, and if you open up the back you can throne on it in beauty! The price? A mere $10,000. And those who wish to turn their homes into zoos without needing to worry about the feeding or natural functions of their animals can buy fluffy white stuffed sheep as dining room chairs, a set costing about $12,000; a writing desk in the shape of a rhinoceros for $24,000; a cocktail bar in the shape of two ostriches, or a really comfortable, deep and soft easy chair in the shape of a huge, coiled snake!

The British furniture manufacturer who went to New York in search of new, up-to-date designs stood pale and shaken after having been shown these models. "Really . . . is nothing sacred anymore?" he murmured.

conclusion

◉ ◉THE YEAR 1968 WAS PROCLAIMED HUMAN
Rights Year. One would have expected at least the Western
press to devote some space to this fact, and to attempt to
rekindle in the public mind a certain enthusiasm for ideals

once so dear to the hearts of men but now diluted beyond recognition in the social institutions of contemporary technical civilization. Instead, perhaps because the less attention paid to the human condition the better, or because human rights are not news, the press and the other mass media pretended we were celebrating an Animal Rights Year and devoted more space and time than ever before to the worship of the animal god, the Pet.

The German philosopher Schopenhauer held that "the trouble with humanity is that it is descended from monkeys and not from dogs." If he lived today he would probably lament that humanity has preserved so little of the unquenchable curiosity, the mental and physical alertness and taste for experiment, characteristic of its simian ancestors. Having created a sick civilization in which machines work, computers think for him, and an elect few decide not only *whether* he shall live or die but also *how* he shall live or die, alienated from himself, dependent and lazy like his canine pets, man reclines on his laurels before his television set and listens to His Master's Voice. But, as if eye and ear conspired to protect the delicate brain from having to make the slightest effort, the picture seldom penetrates except when animals appear on the screen, and the Voice, when it addresses the listener through the medium of commercials, keeps its message short and clear: "Buy! Buy! Buy!"

In the course of time, the *Homo neuroticus* has developed an incurable allergy to words. Experience has taught him that they mean neither what they say nor the contrary, but serve only to camouflage a secret purpose that is usually hostile to him. He reacts to them as he reacts to the other noises that constantly surround him, he shuts them out of his consciousness. Like his "lesser brothers" that have come to play such an important role in his life, he, too, believes only in what he can touch, taste, or smell. The possessions he accumulates, what he eats and drinks, are his: only *things* are real, only *things* are worth fighting for, whether "fighting" means working, begging, cheating, stealing, robbing, or killing. Except in war, and even that is no longer certain, no one can make him fight for what he does not believe in. Human rights? Four freedoms? Gibberish!

If, by some miracle, the have-nots suddenly became aware of the rights that society grants them on paper, and claimed them, society would go bankrupt. And what good is freedom of speech in a world where everyone speaks and nobody listens? What good is freedom of worship in a world where faith is dead? What does freedom from want mean to the few who never wanted for anything, or to the many who have never been, and will never be, free from it? And who, in the Atomic Age, is free from fear?

Brainwashed into accepting that the body is vile, thought subversive, and emotion suspect, the *Homo neuroticus* uses every means at his disposal to hasten his physical deterioration, drowns thought in permanent, noisy activity, and restricts his emotional life to his relationship with animals. The popularity of the dog above all other pets can, perhaps, be explained by the ease with which his unwavering gaze can be interpreted as unconditional adoration. Animal psychologists confirm the belief in the dog's love of his master, but one cannot exclude the possibility that they base their conviction on the very unscientific views expressed in world literature and that they, too, present wish-fulfillment dreams as facts. Even human psychologists who belong to the same species as their patients often misinterpret certain phenomena. How then could a human identify himself with a member of a different species to the extent of pronouncing judgment on its emotions?

Would it be sacrilegious to suggest that what a dog is trying to convey is not love but his despair at his inability to understand the strange being who owns him, his loneliness in a world that has remained alien to him after all these millenia, his longing for the pack and for the old way of life that his genes remember, his absolute dependence on his master for his food, for a warm corner, for his very life, and his ever present fear of being abandoned? If it were so, modern man's relationship to his dog and other animal pets would be much more understandable. For man, too, lives in despair because he cannot understand the golem he created and that now owns him. Man, too, yearns for a long-forgotten way of life that only his genes remember. He, too, has come to depend for all his needs and his very life on society, and he too lives in fear of being abandoned by it.

Whatever the explanation, there is something frightening, something threatening, in the speed with which the cult of pet animals has gained ground throughout the Western World in the last decade or so. It seems as if, by anthropomorphizing the animals he takes into his home and gradually *replacing* his human contacts with animals, man were trying to escape into an other-than-human community, a community that he can control and that, therefore, does not threaten his very existence. There are fewer and fewer people left to love animals *as animals*, with an affection born of curiosity, the appreciation of their differentness and often beauty, and a childlike and uncorruptedly human enjoyment of watching them in their natural state.

Everyone who has read Gerald Durrell's books must have felt that here is a human being who lives *in* his body and *in* his mind, who has not allowed any taboo to impede his growth and who experiences life, adventure, people, and animals "with innocence, truth and love." Gerald Durrell and people like him, whether they collect animals, build houses, work in a bank, paint pictures, wash dishes, or teach school—and how fervently one wishes more of them would teach school— make one realize that hope is not dead. Imposing their own balance on an unbalanced world, they seem, if only for a moment, to straighten it out. They, however, are but tiny oases of sanity in an infinite desert of insanity, always in danger of being buried by shifting sands. Others, perhaps not less clear-sighted but less resistant, stumble along until, exhausted, they make themselves believe that the mirage they see is indeed a river and the upside-down city in the fata morgana a real city with real people.

In this upside-down city, on the gate of which he can read the upside-down inscription *Ego sum via, veritas et vita* that tells him that he is about to enter a world more progressive, more devoted to truth, and more convinced of the sanctity of life than any other, the doubt-weary traveler is received with open arms. True, the arms close about him and hold him fast while the soles of his feet are beaten until, unable to stand on them, he, too walks on his head, but once he has learned the trick he is admitted unconditionally into the community of men and animals unless, of course, the color of his skin, the shape of his nose, the language he speaks, or the god he worships, sets him apart from the majority.

Since the changed posture induces a changed outlook, he will soon adopt the views of his fellow citizens and regard anyone who so much as mentions the possibility of walking on one's feet as an enemy of society, insane, or "red." And if, God forbid, the thought should enter his own mind, he will hop on his head to the nearest psychiatrist and beg to be cured. To preserve what we mistakenly believe to be our sanity, most of us make ourselves accept the fallacy that *upside down is right side up*. And once we have accepted that, there is no reason why we should not proclaim that our Western World, though perhaps not absolutely perfect yet, is the best of all possible worlds.

We will then wholeheartedly agree that some animals are more important than some people. That we owe a debt to animals because we domesticated and exploited them, but that we owe nothing to the black people we colonized, or kidnaped and sold at a profit, and have, ever since, exploited, or to other minorities whom, partly out of kindness, partly because of a manpower shortage, we admitted to our prosperous countries, or to the children we bring into this world, or to the parents who created us.

Unthinkingly we will parrot the meaningless tenet that in an enlightened democracy the freedom of the individual, and his right to his opinions, are sacred. We will applaud the woman who leaves 30,000 pounds in her will for the care and happiness of old horses, and the judge who sends the mother of three children to prison for three months because she owes the local council thirty pounds, causing her children incalculable psychological harm and the council the expense of their maintenance, at least ten times as much as the debt. We will rejoice that to commemorate the one hundredth anniversary of the ASPCA, the United States issued more than a 100 million beautiful new stamps and that, to commemorate the Human Rights Year, issued the police forces with chemical sprays, gas guns, "dum-dum" bullets, and other sophisticated new weapons to be used against the nation's "expendables." Nor will we find it at all strange that Britain's spineless, white supremacist government functioning under the pseudonym "Labour" should have celebrated the Human Rights Year by depriving of their human rights, and British citizenship, a quarter of a million colored people who, because they trusted Britain, have now become stateless refugees to be kicked around by their "superiors."

We will take it for granted that "equality" means that pet animals enjoy equal rights with some people, and more than others. They have a right to food, shelter, care and affection, and when their time comes, a painless, humane death. Our fellow humans who, Our Master's Voice tells us, have equal opportunities and should therefore look after themselves have a right, if they wish, to live in misery and die, long before their time, a painful and unnecessary death.

We will never for a moment doubt that brother love means man's love for his "lesser brothers," and especially for his pets, and not for his fellow men. On the contrary, *that* kind of brother love is suspect, its champions are undoubtedly traitors to their country, or to their class, hypocrites or, at best, just fools, depending on how far that love extends. We will be convinced that those who help us anthropomorphize our pet animals—trainers, veterinarians, groomers, the pet trade, and the pet industry—are infinitely more valuable sections of the community, and thus deserve a much higher living standard, than teachers, who are, everywhere in the West, overworked, underpaid, and discouraged by the blatant disrespect shown them by society. They are responsible *only* for our children, for the shaping of the future, and not for our pets.

Living without a "sense of being," without a constant awareness of ourselves as human beings, we will feel no compunction about destroying millions of people whose humanity is as unreal to us as our own if the Supreme Persuader, whatever his name or nationality, tells us to "do unto others what we do *not* want them to do unto us," although only they seem to know, and keep the knowledge to themselves, how killing and being killed can prevent killing and being killed.

By denying that we are descended from animals and compelling us to suppress, or sublimate, our animal instincts, Christianity may have contributed to the growth of the human intellect, but by creating an insoluble conflict between body and mind, it has finally driven us round the bend, made us schizophrenic and, in the process, has lost some of its power over us. It may well be that our intense preoccupation with animals, our strange need for them, and our adoption of some species into our own ranks, are symptoms of our rebellion against the false consciousness imposed upon us by Christianity. We seem to say animals are also human, but what we really say, although we may not realize it, is that we, too, are animals and that by living in close intimacy with them, we hope to relearn some of the things we have in common with them and have been made to forget. They might teach us to enjoy without guilt the simple pleasures of life—eating, drinking, sleeping, touching, sex—that, because, it is the mind and not the body we mortify, we do not deny ourselves but season with the spice of bad conscience. More important still, their example might revive in us the almost extinguished embers of the instinct of survival.

Unfortunately we cannot forget the present as we have forgotten the past. Nor can we pick out the good in both, jettison the bad, and synthetize past and present into a higher way of life, a world built on the foundation of *veritas et vita* for which we are not yet ready. If one day we shall be what, today, we pretend we are—human beings—it will not be due to our close association with anthropomorphized pet animals. It is much more probable that the "breakthrough from maniac to man," as Arthur Koestler defines it in *The Ghost in the Machine*, will come about in the way he suggests.

Koestler, whose sensitivity allows him to view our world from the "inside," while his scientific mind gives him the power to observe it from the "outside" and whose imagination, which puts him far ahead of us, traces the road we have to follow, can be called a "seer" rather than a "novelist," although his *Darkness at Noon* is truth distilled into literature and more effective and more lasting in its effect than a whole archive of documents and testimonies. Therefore it is anything but science fiction when he foresees the invention of a synthetized hormone, a mental stabilizer that would "have no noticeable effect, except promoting cerebral coordination and harmonizing thought and emotion; in other words, restore the integrity of the split hierarchy." The first step in this direction was taken when the first chemical cure for schizophrenia was attempted. Scientists are probably as aware as he is of the desperate urgency to produce that "mental stabilizer" before we have a chance to commit "genosuicide." There is no time to write works of fiction about what we may well call the "Survival Pill"; there is only time, and even that is not certain, to invent it.

Given a little time, the petishist millions might, perhaps, take a good look at their beloved "familiars" and admit that the evolutionary gap between them and us is too wide to bridge and that instead of trying to narrow it, they should attempt to make it wider. Meditating about the meaning of being human, they might realize that the headhunter in the Brazilian jungle, the Oxford don, the naked savage in Africa, the head of an American advertising agency, the Vietnam child, the Nobel Prize laureate poet, the Russian housewife, the inmate of a mental asylum, the bishop, the prostitute, the murderer, and the judge all belong to the same species as the animal lover. We may love animals in the form of roast beef or pet Pekingese, love them enough to feed one to the other, save them from cruelty, treat them well, spoil them, even feel responsible for them, but our first responsibility is *to our own species*, not merely to ourselves, our families, our countries, our "side" or "race."

We can forget our responsibility to our pets and still go on living, but if we forget our responsibility to our species, black or white, capitalist or Communist savage or civilized, rich or poor, young or old, we shall die an ugly violent death, either at the hands of those we repudiate as "expendables," inferiors or enemies, or together with them, with no one left to mourn.

If we persist in our refusal to face facts and in our belief that we can bend reality to our convenience, we shall, as Tom Lehrer so cheerfully predicts, clutching our pet poodle, parrot, python or panther ". . . all go together when we go!"

selected bibliography

ABEL, ALAN, *Yours for Decency*, Elek Books, London, 1966.

ARDREY, ROBERT, *African Genesis*, Atheneum, New York, 1961.

———, *The Territorial Imperative*, Atheneum, New York, 1966.

BALINT, MICHAEL, *The Doctor, His Patient and the Illness*, International Universities Press, Inc., New York, 1957.

BERNE, ERIC, *Games People Play*, Grove Press, New York, 1964.

BOUDET, JACQUES, *Man and Beast, a Visual History*, Golden Press, New York, 1964.

BRELAND, O. P., *Animal Life and Lore*, Harper, New York, 1963.

BRILL, K. and THOMAS, R., *Children in Homes*, Verry, New Mystic, Conn., 1964.

BROADHURST, P. L., *The Science of Animal Behavior*, Penguin, Baltimore, Md., 1963.

CRAIG, THURLOW, *Animal Affinities with Man*, Country Life Ltd., London, 1966.

CRONIN, H., *The Turn of the Screw*, John Long, London, 1967.

DARWIN, CHARLES, *On the Origin of Species*.

DEMBECK, HERMANN, Mit Tieren Leben, Econ Verlag, Germany, 1961.

DURRELL, GERALD, *My Family and Other Animals*, Viking, New York, 1957.

———, *The Whispering Land*, Viking, New York, 1962.

———, *The Bafut Beagles*, Ballantine, New York, 1966.

———, *The Drunken Forest*, Berkley Publishing Corp., New York.

———, *The Zoo in My Luggage*, Viking, New York, 1960.

DURRELL, JACQUIE, *Beasts in My Bed*, Atheneum, New York, 1967.

ERIKSON, ERIK, *Insight and Responsibility*, Norton, Inc., New York, 1964.

———, *The Challenge of Youth*, Doubleday, New York, 1963.

FRAZER, J. G., *The Golden Bough*.

FREUD, SIGMUND, *Totem and Taboo*, Norton, Inc., New York, 1950.

GALBRAITH, J. K., *The Affluent Society*, Houghton Mifflin, Boston, Mass., 1958.

GRONEFELD, GERHARD, *Weil wir Tiere lieben*, Westerman, Germany, 1964.

GRZIMEK, BERNHARD, *Twenty Animals, One Man*, Andre Deutsch, London, 1963.

GURNEY, ERIC, *How to Live with a Pampered Pet*, New English Library, London, 1966.

HARRINGTON, MICHAEL, *The Other America*, Macmillan, New York, 1962.

HAWKES, JACQUETTA, *History of Mankind*, Pt. I., Mentor Books, New York, 1965.

HERODOTUS, *The Histories*, E.P. Dutton, New York, 1964.

HOSKISSON, J. B., *Loneliness*, The Citadel Press, New York, 1965.

JOSEPHSON, E. and M. (eds.), *Man Alone: Alienation in Modern Society*, Dell, New York, 1966.

KINSEY, ALFRED C., and others, *Sexual Behavior in the Human Male*, Saunders, Philadelphia, 1948.

———, *Sexual Behavior in the Human Female*, Saunders, Philadelphia, 1953.

KOESTLER, ARTHUR, *The Ghost in the Machine*, Macmillan, New York, 1968.

LAING, RONALD, *The Politics of Experience*, Pantheon, New York, 1967.

———, *The Divided Self*, Barnes and Noble, New York, 1960.

LANZMANN, J. and GILBERT, M., *Guide Mi Chien*, Denoel, Paris, 1967.

LLOYD-JONES, BUSTER, *The Animals Came in One by One*, John Day, New York, 1967.

LORENZ, KONRAD, *On Aggression*, Harcourt, Brace, New York, 1966.

———— , *King Solomon's Ring*, T.Y. Crowell, New York, 1952.

MARCHANT, R. A., *Man and Beast*, G. Bell & Sons, London, 1966.

MASON, OTIS T., *The Origins of Invention*, M.I.T. Press, Cambridge, Mass., 1966.

MAXWELL, GAVIN, *Ring of Bright Water*, Dutton, New York, 1961.

McNEILL, WILLIAM, *The Rise of the West*, University of Chicago Press, Chicago, 1963.

MENNINGER, KARL A., *Psychoanalysis and Culture*,"Totemic Aspects of Contemporary Attitudes towards Animals," ed. George B. Wilbur and Warner Muensterberger, International Universities Press, Inc., New York, 1951.

MERY, FERNAND, *Ici les Betes*, Denoel, Paris, 1954.

———— , *Ames de Betes*, Denoel, Paris, 1952.

MICHELET, JULES, *Satanism and Witchcraft*, Citadel Press, New York.

MILNE, L. and M., *The Senses of Animals and Men*, Atheneum, New York, 1962.

MITFORD, JESSICA, *The American Way of Death*, Simon and Schuster, Crest Books, New York, 1963.

MONTANDON, RAOUL, *De la Bete a l'Homme*, Attinger, Switzerland, 1942.

MORRIS, DESMOND, *The Naked Ape*, McGraw-Hill, New York, 1968.

PACKARD, VANCE, *The Hidden Persuaders*, McKay, New York, 1957.

———— , *The Naked Society*, McKay, New York, 1964.

———— , *The Status Seekers*, McKay, New York, 1959.

———— , *The Pyramid Climbers*, McGraw-Hill, New York, 1962.

PARRINDER, E. G., *Witchcraft: European and African*, Barnes and Noble, New York, 1963.

REIK, THEODOR, *The Need to Be Loved*, Farrar Straus, New York, 1963.

ROBB, BARBARA, *Sans Everything*, Nelson, London, 1967.

ROCHEMONT, RICHARD, *Pet's Cookbook*, Knopf, New York, 1964.

SARGANT, WILLIAM, *The Unquiet Mind*, Atlantic Monthly Press, Boston, Mass., 1967.

———— , *The Battle for the Mind*, Pan Books, London, 1964.

SCHALLER, G. B., *The Year of the Gorilla*, University of Chicago Press, Chicago, 1964.

SCHEFF, THOMAS J., *Being Mentally Ill*, Aldine Publishing Co., Chicago, 1966.

SEARLES, HAROLD F., *The Nonhuman Environment*, International Universities Press, New York, 1960.

SUSANN, JACQUELINE, *Every Night, Josephine!* Bernard Geis, New York, 1963.

SWIFT, JONATHAN, *Gulliver's Travels and Selected Writings*, Random House, New York.

TREFFLICH, HENRY, *They Don't Answer Back*, Appleton Century, New York, 1954.

TRESILIAN, LIZ, *The Dog's Horoscope Book*, Arlington Books, London, 1967.

TUNSTALL, JEREMY, *Old and Alone*, Humanities Press, New York, 1966.

TURNER, E. S., *All Heaven in a Rage*, Michael Joseph, London, 1964.

VESEY-FITZGERALD, B., *Enquire within about Animals*, Pelham Books, London, 1967.

WAUGH, EVELYN, *The Loved One*, Little, Brown, Boston, Mass., 1948.

WELLS, H. G., *The Outline of History*, Doubleday, New York, 1956.

WENDT, HERBERT, *Auf Noah's Spuren*, Rowohlt, Germany, 1967.

WHITE, LESLIE A., *The Science of Culture*, Grove Press, New York, 1958.

WHITE, T. H., *The Bestiary*, Putnam, New York, 1960.

WHYTE, W.F., *Street Corner Society*, University of Chicago Press, Chicago, 1955.

WILBUR, G. B. and MUENSTERGER, W., *Psychoanalysis and Culture*, International University Press, New York, 1965.

WOLFF, MICHAEL, *Prison*, Eyre & Spottiswoode, London, 1967.

MAGAZINES

UNITED STATES: *Pet Shop Management; Petford Industry; Pet Industry; Pet Fair.*

ENGLAND: *Pet Trade Journal; Animals Magazine.*

GERMANY: *Zoologischer Zentralanzeiger; Tier Illustrierte; Mag. der Tierfreunde.*

FRANCE: *La Vie des Betes; Betes et Nature.*

Index

249

Maternity Shop for Dogs, 181
Maxwell, Gavin, 224
May, Clarence, 167
Medicaid, 30
Menageries, 13, 14
Menninger, Karl A., 108, 110, 130, 142
Mental Health Research Fund, 85
Mental Health Trust, 85
Mery, Fernand, 82
Metaframe Corporation, 195-196
Mice, 12, 81, 199, 215
    mattresses for, 157
    novelty items for, 197
    as pet food, 113
Middle Ages, 11, 12-13
Midland Bank, 230
Millipedes, 197
Miniature poodles, 146
Mistress-and-dog outfits, 152
Mongooses, 216
"Monkees" (pop group), 178
Monkeys, 8, 55, 172, 185, 198, 216, 217, 218
    books on, 223
    cost of, 198, 218
    markup on, 205
Morris, Desmond, 99
Moscow *Literary Gazette*, 75-76
Motion picture industry, 222-223
Munnings, Violet, 167
Mynah birds, 171
    markup on, 205

Naked Ape, The (Morris), 99
National Anti-Vivisection Society, 85
National Association of Child Protective Agencies, 78
National Canine Defence League, 85
National Cat Club, 147

National Health Service (Great Britain), 28
National Institute for the Deaf, 37
National Society for Mentally Handicapped Children, 85
Nazi Party, 20
Negroes, 45, 48, 148
New Statesman, The, 70
New York Times Magazine, 181-182
New Yorker, The, 80
Newsweek (magazine), 148
Next Development in Man, The (Whyte), 3
Niccoli, Ria, 209
Nonhuman Environment, The (Searles), 39
Norfolk, Duchess of, 167
Novak, Kim, 177
Nuffield, Lord, 56
Nuffield Foundation, 55-56

OBAB Society, 82
Ocelots, 115, 159, 172, 176, 197, 198, 217
    books on, 223
    markup on, 205
Old and Alone (Tunstall), 47
Old Furred and Feathered People's Home, 103-104
Orangutans, 198
Original sin, dogma of, 132-133
Orwell, George, xii, 90
Ostriches, 198
Other America, The (Harrington), 48
Otters, 173
Ovary surgery, 149, 153
Owen, Corinne, 36

P. Lorillard Company, 20

ABOUT THE AUTHOR

Born in Budapest, Kathleen Szasz is well known for her translations from Hungarian, German, French and Spanish. Her research for *Petishism* took her all over the United States and Europe, and she has written a book that cannot, will not, be ignored.